The Fibonacci Effect
Lan Turner's Stock Market Playbook of Strategies

First Edition

ISBN 979-8370473302

Published by PitNews Press, Inc.
271 N. Spring Creek Parkway, Suite A1
Providence, Utah 84332

The opinions expressed in this book are those of the author and do not necessarily reflect the views of the publisher.

Printed in the United States of America.

Table of Contents

To gain access to the free video course call: 800-862-7193.

Tell them you purchased this book, and ask for access to Technical Analysis of the Financial Markets 301.

This is the same online course I teach at Dixie State University.

You can find it for sale online at: LanTurner.com for $399. It's yours free for purchasing this book.

International callers call: 435-752-8026

Welcome to my world!

As you dive into this exciting (and sometimes volatile) world, it's important to understand the primary patterns that all traders are subject to. These patterns include Fibonacci, Elliott Wave, and recurring price patterns like head and shoulders, wedges, triangles, and my personal favorite, "spider webs."

I've published a number of video boot camps that accompany this book and example each lesson in detail. For details about those book camp courses, visit me online at: LanTurner.com

- Education is a crucial factor in successful trading.

- By learning about the markets, tools, and risk management strategies, you can make informed decisions and increase your chances of success.

- Education can come from a variety of sources, such as online courses, books, and mentorship from experienced traders.

- It's important to stay up-to-date on the latest developments in the world of trading.

Understanding the risks associated with different types of trades, as well as learning how to set stop-loss orders and properly diversify your portfolio, can help you better protect yourself and your investments.

Now, I know what you're thinking: "Lan, I've never even heard of these patterns, how am I supposed to trade using them?" Even if you're not familiar with these tools, they can still impact your trading. Markets are dynamic, and most market action is influenced by events, mathematical models, indicators, and trading tools. The more traders who use a specific tool, the greater the chance it will have an impact on market price. It's like a self-fulfilling prophecy.

But here's the thing: many professional traders, myself included, rely on these patterns to make informed trades. In fact, Fibonacci and Elliott Wave are often misunderstood and misused by retail traders, which may contribute to the high failure rate among traders. That's why it's so important to educate yourself and trust your own instincts. Don't just rely on others to give you stock tips - become the person that others look to for advice.

In addition to understanding these foundational patterns, it's also crucial to stay informed about market events and news that may affect the prices of the assets you're trading. Economic indicators, political developments, and other factors can all impact the market. That's why it's important to have a trading plan and stick to it. This will help you make consistent, disciplined decisions and avoid impulsive trades based on emotions.

Finally, when investing for the long-term, proper risk management is key to your success in trading. This means setting stop-loss orders to limit potential losses and not risking more than you can afford to lose. It's also important to diversify your portfolio and not put all your eggs in one basket. By spreading your investments across different asset classes and markets, you can reduce the impact of any single trade on your overall portfolio.

What Kind of Trader Are You?

What is the difference between a Scalper, a Day Trader, an Investor, a Swing Trader, and a Gambler?

Gambler; unfortunately, this is one of the most popular methods of trading, and the preferred strategy by most of our young gen X,Y,Z Reddit crowds. They get a little extra stimulus cash, they open a Robinhood account, and they start picking stocks like they are racehorses at the track, laying it all down on one or two wild bets, based primarily on tips from their Internet friends. (Don't be that guy!)

Scalper: a scalper is a trader who trades on extremely short time frames, sometimes tic-by-tic, and/or 10 second charts. A one-minute chart is a long-term chart for a scalper, since they are making most of their trading decisions based on the movement of the current active price bar, level two data, and the tape.

Scalpers take a lot of small risks using large share size to capture a small move in the market. Scalpers are the piranhas, or sharks of the market, slowly picking the meat off the bones of less skilled or unwitting traders, sharks and piranhas are usually highly skilled and very experienced traders.

Day Trader: a day trader is someone who is looking to get into a trend, and trade that trend throughout the entire morning, or day. Their goal is to take advantage of a rising, or falling market within a single daily time frame, then exit their trade before the trend ends, or the market closes.

A day trader does not make trading decisions based on the last, or current active price bar like a scalper, if the day trader is trading on a one-minute chart, the day trader will only make a new trading decision once per minute, letting the active bar activate his or her exit or entry strategy.

Swing Trader: a swing trader is someone who generally takes long(er) term positions, but this strategy can be executed on any time frame, from minute charts, to daily charts. A swing trader is generally driven by some sort of mathematical trading system, or indicator, a strategy that takes both long and short positions, the trader does not care, in essence, 'swinging' back and forth from longs to shorts.

Position Trader, or Passive Investor; picks a stock, ETF, diversified index fund, or maybe gold, silver, or even crypto currency, they then continue to add funds on a regularly scheduled basis, dollar cost averaging their overall position up and down, investing for the long horizon payoff, generally a five-to-ten-year period. At the end of their timeline, they stop adding, and start withdrawing, increasing their quality of life. Passive Investing is a popular strategy for self-directed IRA retirement accounts.

Active Investor: is a trader who desires to beat the market through their own trading skills, researching fundamental and technical trading opportunities across a broad scope of stocks, in essence, building their own private hedge fund. These investors are continually adding new positions to their portfolio, while pruning losers or poor performers, cutting losers short, and letting winners run, while taking and reinvesting profits along the way.

An Active Investor employees multiple trading strategies and tools, such as options, pairs trading, event trading, spreads, shorting, and the like. An active investor may even use quant-style computerized execution algorithms to help them enter and exit markets more efficiently. In my opinion, Active Investing is one of the most exiting trading methodologies there is, and is what this document was primarily created to address.

Position Trader, or Passive Investor; picks a stock, ETF, diversified index fund, or maybe gold, silver, or even crypto currency, they then continue to add funds on a regularly scheduled basis, dollar cost averaging their overall position up and down, investing for the long horizon payoff, generally a five-to-ten-year period. At the end of their timeline, they stop adding, and start withdrawing, increasing their quality of life. Passive Investing is a popular strategy for self-directed IRA retirement accounts.

In summary:

Scalpers: Scalpers are traders who aim to make small profits by quickly buying and selling securities, often holding their positions for just a few minutes or even seconds. Scalping requires a high level of market knowledge and quick decision-making skills, as well as the ability to handle volatility.

Day traders: Day traders are traders who buy and sell securities within the same trading day. Day traders may hold their positions for a few hours or even just a few minutes. Day trading requires a high level of focus and discipline, as well as the ability to react quickly to market conditions.

Swing traders: Swing traders are traders who hold positions for longer periods of time, typically a few days or even a few weeks.

Position traders: Position traders are traders who hold positions for even longer periods of time, often months or even years.

Active investors: Active investors are investors who actively manage their portfolio, making frequent buy and sell decisions based on their own research and analysis.

Passive investors: Passive investors are investors who take a more hands-off approach to their portfolio, typically buying and holding a diversified portfolio of securities over the long term.

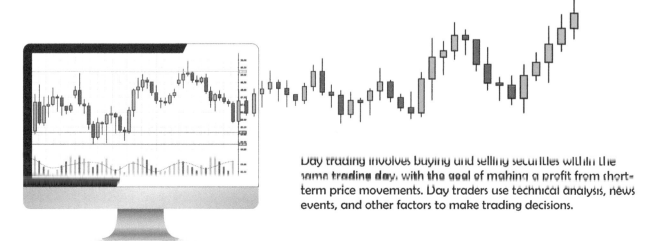

Day trading involves buying and selling securities within the same trading day, with the goal of making a profit from short-term price movements. Day traders use technical analysis, news events, and other factors to make trading decisions.

Where Systems Fail, Methods Prevail

One of the biggest questions I always get is, "If I trade your 'system,' how much money can I make, what's the 'back-test' results on your 'system?'

First and foremost, what I'm about to reveal to you is NOT necessarily a trading system. It's a trading methodology, and as the title says, where systems fail, methods prevail.

What's the difference between a trading methodology and a trading system?

What you are going to learn in this document is the foundational structure for all other trading systems and methods. Whether you're trading the MACD system, the Larry Williams %R System, the Jake Bernstein's 10x8 MAC system, Steve Nissan's Candlestick formation strategies, or the Bulls 'n Bears Wells Wilder system, all these and every other so-called "system" that you can name must adhere to the primary rules of Fibonacci and Elliott Wave; whether the trader, or system designer realizes it or not.

Elliott Wave in itself is not a trading system, Elliott Wave is the foundational structure of how a market moves through price and time. Higher highs and higher lows, which makes for an uptrend (bullish), lower highs and lower lows, which makes for a downtrend (bearish), that's Elliott Wave Theory; every trading system is subject to those rules.

> Now, can you buy when a market changes directions from a bearish Elliott Wave to a bullish Elliott Wave on a classic 123/ABC bottom formation or when a level of support or resistance is breached? Yes, certainly, but that in itself is not a system, it is a methodology.

> Most "systems," will try to identify that change in trend or breach of support and/or resistance for you, and throw some sort of computerized buy or sell signal, but you as a trader must understand the foundational structure of markets so that you understand why that mathematical model, or system, gave you that arrow.

Now, what you do with that information, or trading signal, determines your outcome. Do you systematically buy each time you get a buy signal, and systematically sell every time you get a sell signal? I can tell you from personal experience, that's a quick way to give up your holdings to someone else.

Once you understand the foundational structure of market dynamics, and of how markets move through price and time, you can use that information to structure your trading to any number of strategies, or systems, whether trading Stocks, Futures, Forex, or Options.

There are thousands of systems designed for trading every type of market that you can imagine. We, as small speculators, are looking for trending markets, we're trend traders, we look for and anticipate markets to make higher highs and higher lows, we follow the rules of Elliott Wave theory.

If a stock doesn't act right, don't touch it. Not all markets move through Elliott Waves and adhere to our rules at all times, many stocks seem to have no rhyme or reason to their advances and declines, making them nearly impossible to trade profitably.

I tell traders all the time, don't feel bad that you missed out on a huge run in the market in a stock that didn't give you a proper signal setup, that run was not for us, that was for someone else who trades a different strategy, or system. Wait, be patient, our turn will come soon enough.

> Always remember, the big money comes from letting the market run. I've seen too many traders hold onto losers, and cut winners short. They're brave when they should be scared, and they're scared when they should be brave.

When you're making money, be brave, and stay in the market, when you're losing money, be scared, and get out; learn to read the charts, learn how to count and measure, (this gives you confidence to hold through draw-downs.), then look to the overall long-term trend.

> Our goal is to keep a stake in the position through the entire move of the market, if possible, from A1 to X3, but be mindful and also take small profits along the way, then look for your final exit at the end of the third drive, or X3.

Successful trading takes skill, patience, and nerves of steel. It's not something that you will master overnight, and it's not something that will happen with every trade. However, when you do make a successful trade, you will know that you have done it right. As the saying goes, "It only takes one good trade!"

My advice to you is to have patience when you're winning. I can't tell you how many times I've taken a profit only to watch the market move even further in my favor. "Cut losers short and let winners run" is more than just a catchy phrase - it's the first law of trading.

When trading, it's important to remember that you are not trying to catch the very bottom of a rebound or exit at the very top. These are what we call the appetizers and dessert of trading. As a trader, your focus should be on the meat and potatoes - the big move in the middle. Trying to catch the ultimate top or bottom is a fool's errand. Instead, focus on the main course and let the smaller moves take care of themselves.

One key to success in trading is to have a clear, defined strategy and stick to it. This means setting specific goals, identifying your risk tolerance, and developing a plan for making trades based on these factors. Having a strategy can help you make consistent, disciplined decisions and avoid impulsive trades based on emotions.

When investing for the long-haul, it's also important to have a long-term perspective and not get too caught up in the day-to-day fluctuations of the market. While it's important to stay informed and react to market conditions, it's also crucial to have a big picture view of your investments and not get too caught up in short-term noise. By focusing on your long-term strategy, you can make more informed, calculated decisions that are more likely to lead to success.

The Five Rules of Highly Successful Traders
Plan your trade, and trade your plan.

Learning what to count, what to measure, setups, triggers and how to exit a market when you're either right, or wrong, is the key to finding success in these markets, this is the foundation of what trading is all about, and the concepts we'll be focused on throughout this document.

That said, this document is just a primer to get you started, once you understand these concepts, we'll need to then take you to the next level, where you'll learn numerous different strategies that take advantage of these concepts, such as options, contracts, lots, and various combinations of all the above; strategies with names like Flea Flicker, and The King Tut!

> A student once said, "Wow, I love your system!" I replied, "Taking credit for this would be like Isaac Newton taking credit for gravity, all I'm doing is opening your eyes to the true nature of the markets; but, I will allow you to give me credit for doing that."

> Technical analysis is the process of using geometry and mathematical probabilities to help determine the best entry and exit points. I call it SWAG, (Scientific Wild-A$$ Guess.)

Nobody knows where the markets going to be at any given time in the future, but technical analysis is the best means of helping to determine just that. Let's always make sure that when we trade, that we make our wild-a$$ guesses as scientific as possible.

Trading Strategy Fundamentals (Our Five Rules!)

1. Count; What do we count?
   We count the waves of the market, what's known as Elliott Waves, based on price action that follow a predictable pattern.

2. Measure; What do we measure?
   We measure the Elliott Waves using a ruler that's based on the Fibonacci scale.

3. Setup; What is a setup?
   A setup is a recurring price pattern that give us a clue as to where the market might go next.

4. Trigger; What is a trigger?
   The trigger is price action within the market that triggers our entry order. Common trigger points for entry include breaking through resistance levels, reaching key support levels, or crossing over moving averages.

5. Follow through to exit.
   Follow through is how we exit the market, whether we're wrong or right, and using Stop Loss Order strategies to maximize our profit potential and reduce risk.

Basic Terminology

What is a Bull Market? A Bull Market is a market where prices are on the rise. If someone says they are Bullish, they anticipate a rise in price.

BEAR MARKET
Pessimism Markets Fall

BULL MARKET
Optimism Markets Rise

What is a Bear Market? A Bear Market is a market where prices are on the decline. If someone says they are Bearish, that means they anticipate a fall in price.

Many trading systems, or indicators, try to identify when a market changes from Bullish to Bearish, and from Bearish to Bullish, there are many different mathematical models to help determine this, some work better than others, but all have been created for this one purpose.

Technical analysts have specific rules they follow to determine, with an absolute degree of

If I'm bullish, I'm anticipating a rise in price.

If I'm bearish, I'm anticipating a fall in price.

certainty, when these events occur. You'll often hear a market analyst pronounce with great authority that a market has just changed from Bullish to Bearish, and in fact, using technical analysis rules, a trader can determine the exact minute in which these changes occurs; what they can't tell you is how long the trend will last.

In this document we're going to study the primary rules of technical analysis. There have been many books written on technical analysis, and there is no way, in this short 'cheat sheet,' we could cover all the rules that go into being a technical analyst, but I hope to give you a glimpse into that world, and spark your interest in further study.

In the world of finance, there are two basic camps of thought.

Fundamental analysis, and technical analysis; fundamental analysis is the study of why a specific market might rise or fall, such as news events, earnings releases, restructuring of board members, partnerships, contract cancellations, or even government reports, such as non farm payroll, or unemployment reports.

On the other hand, there is technical analysis, which is the study of charts and price, such things as levels of support, resistance, recurring price patterns with names like head and shoulders formations, triangles, wedges, support and resistance, technical analysis also includes the use of mathematical models like MACD, RSI, and Stochastics. A technical analyst believes that all necessary fundamental information needed to trade is already in the chart, represented by price.

In my opinion, both methodologies are imperative to creating a successful trading strategy. The fundamentals of the market drive the long term trends, while the technicals drive the short-term trends, and provide the setups and triggers for entry of the overall long(er) term fundamental trends.

By combining both fundamental and technical analysis, traders can get a well-rounded view of the market and make more informed trading decisions.

Trading Signals and Setups

A bull market is a financial market characterized by rising prices, typically in stocks, bonds, or other securities. In a bull market, investors are generally optimistic about the state of the economy and believe that asset prices will continue to rise, leading to a sense of confidence and enthusiasm among traders. Bull markets often occur during periods of economic expansion, when unemployment is low, and corporate profits are growing. In contrast to a bear market, which is characterized by falling prices, a bull market is typically seen as a positive sign for the overall economy and can encourage more people to invest in the stock market. It is important to note, however, that bull markets eventually come to an end, and it is crucial for investors to be aware of the potential risks and to diversify their portfolio to minimize potential losses.

A bear market is a financial market characterized by falling prices, typically in stocks, bonds, or other securities. In a bear market, investors are generally pessimistic about the state of the economy and believe that asset prices will continue to decline, leading to a sense of caution and hesitation among traders. Bear markets often occur during periods of economic recession or slowdown, when unemployment is high, and corporate profits are declining. In contrast to a bull market, which is characterized by rising prices, a bear market is typically seen as a negative sign for the overall economy and can discourage people from investing in the stock market. It is important to note, however, that bear markets eventually come to an end, and it is possible for asset prices to recover and begin rising again. It is crucial for investors to be aware of the potential risks and to diversify their portfolio to minimize potential losses.

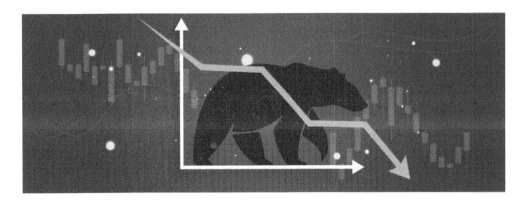

Price Bars
What constitutes a chart?

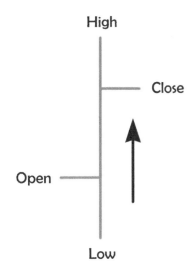

As a technical analyst, we look at price, which in my opinion, is the single most important piece of information you can have or know to help you make your trading decisions. Price is everything! What is the current price, what was the price yesterday, the day before, or even a week, or month before today? These are the most important questions you as a trader can ask. All pertinent fundamental information is already built into price; price is a reflection of market sentiment.

Price is represented in numerous ways, but the two most common methods are through price bar representation. Each chart is made up of a series of price bars, in this example, we're looking at two different styles of price bars, it really doesn't make much difference which one you use, it is, for the most part, just personal preference.

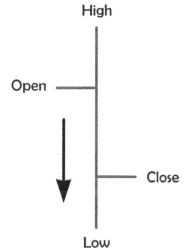

In this example, we have what we call OHLC price bars, we also have Candlestick Price bars. Both represent the Open (O), the High (H), the Low (L), and the Close (C), or O,H,L,C., for a specified amount of time.

Any, or every time frame can and is represented by these price bars. They can represent one minute, ten minutes, 30 minutes, 60 minutes, daily, weekly, monthly, it does not matter, each price bar represents the O,H,L,C for that time frame. String them together, and you get the market price history for that time frame.

String together a bunch of one minute price bars, we call this a one-minute chart, where each bar represents the O,H,LC for each minute. Same for Hourly, same for Daily. There are many technical analysis techniques based around how these bars string together to make recurring price patterns; many people like to trade what are known as, 'candlestick patterns,' which are usually one to three bar formations made up of candlestick bars. (Track 'n Trade has a tool that can automatically identifies these patterns for you.)

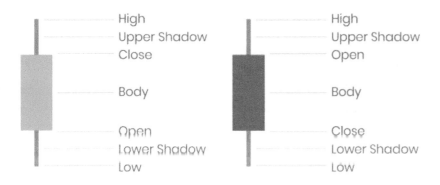

The color of the candlestick body itself is significant, it's the relationship between the open and close prices. This information can be useful for identifying trends and when making trading decisions. Red for bearish, green for bullish.

Sometimes we see candlestick patterns with solid and hollow bodies. This is just to help the trader with black 'n white charts. A solid body represents a market that closed higher than it opened, while the open body means it closed lower.

In later chapters we'll discuss different types of candles, such as Heiken-Ashi.

Time of day can be our single most important trading strategy:

Day trading involves buying and selling financial instruments within the same trading day, and it can be a lucrative strategy for traders who are able to identify and capitalize on short-term price movements. One question that many day traders have is what is the best time of day to trade?

There is no one-size-fits-all answer to this question, as the best time to trade will depend on a variety of factors, including the specific financial instruments you are trading, your trading strategy, and your own personal schedule. However, there are some general patterns that can be observed in the markets that can provide some guidance.

One of the busiest times for day trading is typically the opening and closing hours of major financial markets, such

as the New York Stock Exchange and the London Stock Exchange. During these times, there is typically a high volume of trading activity, which can lead to more liquidity and potentially more opportunities for traders.

Another factor to consider is the time of day when major economic news releases or events occur. These events can have a significant impact on market prices, and traders who are able to react quickly to news events may be able to capitalize on price movements.

Ultimately, the best time to day trade will depend on your own personal circumstances and trading goals. It may be helpful to experiment with different times of day and observe how the markets behave to determine what works best for you.

Watch the 2:30 PM mark, I've noticed that many times, this is the actual beginning to Power Hour, making "Power Hour" one and a half hours long.

Also watch the 10 minute mark before the close, this seems to be a key exit point for many automated trading systems, you'll often see a large amount of trading activity right at the 10 minute mark, where trading systems start liquidating their positions in preparation for the end of day.

Chicago vs New York

Why Trade Futures?

There are a number of Financial Exchanges that a trader can trade on. Most traders only consider trading through the New York exchanges, such as the NY Stock Exchange, and the NASDAQ.

Most traders have no idea about the advantages of trading through other exchanges such as the exchanges in Chicago; the Board of Trade, and the Mercantile exchange. Here's a list why you might want to consider trading through Chicago rather than New York. (They're competitors.)

Trader's are unaware that you can trade all kinds of wonderful markets through Chicago, such as Crude Oil, Natural Gas, Wheat, Soybeans, Corn, Live Cattle, Live Hogs, Sugar, Orange Juice, and my favorite, all four of the major indexes, S&P500, DOW, NASDAQ, and Russell 2000. (These are just a few of the markets Chicago offers, there are many more fun things to trade!)

Here's 20 reasons why you might want to consider trading through Chicago, rather than New York.

No pattern day trading rules: In the stock market, traders who make more than three day trades in a rolling five-day period are subject to the pattern day trader rules, which requires a minimum account balance of $25,000. This rule does not apply to the futures market. Make as many trades as you want in one day, penalty free!

No minimum account balance: Many futures brokers do not require a minimum account balance to open an account, which makes it accessible to traders with a small amount of capital. (Extremely tight spreads, easy in and easy out of markets.)

Trade with unrealized gains: In the stock market, traders must sell shares to realize their gains, which can result in taxes and transaction costs. In the futures market, traders can hold onto their positions and even trade using their unrealized gains.

No waiting to clear: In the stock market, trades can take one to three days to clear, which can be inconvenient for traders who need to enter or exit positions quickly.

Leverage: Futures contracts typically offer higher leverage than stocks, which means traders can control a larger position size with a smaller amount of capital.

Contract sizes: The futures market offers a variety of contract sizes to suit the needs of many different traders, including beginners.

Micro-sized contracts, also known as "micro lots," allow traders to control a smaller position size with a smaller amount of capital; excellent for beginner traders.

Mini-sized contracts, also known as "mini lots," are slightly larger than micro-sized contracts and may be suitable for traders with a slightly larger amount of capital.

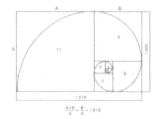

Standard-sized contracts are the largest and may be suitable for traders with a larger amount of capital, and commercial entities with a higher risk tolerance.

This can be beneficial for traders who want to tailor their position size to their risk appetite and capital availability. This flexibility can allow traders to find a contract size that fits their needs and trading style.

Short selling: Futures contracts can be sold short, which allows traders to profit from falling prices without fees, interest or penalties. This is often times not possible in the stock market, where short selling is restricted, and penalized with fees, interest and dividends that must be paid by the trader.

Trading hours: The futures market is open for trading 24 hours a day, five days a week, which can be convenient for traders in different time zones.

Tax benefits: Trading futures may offer certain tax benefits compared to trading stocks. For example, futures traders can elect to have their profits treated as 60% long-term capital gains and 40% short-term capital gains, which may result in a much, much lower tax rate.

Margin: Futures traders maintain a margin account, which is a type of collateral that ensures they have the financial resources to cover any potential losses on their trades. This can make it easier to enter and exit trades quickly, as there is no need to sell shares to cover short positions.

Volatility: The futures market can be more volatile than the stock market, which can create opportunities for traders who are able to capitalize on price movements.

Diversity: The futures market offers a wide range of contracts to trade, including commodities, currencies, and indexes which allows traders to diversify their portfolio.

Liquidity: The futures market is highly liquid, which means it is easy to enter and exit trades without affecting the price significantly. This can be beneficial for traders who need to move in and out of positions quickly.

The application of Fibonacci retracement in financial markets is based on the assumption that markets have natural tendencies to retrace certain percentages of a move, after which they will continue to move in the original direction. Traders may use these levels as potential entry or exit points for trades.

Fibonacci sequence and its derivatives, like Fibonacci retracement, are used as a technical analysis tool in financial markets. They are used by traders to identify potential levels of support and resistance, and as a result, they have an EFFECT on the market.

Therefore, Fibonacci sequence and its derivatives can be said to AFFECT the financial markets in the sense that it is used as a tool to make trading decisions.

Low costs: Trading futures typically has lower costs compared to trading stocks, including lower commissions and exchange fees. Many traders believe when they trade stocks through the New York markets, they're paying no commissions. This is a fallacy, the stock exchanges and brokerage firms simply hide their commission inside the spread, as well as other clandestine techniques called front running, this is how they extract their commissions. This is not so in the Chicago futures exchanges. There is no front running, and we have super tight spreads. That said we do have commissions, but they can be negotiated with your broker depending on how often you trade. (This is a good thing, up front and honest.) This also facilitates much faster and cleaner order flow, since your orders are not being sold to another firm to be filled.

Regulation: The futures market is federally regulated, which provides traders with a greater level of protection against fraud and manipulation. (Unlike Crypto and Forex.)

Expertise: Many traders who specialize in the futures market have a deep understanding of the underlying assets and market conditions, which can be beneficial for those looking to learn from experienced traders. (Futures brokerage firms are generally run by elite teams of passionate and experienced traders, unlike stock firms who generally hire kids out of college with no experience.)

Technical analysis: Many traders in the futures market rely on technical analysis to make trading decisions, which involves studying charts and other data to identify patterns and trends. The futures market adheres well to the rules of technical analysis, making it work well for technical traders.

Fundamental analysis: Futures traders also use fundamental analysis to make trading decisions, which involves analyzing economic and market conditions to determine the value of an asset.

Speculative trading: The futures market offers opportunities for speculative trading, which involves taking positions based on the potential for price movements rather than the underlying value.

Hedging: The futures market is often used by producers, manufacturers, and other market participants to hedge against price fluctuations in the underlying assets. This can help reduce risk and stabilize income.

Expertise: Many traders who specialize in the futures market have a deep understanding of the underlying assets and market conditions, which can be beneficial for those looking to learn from experienced traders. Futures traders are kind hearted loving people willing to reach out and help new traders, where stock traders are the dregs of the underworld, cutthroat, unwilling to share tactics and strategies. I'm joking of course! ;-) (If you actually got this far, you're ready to start trading futures.)

> NOTE: Now, just because I spent the last three pages explaining to you why I love Futures, does not mean that the education that you'll receive by reading this book won't work in other markets such as Stocks, Forex, and Crypto, it certainly will.

Five Steps To Getting Started Trading Futures For A Living! Part Time, or Full Time

 ## Get a Live Trading Platform

This is the single biggest decision of your trading career, getting the right software will be the absolute difference between success and failure.

Rule 1: Never try to day trade with web based charts and order forms.

Rule 2: Never try to day trade with cheap crappy free software. (It's free for a reason.)

Rule 3: Invest in a high quality platform that you install on your PC.

Rule 4: Never ever try to day trade through your cell phone.

Rule 5: If you're not willing to invest in proper tools of the trade, then don't even start.

Rule 6: The free software provided by your broker is probably a piece of shit.

Remember, my profits come from your pockets. Don't make it easy for me to take your money, and by doing any of the above listed items, you're setting yourself up for failure. If you're going to do it, do it right, or don't do it at all. Trading is difficult enough without starting out with one hand tied behind your back.

Personally, I like software platforms that are dedicated to the market I'm trading. There are enough differences between Stocks, Futures, and Forex that I don't want the same platform trying to manage all three markets through a single interface; causes way too much confusion, confusion causes losses. (I don't personally trade crypto, but these strategies all work just the same in crypto as they do in stocks, futures, and forex.)

 ## Software Choices

There are several good trading platforms on the market. Here's three of my favorites, pick one of these and you'll be good to go. (None of these platforms are free, but the best software never is.)

Platform 1: Track 'n Trade Live Futures. **This is the software I use. It's specialty software dedicated to trading the futures market. (They also have a dedicated Stocks & Forex versions.)**

- Track 'n Trade offers a fully functional two week trial, allowing you to try it before you buy.

    o Get a free two week trial which includes live data at: Tools4Traders.ORG

- It has programmable "Bots," allowing you to quickly and easily create custom order tools, OTO & OCO, (One-Triggers-Other, One-Cancels-Other) No coding required.

- It has a visual interface, allowing you to actually trade directly on the chart. (You never enter your orders through a cumbersome order box. You simply drag 'n drop orders on the screen, and move them to the price levels you want. I'd say it's amazing, but that would be cliché', so I'll just say, I love it.

- It has all the necessary indicators, Fibonacci & Elliott Wave tools necessary to perform your technical analysis.

- Once you purchase the software & subscribe to your live data feed, you never have to pay for another software upgrade again, all software upgrades to new versions are free for active traders. (Saves a lot of money never having to buy new version upgrades.)

Platform 2:eSignal. This is a pretty popular platform, but it's really expensive, almost three times the cost of Track 'n Trade per month, and lacks many of the features in Track 'n Trade that I love most.

- It's not a visual interface, you must enter your orders via an order entry dialog box, and your orders never show up on the chart.

- You can place your orders through special shortcut key press combinations on the keyboard. (Pain in the arse.) It's much more cumbersome, but once you get the hang of it, can be relatively fast.

- It has some special features some traders really like, such as cascading charts. (I hate cascading charts personally, they're hard to manage.)

- It also has a descent set of indicators and technical analysis drawing tools.

- Be prepared to purchase new software versions and updates

Platform 3: Trade Station. This is the most expensive and complex trading platform on the market. The company that creates it is huge, so large in fact, they're traded on the New York Stock exchange. (Although impressive, that's not necessarily a selling point.)

- This platform is extremely expensive. Way, way overkill for the kind of trading we do. This is basically an institutional trading platform for large speculators and commercial traders.

- They do not offer a trail. You can't try it before you buy it.

- It's very old, and complex, you'll need at least a year of training to figure it out.

- It does everything you can imagine, including live news feeds and commentary.

- It covers all markets through one user interface. (Something I don't like.)

- It requires you to write computer code to make it automate anything at all.

  o If you're not a programmer, move along, these are not the droids you're looking for.

- It does NOT have drag 'n drop orders, although it does show markers on the screen where you placed your orders.

- Be prepared to continually purchase new software updates.

There are many other trading platforms out there, but if they did not make my top three list, you can pretty much be sure they're not as good as these. (Each of these three have won Stocks 'n Commodities Annual Reader's Choice Award.) They're all three very popular.

All my trade examples, videos, and educational cheat sheets are created using the Track 'n Trade platform. If you want my help, I recommend you use the same platform I use.

 # Getting a Brokerage Account

A brokerage account is very similar to a bank checking account. You place your money in that account, and it's not at risk until you place an order; it also does not earn any interest. The growth of that account comes from your trading activity.

Track 'n Trade and eSignal are not brokerage firms, they are software developers who develop software for the financial industry, primarily for professional day traders.

When you install Track 'n Trade, you can open your Futures trading account directly through the software by clicking "Open Live Account," which will connect you to their recommended brokerage firms. (The firm I'm with is Gecko Financial Services, and is the Futures brokerage I recommend.)

Both Track 'n Trade and eSignal Stocks version use Tradier as their clearing firm, which is where I have my stock/options trading account, and how I trade my LEOs.

TradeStation on the other hand is a brokerage firm themselves, so you would open your trading account directly through TradeStation for both futures and stocks.

 # You Need a Trading Plan

You need to decide what type of trader you want to be. Ask yourself these questions.

- Are you a scalper?
  - ○ Very short trading time frame, seconds to minutes.
- Are you a day trader?
  - ○ Long(er) time frame than scalper, usually minutes to hours.
- Are you an investor?
  - ○ Long(er) term trades, weeks to months, to years.
- Are you an options trader?
  - ○ Options can be traded on any time frame, day trade, short-term, to long-term.
  - ○ Long term options, nine months or more are considered LEAPs. I call them LEOs, (Long-term Equity Opportunities.)

If you're reading this document, you're probably interested in Day Trading, and Scalping. That said, let me say, what I like to do is something I call Scalp 'n Trail, which is a combination of Scalping and Day Trading. Then, once I've made enough money doing that, I withdraw my profits and purchase LEOs in the Stock Market.

If you want to do what I do, you'll need Track 'n Trade Live Futures to Scalp 'n Trail, and Track 'n Trade LIVE Stocks to trade LEOs.

I never day trade stocks, I only Scalp 'n Trail futures. (Visit the home page to get my trading book.)

I like short term options in futures, but like to buy LEOs in the stock market.

 # You Need Education

The best education you can get is to download and install Track 'n Trade Live Stocks & Futures and start practicing in the live Demo Account(s).

The demo account is free for the first two weeks, and then it's included when you purchase the software and subscribe to your live data feed. This way you can continue to practice before committing real money to the market.

- We teach a number of streamlined online courses, you can <u>find them listed here</u>.

Once you have the software, you'll need to learn two things:

You'll need to learn how to use the Track 'n Trade software. You'll need to watch the "How To" videos in the help menu. There's going to be a learning curve, much less of a learning curve with Track 'n Trade than with any other software. Track 'n Trade is the easiest to learn.

Even though you have the software, you still need some step by step guidance on how to get started trading. This is the book you need for that. (Once you read this book, you will of course want to continue expanding your knowledge by reading many more books as well.)

I regret nothing in life but the things I have not done.

- Coco Chanel

Rule 1

Elliott Wave Theory
Why is Elliott Wave Important?

Lan Turner's Crash Course In Trading

Stocks * Futures * Forex

Introduction to Elliott Wave
Step 1: Count, What do we count?

Elliott Wave theory is a popular technical analysis method used by traders to identify and analyze market trends and patterns. Developed by Ralph Nelson Elliott in the 1930s, the theory suggests that market prices move in repetitive waves that can be identified and used to make informed trading decisions.

According to Elliott Wave theory, market prices move in a series of five waves in the direction of the trend, followed by three waves in the opposite direction, forming a complete cycle. The five waves in the direction of the trend are known as "impulse waves," while the three waves in the opposite direction are known as "corrective waves."

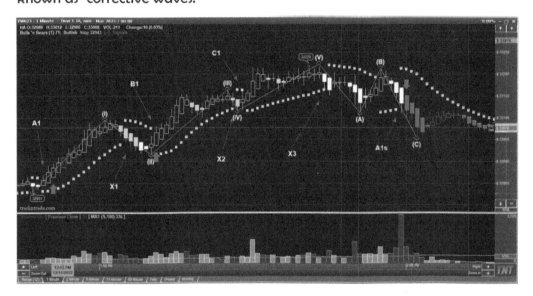

Elliott Waves have three major drives, A1, B1, C1, followed by two counter drives A-B-C.

Why do we see this recurring pattern so often? Because large banks and hedge funds make this happen through what's known as the Wyckoff Theory. Something we'll discuss in further chapters.

Traders who use Elliott Wave theory look for specific patterns and structures in the market to identify the stages of the wave cycle and make predictions about future market movements. By analyzing the size, shape, and duration of the waves, traders can make educated guesses about the likelihood of a trend continuing or reversing.

One of the key principles of Elliott Wave theory is the idea that markets move in cycles, with each cycle being a reflection of the collective psychology of market participants. According to the theory, market participants move through a series of emotions, from fear and pessimism at market bottoms to greed and optimism at market tops. These emotional swings, in turn, drive the cyclical nature of market movements.

Elliott Wave theory is a complex and nuanced approach to technical analysis, and it requires a deep understanding of market trends and patterns to be effective. It is important for traders to carefully study and understand the theory before attempting to use it in their trading strategies.

Overall, Elliott Wave theory is a powerful tool for traders looking to identify and analyze market trends and patterns. By understanding the underlying principles of the theory and learning how to identify and analyze wave patterns, traders can make informed decisions and potentially improve their trading results.

Trading Signals and Setups
What is an Elliott Wave?

An Elliott Wave is nothing more than two overlapping ABCD patterns. Higher highs and higher lows, which is the foundational keystone to all trading patterns, signals and setups. (Go back and review our diagram of a bull market and bear market, can you identify the Elliott Wave patterns in each?)

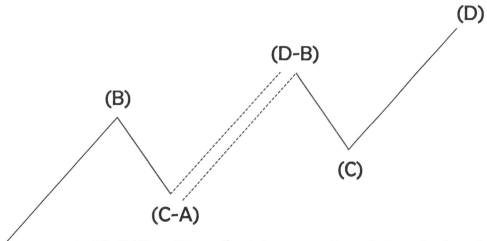

In Elliott Wave theory, fractals are a pattern that can be found within the larger Elliott Wave structure. A fractal is a pattern that is self-similar, meaning that it can be divided into smaller parts that are similar to the whole.

In the context of Elliott Wave theory, a fractal is a sequence of five waves that exhibits the same pattern as the larger Elliott Wave structure. In other words, the five-wave pattern of a fractal is similar to the five-wave pattern of the larger Elliott Wave structure.

Elliott Waves are "fractal," which means large Elliott Wave patterns are made up of smaller Elliott Wave patterns; we count Elliott Waves like this.

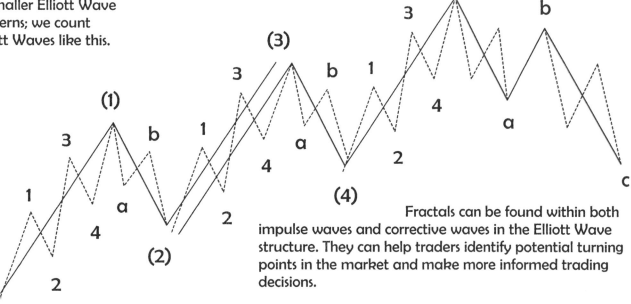

Fractals can be found within both impulse waves and corrective waves in the Elliott Wave structure. They can help traders identify potential turning points in the market and make more informed trading decisions.

For example, if a trader is looking at a chart and sees a five-wave pattern that looks like an impulse wave, they may consider this a bullish sign and look for opportunities to buy. On the other hand, if the same trader sees a five-wave pattern that looks like a corrective wave, they may consider this a bearish sign and look for opportunities to sell.

Trading Signals and Setups
What is an Elliott Wave?

When we count the waves of the Elliott Wave, we count as outlined in the diagram below.

It's important to remember, that we never trade the pull-back, or counter trend, we only trade with the trend; only trade from X to 1, 2 to 3, and 4 to 5. Never short, or try and trade 1 to 2, or 3 to 4.

A continuation of the Elliott Wave pattern is the ABC retracement back from the five (5) point; taking a short position off the 5th bullish wave is a very popular strategy. (We anticipate the market falling back to the four (4) point, or half of the overall three drive pattern.

Each long(er) term Elliot Wave pattern is created from smaller waves within each leg. Elliott Wave patterns can be found on every time frame, from minute charts, to daily, weekly and even monthly charts. (Day traders, and scalpers will trade Micro Elliott Waves, tiny moves on a one minute chart.)

I prefer the method of identifying the pattern on a long(er) term chart, and then applying our entry strategies on a short(er) time frame chart. This is known as a top down approach.

Depending on which time frame you intend to execute your trade on, for example, you may trade on a one minute chart, therefore your 'long-term' view would be a five (5) minute or maybe fifteen (15) minute chart.

Once the trade is executed on the short term time frame, and stops have been brought to break-even, the prudent trader may choose to move out to a long(er) term chart to continue execution of the trade.

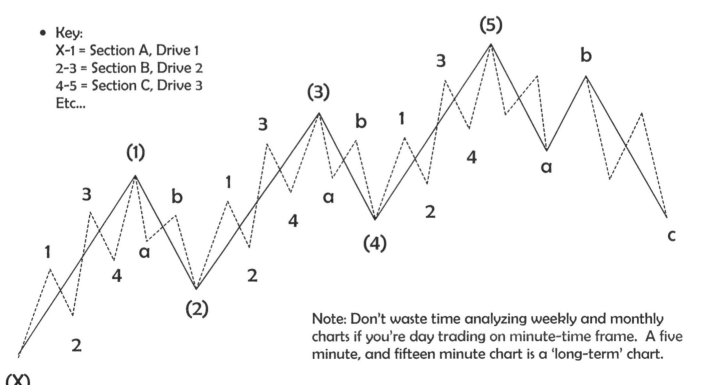

- Key:
  X-1 = Section A, Drive 1
  2-3 = Section B, Drive 2
  4-5 = Section C, Drive 3
  Etc...

Note: Don't waste time analyzing weekly and monthly charts if you're day trading on minute-time frame. A five minute, and fifteen minute chart is a 'long-term' chart.

Elliott Wave Rules & Regulations
Rules of the Road.

Now, Ralph asserted (his full name is Ralph Elliott), Ralph asserted that markets move in wave patterns, and that markets generally, statistically speaking, move through a series of higher highs, and higher lows up to the FIFTH wave, then they turn around and rebound back down through the A-B-C retracement, or counter trend wave pattern.

Now, I'll add, this does not mean that markets cannot go to the 6th, 7th, 8th or higher wave counts, they certainly can, and often times do, and it also does not mean that markets can't stop at the third wave, which they also very often do. Remember, the fifth wave, or third drive is the average.

Ralph's assertion was that markets make three distinct drives to the fifth point. Drive 1: X-1, Drive 2: 2-3, and Drive 3: 4-5 (You'll often hear me refer to this as the 'three drives to the top,' pattern.) Higher highs and high lows; remember, everything we're learning here can be turned upside down and counted from top down, rather than from bottom up.

Basic Elliott Wave Rules:

1. Rule 1:   Point 2 must remain higher than X.

2. Rule 2:   Point 3 must be higher than Point 1.

3. Rule 3:   Point 4 should stay above Point 2, but sometimes it's allowed to fall below Point 2, but cannot fall below X. (I know, I know, weird rule, but that's what Ralph allowed for, seems to be the one rule that breaks all the other rules.)

4. Rule 4:   Point 5 must be higher than Point 3

5. Rule 5:   Point B must be lower than Point 5

6. Rule 6:   Point C must be lower than Point A

7. Rule 7:   We like to see Point 4 stay above Point 1, and Point a above Point 3.

Establishing a new X (beginning) point is where most traders struggle. Use this rule of thumb; when Day Trading, start the new A1, X Point setup with the first signal after the morning bell.

You can re-establish a new A1, or X Point after any major pull back against the major trend as indicated by the Bulls 'n Bears indicator; a pull back into red if bullish, or a rebound into green if bearish.

We should also start looking for a rebound at the 50% to 61.8% Fibonacci levels, which if we look close at our count, should be an X2-A1; if that fails, then we would look for a new rebound at the bull fifth wave extension, which would be X3-A1. (Which will be discussed in detail during Rule 1.)

Long-term Point of View

As exampled in previous pages, an Elliott Wave is simply two ABCD patterns in a row, combined we see three distinct sections of the pattern; A Section, B Section, and C Section.

In a "perfect world" we would see three buying opportunities within each section of the Elliott Wave, of course we rarely have a perfect world when it comes to the markets and trading, therefore making adjustments to this pattern is a constant process.

It's not uncommon to see patterns with more than three buying opportunities within each leg, for example, you could see B4, B5 in the second leg, while only seeing C2 in the third leg.

It's also possible to see a section D, with D1, D2, and D3, or an E section with E1, E2, and E3, but D and E sections are rare, and we, as small speculators usually avoid trying to establish new entry positions in D, and E sections due to their low probability of success. Of course, if we're already in the market from an initial entry from one of the previous sections, A through C, we certainly will continue to hold our positions and practice solid risk management strategies to take advantage of rising markets and taking profits on market failure.

This is the primary skill you need to learn, learn to count, if you can't properly count the market signals as exampled here, you're not ready to trade.

Practice doing this in a real-live market as prices progress through price and time, it's easy in hindsight, not so easy on the fly, but will soon becomes second nature.

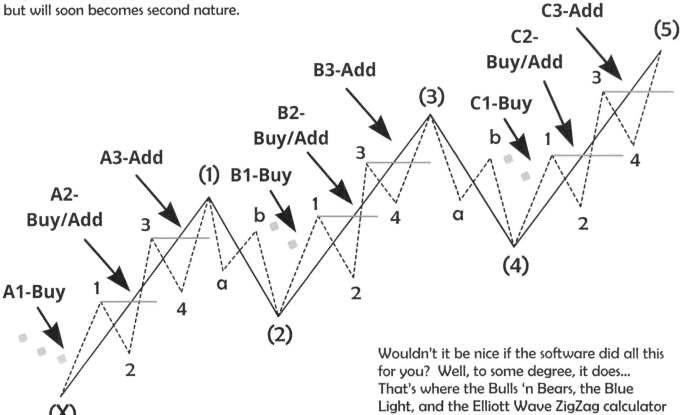

Wouldn't it be nice if the software did all this for you? Well, to some degree, it does... That's where the Bulls 'n Bears, the Blue Light, and the Elliott Wave ZigZag calculator come to the rescue.

In summary, Fibonacci numbers and the Elliott Wave theory are two popular tools used by traders to identify and analyze market trends and patterns. Fibonacci numbers are a sequence of numbers that is commonly used to identify potential levels of support and resistance in the market, while the Elliott Wave theory suggests that market prices move in repetitive waves that can be identified and used to make informed trading decisions. While these tools can be used separately, they can also be used together to provide a more comprehensive view of the market and help traders make informed decisions.

Fibonacci numbers and the Elliott Wave theory are two popular tools used by traders to identify and analyze market trends and patterns. While these tools are often used separately, they can also work hand in hand to provide a more comprehensive view of the market.

Fibonacci numbers are a sequence of numbers that is commonly used in technical analysis to identify potential support and resistance levels in the market. The sequence starts with 0 and 1, and each subsequent number is the sum of the two previous numbers (0, 1, 1, 2, 3, 5, 8, 13, etc.). These numbers can be found in a variety of natural phenomena, including the number of petals on flowers and the arrangement of branches on trees.

In the context of trading, Fibonacci numbers are often used to identify potential levels of support and resistance by dividing the vertical distance between two points on a chart by a Fibonacci ratio. The most commonly used Fibonacci ratios are 61.8%, 50%, and 38.2%. These ratios are derived from the Fibonacci sequence and are believed to indicate potential areas where the market may reverse direction.

Elliott Wave theory is a technical analysis method that was developed by Ralph Nelson Elliott in the 1930s. It suggests that market prices move in repetitive waves that can be identified and used to make informed trading decisions. According to the theory, market prices move in a series of five waves in the direction of the trend, followed by three waves in the opposite direction, forming a complete cycle.

One of the key principles of Elliott Wave theory is the idea that markets move in cycles, with each cycle being a reflection of the collective psychology of market participants. By analyzing the size, shape, and duration of the waves, traders can make educated guesses about the likelihood of a trend continuing or reversing.

While Fibonacci numbers and the Elliott Wave theory can be used separately, they can also be used together to provide a more comprehensive view of the market. For example, a trader may use Fibonacci levels to identify potential support and resistance levels and then use the Elliott Wave theory to confirm whether the market is likely to continue in its current direction or reverse.

Overall, Fibonacci numbers and the Elliott Wave theory are powerful tools that can be used separately or in combination to help traders identify and analyze market trends and patterns. By understanding these tools and how to use them effectively, traders can make informed decisions and potentially improve their trading results.

The Bulls 'n Bears
What is the Bulls 'n Bears Indicator?

This is a tough section to teach, because I need to teach you about Fibonacci and Elliott Wave before you can understand the Bulls 'n Bears Indicator, but I can't teach you the fundamental principles of Fibonacci and Elliott Wave without the Bulls 'n Bears Indicator. So how's that for a solid Catch 22? (This is why it's important to read this book six times.)

> I have to start somewhere, so we're going to start with an overview of the Bulls 'n Bears Indicator first, then I'll fill in the blanks as we delve deeper into these tool as we move through the rest of the material.

The Bulls 'n Bears is the fundamental foundation of everything we're going to be discussing, it is the concrete of our entire trading strategy.

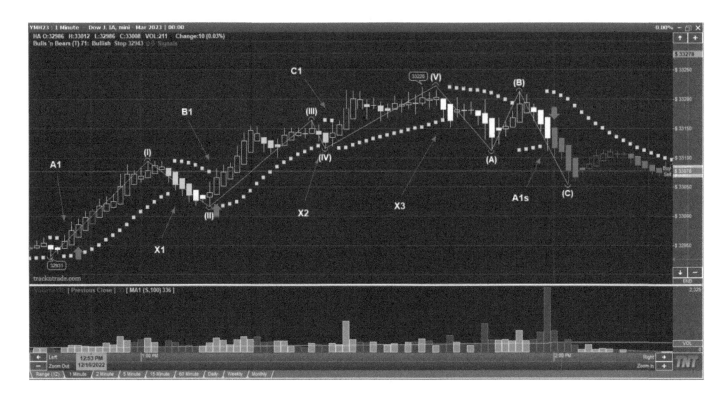

Turning on the Bulls 'n Bears indicator color codes the market, it's like turning the lights on in a dark room, I don't know how anyone can trade without it. (These are your cheat codes.)

In this example, the Bulls 'n Bears indicator is what's turning the price bars red, yellow and green; red for bearish, yellow for neutral, and green for bullish.

The yellow, or neutral bars are really the key to understanding the Bulls 'n Bears indicator; yellow bars represent the neutral zone between a bullish trend, indicated in green, and a bearish trend, indicated in red.

The neutral, or yellow zone is what we call the Fibonacci Sweet Spot, (covered in Rule 2). And, the red arrows indicate that the market is changing from neutral to bullish, or from neutral to bearish; knowing this is key.

The Bulls 'n Bears Blue Light System

What is the Bulls 'n Bears Blue Light System? The Blue lights are mathematically calculated trend lines, again, more cheat codes to the market. The Blue Lights tell us where to draw our trend lines, and where each leg of the Elliott Wave patterns starts and ends.

Optimally, we want the market to cross over our hard, hand drawn trend lines at the same point as it crosses the Blue Dots. It's these crossover points, or the breaking of a trend lines, that indicates a trend reversal and is considered a decision point for entry or exit.

When we combine the Bulls 'n Bears Red, Green and Yellow bar system with the Blue Lights, we have a complete 1-2-3 knock-out-punch, making almost all other indicators secondary, or basically worthless, since indicators are trying to just show you these exact same turning points. (You can stop hunting for that holy grail of indicators, because now you have the cheat codes.) Also notice, in a perfect setup, the entire three drive Elliott Wave pattern happens between the Bulls 'n Bears arrows. (It's also not uncommon to see yellow bars between each individual (counter-trend) drive, we call these dip trade opportunities.

Elliott Wave Section A (Drive 1) starts at the Blue Light crossover labeled A1

Elliott Wave Section B (Drive 2) starts at the Blue Light crossover labeled B1

Elliott Wave Section C (Drive 3) starts at the Blue Light crossover labeled C1

X3 is where we anticipate a complete trend reversal from Bullish to Bearish.

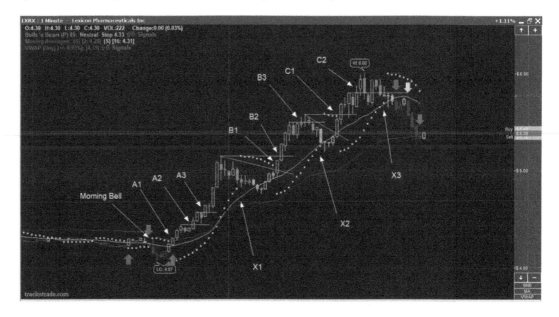

In upcoming chapters, we'll be learning more about how to use Fibonacci and Elliott Wave market structure to help us define our risk vs. reward ratios and goals.

Using these points along the trend are where we can make predictions of where markets will be in price and time, and this is how we calculate our risk vs. reward ratios, as well as determine additional entry and exit strategies. This is powerful stuff when trading options in particular, where it's important to calculate the amount of intrinsic value we need.

We have other tools to help with these calculations, but the Bulls 'n Bears is our primary tool.

Trading Signals and Setups
Leg one of the Elliott Wave; a close-up look.

Leg one would be identified by using letters A1 - A2 - A3 (Sometimes A4 - A5, etc..)

A1 is the first break of the first 'Bullish' Blue Light crossover.

- This leg is a reversal pattern from a bearish formation, often seen as a 123 bottom formation, or head and shoulders formation; it is sometimes difficult to identify, and is often times missed. We usually find this first break-out pattern on the opening bell, or first part of the day. (When looking at intra-day time frames.) or, the trend low on long(er) term charts. (Watch for Bulls 'n Bears arrows to indicate the start of a new trend; I call this the reset.)

- This is the first leg of the overall long(er) term bullish Elliott Wave, and would be considered the first leg of the first ABCD pattern.

- A1 is our initial entry, if we get stopped out on A1, we can re-enter the market on A2. A2 and A3 patterns are generally considered "add-on" entry points or fractal chart patterns.

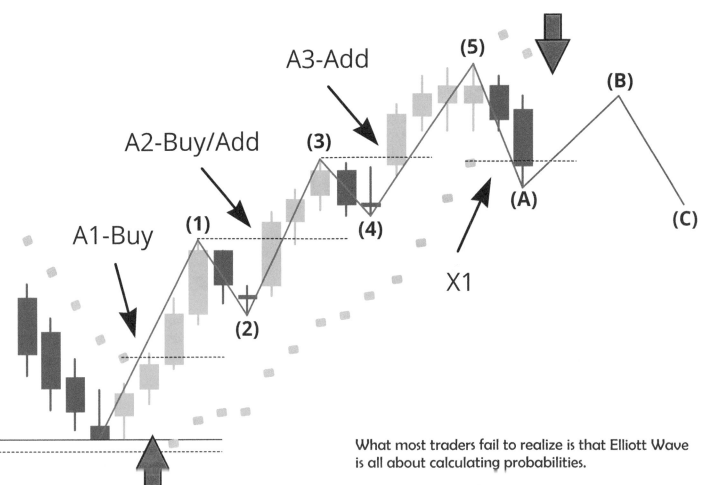

What most traders fail to realize is that Elliott Wave is all about calculating probabilities.

The lower the number, both numeric as well as alphanumerical the better, resulting in a higher probability of success.

Trading Signals and Setups
Mathematical Elliott Wave Models

There are several overlay indicators that can help in identifying Elliott Wave patterns. My favorite is the Track 'n Trade Bulls 'n Bears Blue Light System, the other is the Parabolic Stop and Reverse or PSAR indicator; both of which were written by Welles Wilder, along with the ATR, another favorite.

Each leg of the Elliott Wave is defined by a set of trailing dots. (Blue in the case of the Bulls 'n Bears, red in the case of the PSAR, and yellow in the case of the ATR; within the Track 'n Trade platform.) The PSAR is more aggressive whereas the Blue Lights are usually less so, and the ATR even less so again.

We generally see a 'long' set of dots, which identifies the trend, followed by a short set of dots, which identifies the counter trend.

As trend traders, we want to enter the market at the bottom of, or pull back of the counter-trend, in an attempt to go long the trend, or next 'long-set-of-dots." Drives 1, 2, & 3.

It's common to see three long sets of dots in a row, which identify the three legs, or drives of the Elliott Wave.

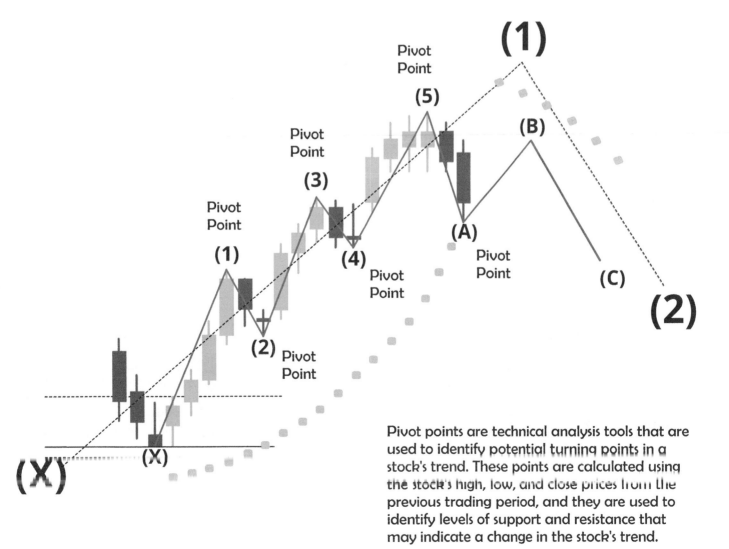

Pivot points are technical analysis tools that are used to identify potential turning points in a stock's trend. These points are calculated using the stock's high, low, and close prices from the previous trading period, and they are used to identify levels of support and resistance that may indicate a change in the stock's trend.

Mathematically Calculated Trend Lines

In my opinion, the trend line is the single most important setup and trigger we have in trading. All recurring price patterns are designed around the simple trend line, while all technical triggers for entry are the breaking of a trend.

My strategy revolves around drawing trend lines in relation to the Bulls 'n Bears Blue Light, (Use PSAR as a substitute if you don't have the Bulls 'n Bears Blue Light system.) I want the hard, or natural trend line of the market to match as closely as possible to the crossover of the Blue Light, the closer the better. Here's a couple of examples.

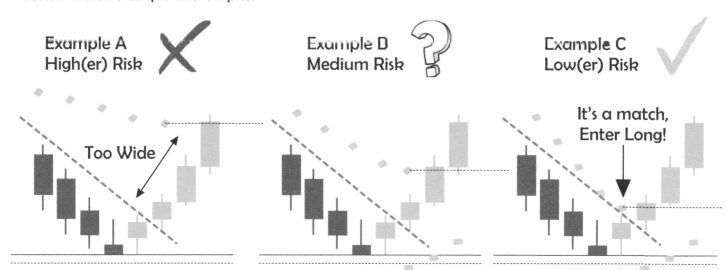

The quality of a signal can be gauged by how far apart those two corresponding trend line tools are one from the other. If there is a large gap between the hard trend line, and the mathematical trend line, then I'm less likely to take the trade, if they match one-for-one, that's where I'm likely to take a larger position size, or risk.

Using the Speed Fan tool (I call this my Spider Web), can better help us see entry signals. The first at the natural crossover of the breaking of the counter trend, (I), or above the first yellow, neutral bar (II), also a Dip Trade, or crossing the Blue Light or PSAR, (III), the horizontal breaking of the previous high, (IV). (Each one is considered a valid signal.)

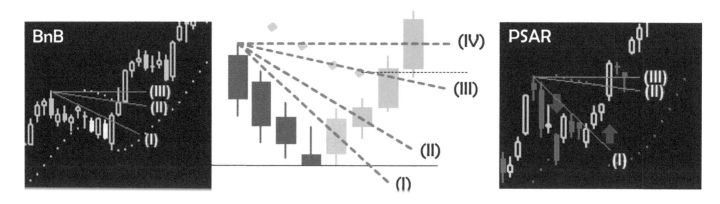

* Sometimes we use four lines, sometimes we use three, sometimes two, it depends on the trend of the market. (Three is most common.)

Trading Signals and Setups Dip Trades (Buy the Dip!)

What is a "dip trade?" Buying the micro-pull-back between numbers 1 and 2, and 3 and 4, is referred to as buying the dip.

Buying the dip looks easier than it is.

Buying the 2 point, and the 4 point of a trend is difficult, often referred to as catching a falling knife. If done properly, which is a relative term, it can add additional profits to one's trade, but it comes with a much greater risk of loss. What if the market never does rally once again and just continues to fall? (This is where we sometimes execute The Flea Flicker.)

The trick to this strategy is to not try and catch the absolute bottom, or to guess where the bottom is, but to anticipate a rise in price above the first price bar to break a new high.

We use several key tools and strategies to help us with this, one is the Speed Fan, seen here labeled **i**, and **ii**, (For fun, you'll hear me refer to the speed fan lines as my spider web, since that's what it looks like to me, you'll see it later examples exactly what I mean.)

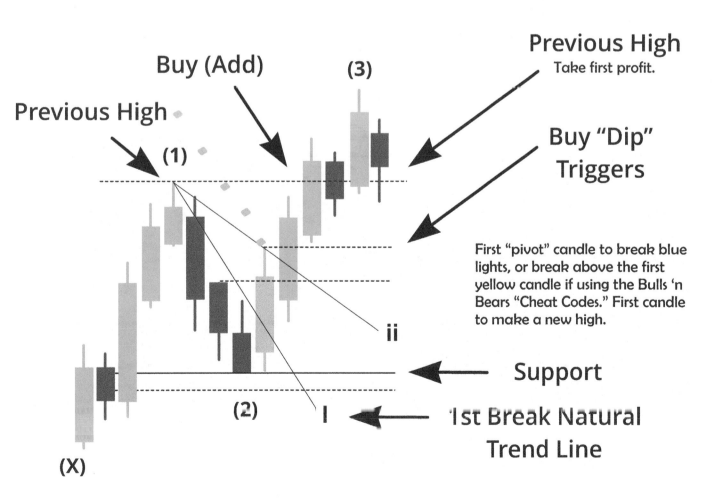

Previous High

Buy (Add)

(3)

Previous High
Take first profit.

Previous High

(1)

Buy "Dip" Triggers

ii

First "pivot" candle to break blue lights, or break above the first yellow candle if using the Bulls 'n Bears "Cheat Codes." First candle to make a new high.

Support

(2)   I   1st Break Natural Trend Line

(X)

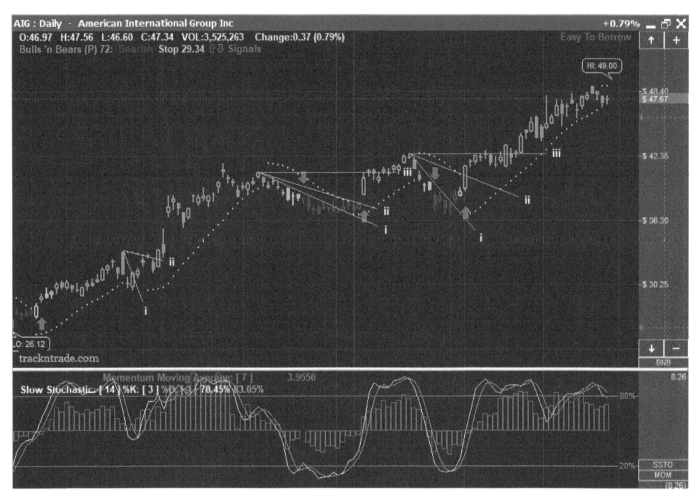

Example of natural pull backs against the prevailing trend, The breaking of the natural trend line, followed by the breaking of the Blue Lights, then the breaking of the previous high.

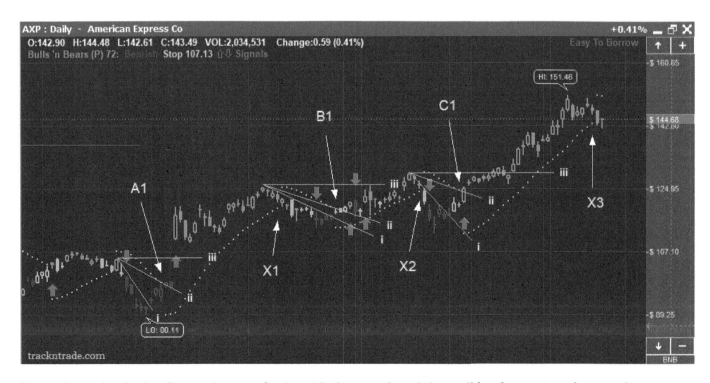

Notice how the A1, B1, C1 correlate perfectly with the trend and the pull backs against the trend.

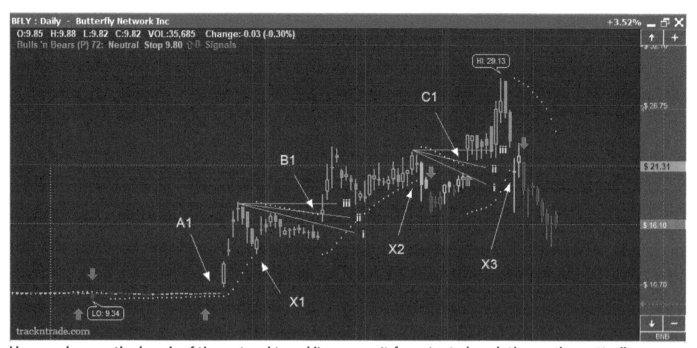

You can buy on the break of the natural trend line, or wait for price to break the mathematically calculated trend line, the Blue Light system.

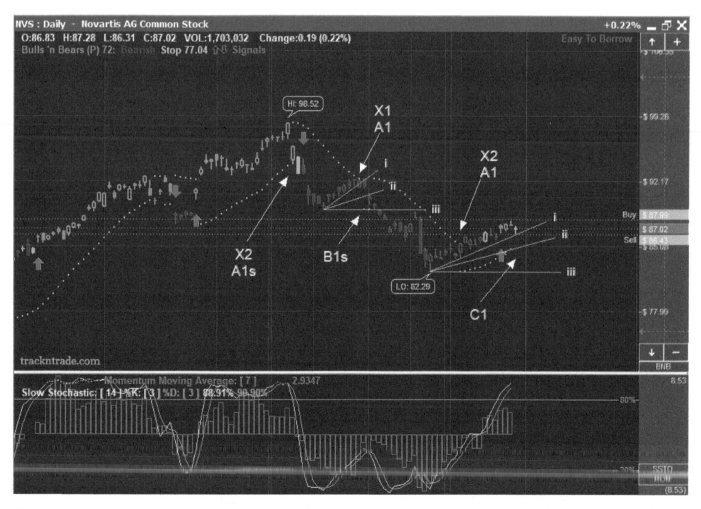

These strategies work well for going long, and in fact, they may work even better when going short. I personally prefer shorting the market to taking it long, as markets seem to fall faster than they rise.

Gaging Entry Signal Quality.

Most new traders never consider the quality of the entry signal they're taking, in their minds, a buy signal is a buy signal, and they never take into consideration the idea that one signal might have a higher probability of success than another.

In this example, you can see how I rank and gauge my entry signals by quality and grade.

Some signals have a higher probability of success than other signals, and some high probability signal have high, medium and low quality of the entry set-up, therefore we don't consider each entry signal equal one to the other.

For example, we might put 1000 shares, or maybe three to five futures contract on an A1 signal, while only putting 100 shares, or a single futures contract on a C3 signal. Both signals are buy signals and fall within our parameters for entry, but the A1 signal warrants a much higher share size due to the fact that we have experienced a much higher level of success when trading this signal.

I've created numerous iterations of my signal grading scale and will surely continue to make changes in the future, feel free to use my signals and grades as a template, and make changes for your own purposes as you perfect your personal trading plan, style, and strategy.

A Drive Trigger Definitions

Ai   =   Initial crossover, breaking of the initial hard trend line; consider starting The Flea Flicker.

Aii   =   Potential Dip Trade entry; breaking above the first yellow, BnB bars.

A1   =   First set of Blue Dots/Lights after a market trend reversal (Possibly an X3) The A1 setup is usually the best setup for a new position, especially when trading options, but it's also the most overlooked or missed signal, since it is the first entry signal for a new trend. (Remember, premature breakouts are often false breakouts.)

Wait for the signal, (often times accompanied by the Bulls 'n Bears arrow), don't try to preempt it, computerized systems only take the signal, and you need them to join the trade, which is what will help move the market higher; computers don't jump in early, humans do.

We usually find this signal shortly before the morning bell in futures, and shortly after the morning bell in stocks. It's obviously much easier to identify the A1 'after-the-fact,' therefore we can use it as a key setup for identifying the next A2, A3, or B1 setups. (If a market is going to break higher, it will do it at the signal.)

A-2   =   This setup is a break above the first micro-pull back, or first fractal Elliott Wave pattern, we often refer to this as a 'pivot point.' If you miss the A1 entry, this is usually a great place to enter the market for the first time, otherwise, use it to add onto your already long A1 entry.

A-3 = This is a break above the second micro-pull back, (pivot point) or second fractal wave. If you got stopped out, this is a good re-entry location, or add onto an already existing position. Be careful, if using this as a new entry, as it is a low probability entry, since the market is possibly approaching the apex of the first leg of our long-term Elliott Wave, and we'll be expecting our first counter trend shortly thereafter.

B Drive Trigger Definitions

Bi = Initial crossover, breaking of the initial hard trend line; consider starting The Flea Flicker.

Bii = Potential Dip Trade entry; breaking above the first yellow, BnB bars.

B1 = First short set of Blue Dots after the first long set of Blue Dots. This is usually my best and favorite entry point, as it's a new fresh crossover of the Blue Light system after the market has already proven it is in a strong new trend. We find this entry trigger on the second leg of the long term Elliott Wave pattern shortly after the first counter trend pull back.

B2 = This setup is a break above the second Section B micro pull back, (pivot point) or first fractal Elliott Wave pattern. If you miss the B1 entry, this is usually a great place to enter the market for the first time, otherwise, use it to add onto your already long A1, or B1 entry.

B3 = This is a break above the second micro-pull back, (pivot point) or second fractal wave. If you got stopped out, this is a good re-entry location, or add onto an already existing position. Be careful, if using this as a new entry, as it is a low probability entry, since the market is possibly approaching the apex of the second long-term Elliott Wave, and we'll be looking for the second Elliott Wave counter trend shortly thereafter.

C Drive Trigger Definitions

Ci = Initial crossover, breaking of the initial hard trend line; consider starting The Flea Flicker.

Cii = Potential Dip Trade entry; breaking above the first yellow, BnB bars.

C1 = Second short set of Blue Dots after the second long set of Blue Dots. We're now heading into the final stretch as we look for the market to make it's third and final drive, and apex at the peak of the 5th wave of the Elliott Wave. C1 is our first entry trigger into the third drive.

C2 = This setup is a break above the third Section C first micro pull back, (pivot point) or first fractal Elliott Wave pattern of the third drive. If you miss the C1 entry this is usually a great place to enter the market for the first time within the third drive, otherwise, add onto your already long A1, B1, or C1 entry.

C3 = This is a break above the second micro-pull back, (pivot point) or second fractal wave. If you got stopped out, this is a good re-entry location, or add onto an already existing position. Be careful, if using this as a new entry, as it is a low probability entry, since the market is approaching the apex of the third long-term Elliott Wave, and we'll be looking for a full 50% to 61.8% retracement of the overall total Elliott Wave three drive pattern soon. Warning, we do not want to be taking on big positions at this time.

Note: Just because we generally don't see market expansions beyond the third drive, does not mean that the market can't make a fourth D section drive, or even and E section drive, and beyond, it certainly can, but they are rare, and we as small speculators generally don't want to take on that additional risk.

If you choose to trade pattern break-outs, do so with your eyes wide open, realizing where you're at in the count, and make sure to label each pattern, setup, and trigger so you know your risk and probability for each trade; also remember, don't over-trade. If you're jumping in and out of the market at different locations other than these identified trigger points, you will be taking on additional risk unnecessarily.

I want to reemphasize, our goal is to enter at A1, take profits along the way, X1, X2, etc., with final exit at X3. (X3 is a great place to consider reversing course, and taking a short position.)

Important note:

Triangles, wedges, pennants are other recurring price patterns, such as head and shoulders can be observed in the markets. Triangles are formed when a security's price action forms a pattern that looks like a triangle, with the upper and lower trend lines converging. Pennants are similar to triangles, but are smaller in size and typically form over a shorter time frame. Both triangles and pennants can be either bullish or bearish, depending on the direction of the trend and the breakout of the pattern.

Elliott Wave theory maintains that these recurring price patterns, such as head and shoulders, wedges, triangles, and pennants, are all part of larger, more complex Elliott Wave patterns. By identifying and analyzing these patterns, traders can make more informed decisions about the market and potentially profit from price movements.

Trading Signals and Setups

Dip Trades

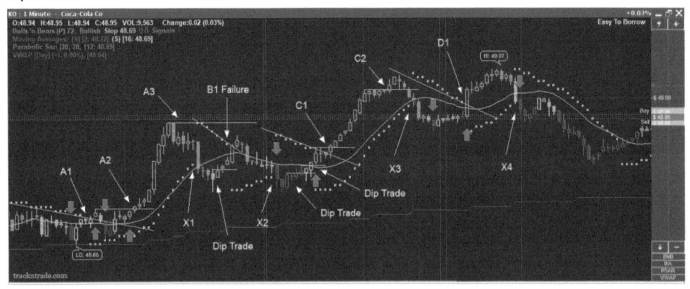

It is important to follow a trading plan to completion, even if it seems like the pattern has failed. Continuing to label the trend along the way can help traders stay on track and avoid losing track of their strategy. Some traders may feel that the market is moving too fast to make these notations, but it is important to do so in order to stay on track. If the market is moving too fast to make these notes, it may be a good idea to sit out that particular trade.

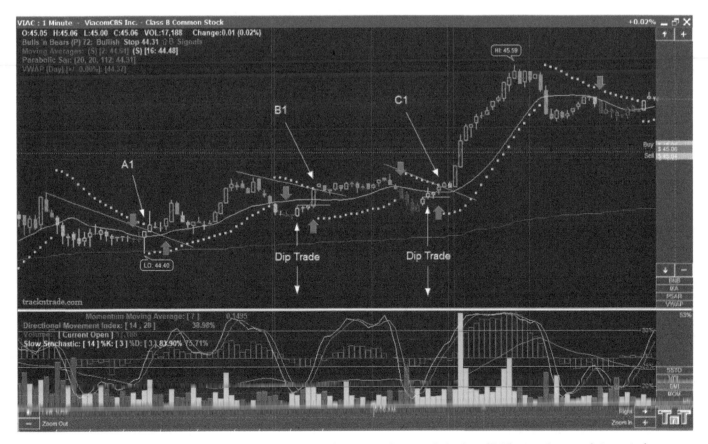

Oscillating indicators, such as Stochastics and the Relative Strength Index (RSI), can be useful tools for helping to identify dip trades, or opportunities to buy into a downtrend at potentially oversold levels.

X, X1, X2, and X3

Reversal Formations; what are reversal formations and how do we trade them?

A reversal formation is when a trend, for one reason or another, whether that's a fundamental reason, or strictly technical reason, changes and begins to trend in the opposite direction.

Trend reversals are major events. Think of a trend like this, "A trend in motion generally stays in motion." You've heard it said a million times, "The trend is your friend until it bends or ends." A trend reversal is a major market event, "It's a big deal!"

It's difficult for a market to turn, switch all it's momentum, and to begin trending in the apposing direction. I know what you're thinking, you're thinking, "If changing direction is so difficult, why does the market do it every time I get in?"

What we're talking about here is not whipsaw, or micro pull backs, what we're talking about is a clear and concise market trend reversal, where the majority of traders start taking short positions, rather than long positions; or visa-versa.

Within this pattern, we also have three primary points where we look for a complete trend reversal, we label them X1, X2, and X3; you'll notice that these are the rebound points, or counter trends within the overall long(er) term trend; the higher the X number the more likely the trend will experience a complete trend reversal.

I want to reemphasize, our goal is to enter at A1, take profits along the way, X1, X2, etc., with final exit at X3.

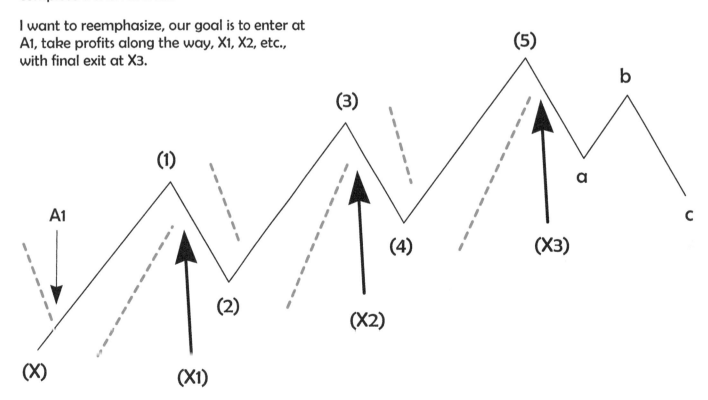

What are the probabilities?

Everything we do in trading is based on probabilities. As I said earlier, nobody knows where a markets going to be in price and time in the future, which is why we must count, measure, and project.

Using our methodology of counting and measuring, we know from past experience that lower numbers, both numerical as well as alphanumerical, have a higher probability of success, while higher letters & numbers have a lower probability of success.

Here's a quick reference guide to my Elliott Wave probabilities Count System.

A1, B1, C1: High(est) Probability
This is a great place to enter a new trading position, either shares, contracts or options. Obviously, A1 is better than B1, while B1 is better than C1.

A2, B2, C2: Medium Probability
This is a great place to enter a new trading position if we missed the first entry signal. Even better, this is a great place to add onto our already existing position.

A3, B3, C3: Low Probability
This is a great place to add on small share size to an already existing position, but not a great place to add a new position, as the trend often does not progress enough to move stops to above break even. (See my Pyramid Strategy, enter smaller and smaller shares up the scale.)

X1, X2, and X3. These are reversal formations, and where trends end, or start. If trading long, we will often call them X1-A1s, or X2-A1s, or X3-A1s (The 's' stands for Short), because each time a market breaks to the downside, creating an X1, X2, or X3, it has the potential of being a new bear trend; following the rules of Elliott Wave, theoretically, this should happen most often at X3-A1s.

If the trend ends at X3, the likelihood of it being a new A1s in the apposing direction (short) is a much higher probability than would be an X1-A1s, or X2-A1s. (When trading, we have to label both longs and shorts at the same time, as markets move through price and time, we do that like this, X1 represents the long count, while A1s represents the short count.) We don't label the long side with an "L", it's assumed, we only label the short signals with the letter "S".

> X1-A1s: Low Probability of a Reversal
> X2-A1s: Medium Probability of a Reversal
> X3-A1s: High Probability of a Reversal

Trading is a process of probabilities, which means that it involves making decisions based on the likelihood of a particular outcome occurring. This can be based on a variety of factors, such as technical analysis, fundamental analysis, market conditions, and the trader's own risk tolerance and trading strategy. In order to be successful, traders must be able to identify and analyze these probabilities in order to make informed decisions about when to enter and exit trades.

What are the probabilities?

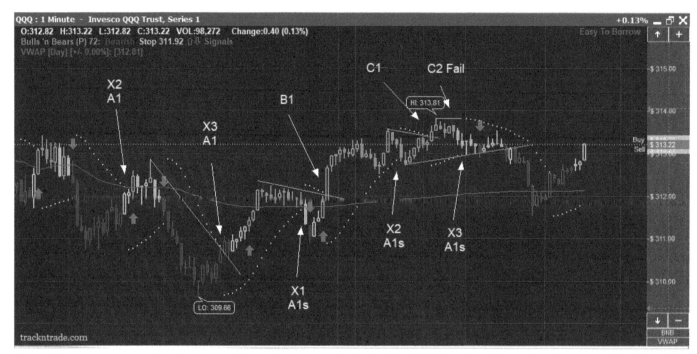

Trend lines are a popular tool used in technical analysis to identify the direction of a trend and to identify potential support and resistance levels. A trend line is drawn by connecting two or more points on a price chart, and it can be used to identify the slope of the trend and to forecast potential price movements.

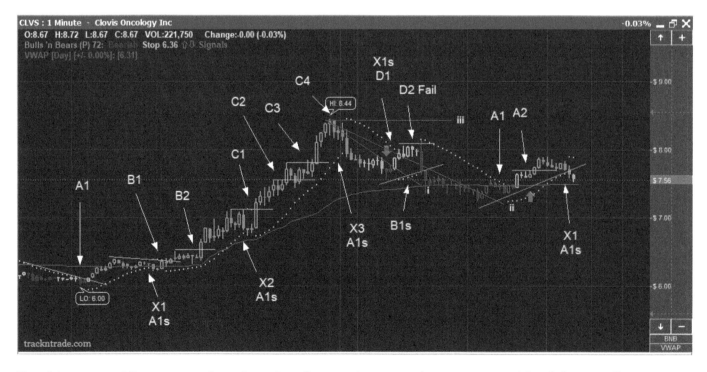

Breaking a trend line occurs when the price of a security or market moves outside of the trendline, indicating a potential change in the direction of the trend. This can be a bullish or bearish sign, depending on the direction of the trend and the direction of the breakout. For example, if a stock is in an uptrend and breaks above a resistance trend line, it may be a bullish sign and indicate further upside potential. On the other hand, if a stock is in a downtrend and breaks below a support trend line, it may be a bearish sign and indicate further downside potential.

What are the probabilities?

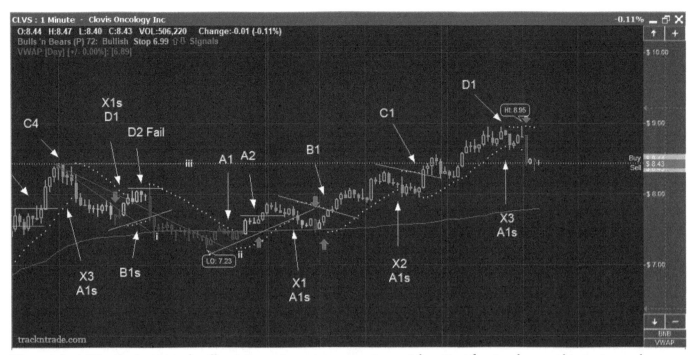

The probability that a trend will continue is an important consideration for traders and investors when making decisions about your positions. There are several factors that can influence the probability of a trend continuing, including market conditions, fundamental factors, and technical indicators.

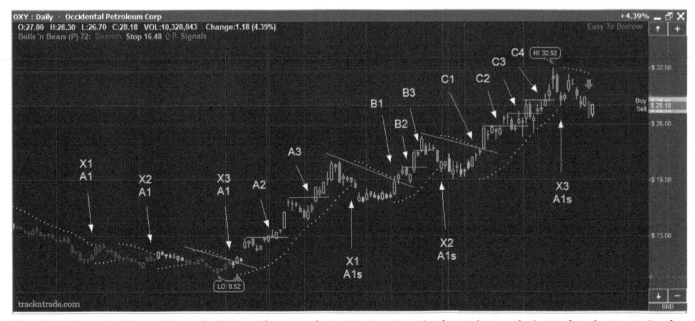

Another way to assess the probability of a trend continuing is to look at the underlying fundamentals of the market or security in question. Factors such as economic conditions, company financials, and industry trends can all influence the likelihood of a trend continuing.

Overall, it is important for traders to consider a variety of factors when evaluating the probability of a trend continuing, and to use this information in conjunction with your trading strategy and risk management plan. When day trading in particular, we need to pay close attention to the fundamental driving factors of the current market. This is generally done through government reports, which are the most reliable means of determining points throughout the day that a market might burst and run.

Trading Signals and Setups

X, X1, X2, and X3

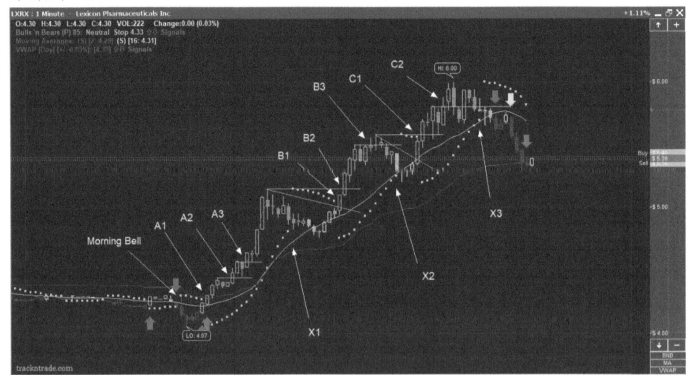

Notice how the entire three drive Elliott Wave occurred between the Bulls 'n Bears Red Arrows. Traders who are able to identify and capitalize on these single long drives through the trend can potentially achieve significant profits, as the market can continue moving in the direction of the trend for an extended period of time. However, it is important to note that these trends can also be volatile and prone to reversals, use caution when taking positions in volatile markets.

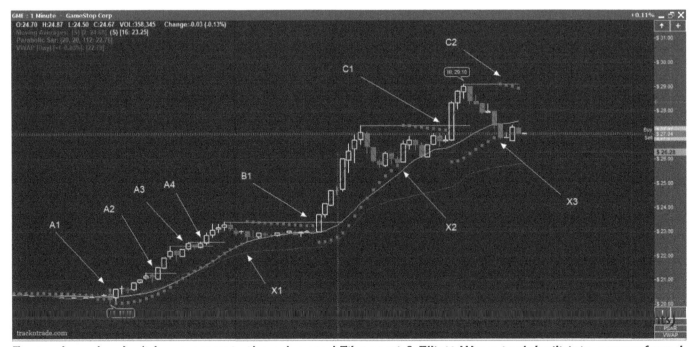

For traders who don't have access to the advanced Fibonacci & Elliott Wave tools built into our preferred trading platform (Track 'n Trade LIVE) then using the PSAR can be a decent substitute.

X, X1, and X2 Continued...

During an uptrend, X is our starting point, identifying the lowest point of the anticipated trend. Many times this point is not identified until after-the-fact, early identification along with catching a trade on it is difficult. If you're a day trader we simply anticipate X being the first low/high of the new day, prior to the breaking of the Blue Light, or PSAR; in a long(er) term trend, the lowest/highest point of a new trend once the trend has been confirmed via a reversal pattern such as a head and shoulders, or 123/abc formation.

The X1 and X2 Dip Trade.

X1 represents the first pull-back, or rebound of the overall trend, this pull back must break the Blue Light, or PSAR system, which gives us the setup for the next leg, or B1/C1 break. In a "perfect world," we expect the market to pull back far enough to produce Yellow Bars from the Bulls 'n Bears indicator, or a complete Candle to close below the price of the last Blue Light or PSAR. (Since, in theory, this is where you would have been stopped out, this is also your new target for re-entry on the X1, or X2 dip trade. (Do not try and Dip Trade X3).

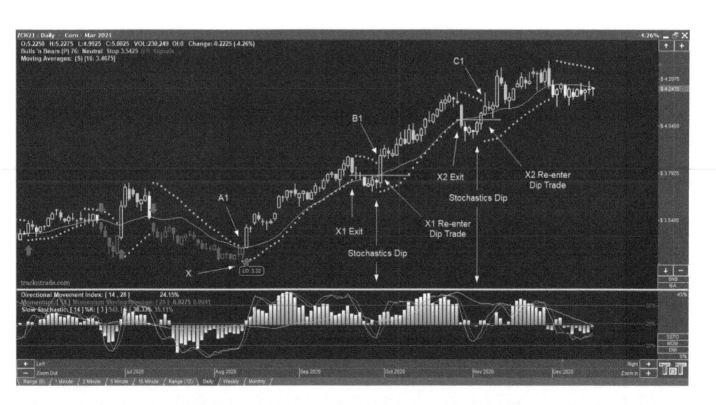

Be mindful, we don't see these opportunities with every pull back, sometimes they're either too shallow, too deep, or too long, or too short; watch just for the setup you like best.

It is important to be mindful of waiting for just the right setup when trading because taking unnecessary risks can lead to significant losses. By being patient and waiting for the right opportunity to arise, you can increase the likelihood of making a successful trade and minimize the risk of incurring significant losses.

Don't Chase the Elliott A1

What is the A1? The A1 is the very first breakout of a new trend, and often the most difficult point along the Elliott Wave to identify. This is why I'm constantly driving home the point that we often miss the A1, or first drive of the Elliott Wave.

Markets have a lot of false breakouts, or new A1's. A quick way to give up your holdings to someone else is to continually chase the A1 break-outs. Many traders constantly take every buy signal from their favorite indicator in an attempt to catch a new trend, only to have that break-out fail.

Trying to catch a narrow sideways channel breakout in anticipation of it being a new A1 drive can be devastating to your account. Experience several narrow channel false breakouts in a row, and you'll end up spending the rest of the day, or week, working to recover your losses. (Ask me how I know.)

The key here is NOT to trade during quite sideways markets in anticipation of a breakout and new trend. Don't do that! Wait, wait, wait. Be patient and watch for a strong A2, or even wait for the B1. Chasing breakouts (false breakouts) can be the death nail to a traders account.

Wait for a market to prove itself first. Before you enter, make sure it's already trending, moving, and shaking. You should have the feeling of FOMO, (Fear of missing out) because the market is moving through a beautiful A1 trend, and you missed it. That's what you want! Then, when the B1 comes along, you'll have a much higher probability of success.

We often say, A1 is the hors d'oeuvres, B1 is the meat and potatoes, while C1 is the desert. We're here for the meat and potatoes, let someone else have the hors d'oeuvres and desert. The fact is, new trends often fail.

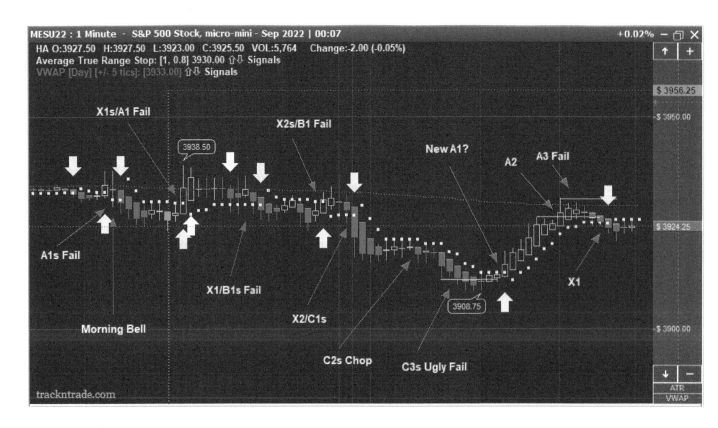

Only Trade X2 and/or X3 Patterns

Elliott Waves, comprised of two overlapping ABCD patterns, generally conclude at the X3 point along the trend. In weak markets, the trend will fail at X2 or possibly even at X1.

New traders struggling with the concept of Elliott Waves or during choppy markets might want to consider the strategy of only entering counter-trend trades at the X2 or X3. In previous discussions, we've primarily discussed entering the market only at A1, B1, and C1 along the trend with the expectation of a continuation. This discussion will provide a solid argument for only trading the X2 or X3 counter-trends.

It's common knowledge that markets fall faster than they rise; take the escalator up and the elevator down, as it's often said. (Traders bail out of markets, they don't bail in.) In this strategy, we only take short positions against the prevailing up trend at the highest probability areas of a trend reversal.

The probability that a market will make a reversal at X1 is low. The probability that it will reverse at X2 is medium and that the trend will likely experience a complete Fibonacci 50% to 61.8% reversal at X3 is high. (If you see X4, or X5, be mindful that these signals are weak. Any X above X3 is a warning sign that the markets are not playing fair or friendly; buyer beware.)

Taking only the highest probability trades at X2 and X3 is a solid trading strategy that could pay off in spades if you have the patience and discipline to map out the Elliott Wave pattern as they occur, then only enter on the highest probability moves. Here are several examples of where markets flushed at X2 & X3 and then retraced through the Fibonacci ruler, a common occurrence.

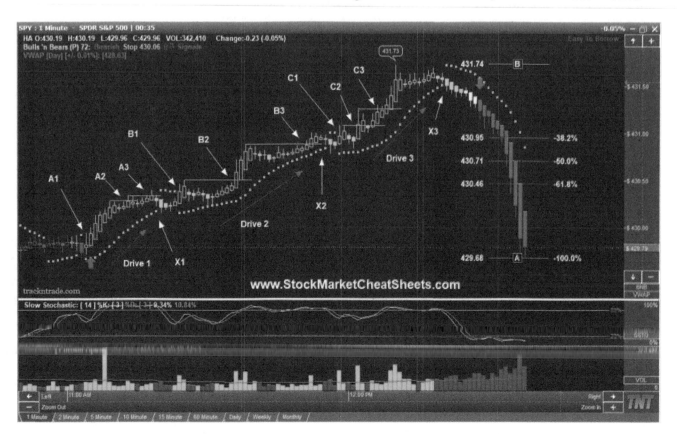

Trading only the X2 and/or X3 reversal points along the trend works hand-in-hand with our three strikes you're out risk management rules. Since this strategy only has three exit/entry points along a traditional Elliott Wave, it can significantly reduce the number of trade signals you receive and help eliminate confusion.

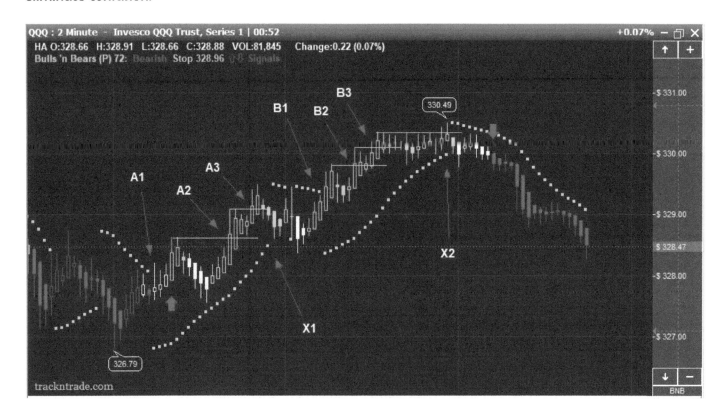

Using a strategy that only has a few defined entry and exit points, such as Elliott Wave, can be beneficial as it can significantly reduce the number of trade signals you receive, which can help to eliminate confusion and allow you to focus on the most high-probability opportunities.

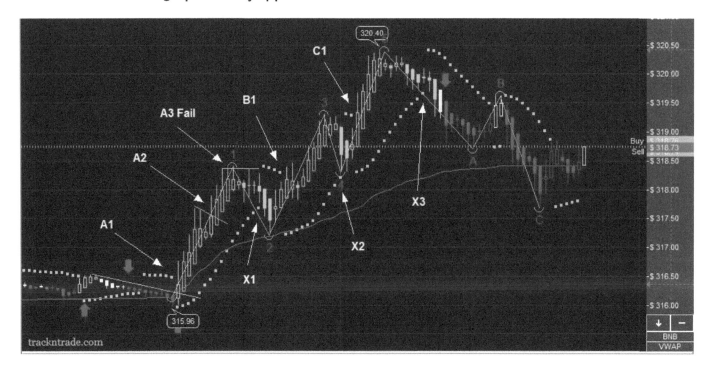

Key

This page is a summary, or key to our trading system signals, the probabilities, and a short description of possible strategy and expected outcome. Always remember, the higher the Alpha Numerical system, the lower the probability of a continuation of the trend.

Ai   Initial crossover, breaking of the initial hard trend line; Start Flea Flicker.
Aii   Dip Trade; breaking above the first yellow, BnB bars.
A1   Initial entry into a new Elliott A Wave, crossing the Blue Lights.
A2   First Pivot; enter if missed the A1 entry, else, add onto our initial position.
A3   Second Pivot, third entry, don't add new position, only small add, or quick scalp.

X1:   Exit Drive A, Stops on the hard trend line, and/or the Blue Light; this is also a potential support level of the next B Wave, Start Flea Flicker; low potential trend reversal; A1s.

Bi   Initial crossover, breaking of the initial hard trend line; Start Flea Flicker.
Bii   Dip Trade; breaking above the first yellow, BnB bars.
B1   Initial entry into a new Elliott B Wave, crossing the Blue Lights.
B2   First Pivot; enter if missed the B1 entry, else, add onto our initial position.
B3   Second Pivot, third entry, don't add new position, only small add, or quick scalp.

X2   Exit Drive B, Stops on the hard trend line, and/or the Blue Light; this is also a potential support level of the next C Wave, Start Flea Flicker; medium potential trend reversal; A1s.

Ci   Initial crossover, breaking of the initial hard trend line.
Cii   Dip Trade; breaking above the first yellow, BnB bars.
C1   Initial entry into a new Elliott C Wave, crossing the Blue Lights.
C2   First Pivot; enter if missed the C1 entry, else, add onto our initial position.
C3   Second Pivot, third entry, don't add new position, only small add, or quick scalp.

X3   Exit Drive C, multi-stop strategy on the hard trend line, and/or on the Blue Light; high probability of a trend reversal; A1s.

A1s,B1s,C1s: All the previous key setups can also be used to count bearish trends, we specify a bearish setup with a small letter "s", for short.

A4,A5,A6, B4,B5,B6, C4,C5,C6:   These Pivot Points can occur, but are rare. Trade them sparingly, possible add on to existing positions, or quick scalp.

D,E,F Elliott Wave Sections: These Waves can occur, but are very rare. (Low probability)

To reemphasize, our goal is to enter at A1, add-on at A2, and A3, Exit at X1. (Often times we miss A1, because we don't want to chase the A1's.) We then want to enter at B1, add-on at B2, and B3, Exit at X2. Then reenter at C1, add-on at C2, and C3, then exit all at X3, and consider taking a reversal position.

Dip Trades, don't forget the dip, (spider web) early entries can be taken at the natural breaking of the counter-trend pull-back trend as the first candle breaks a new high. Another entry can be taken at the breaking above the first yellow rebound candle, or at the crossing of the Blue Lights, (mathematical modeled trend line.)

Some traders will wait, and buy on a break above the previous high. (I'm not a fan of waiting that long. I usually want to be taking profits by that point, then adding into, or dollar cost averaging into my winning trade as the market breaks above the previous high.

Elliott Wave Key (Longs and Shorts)

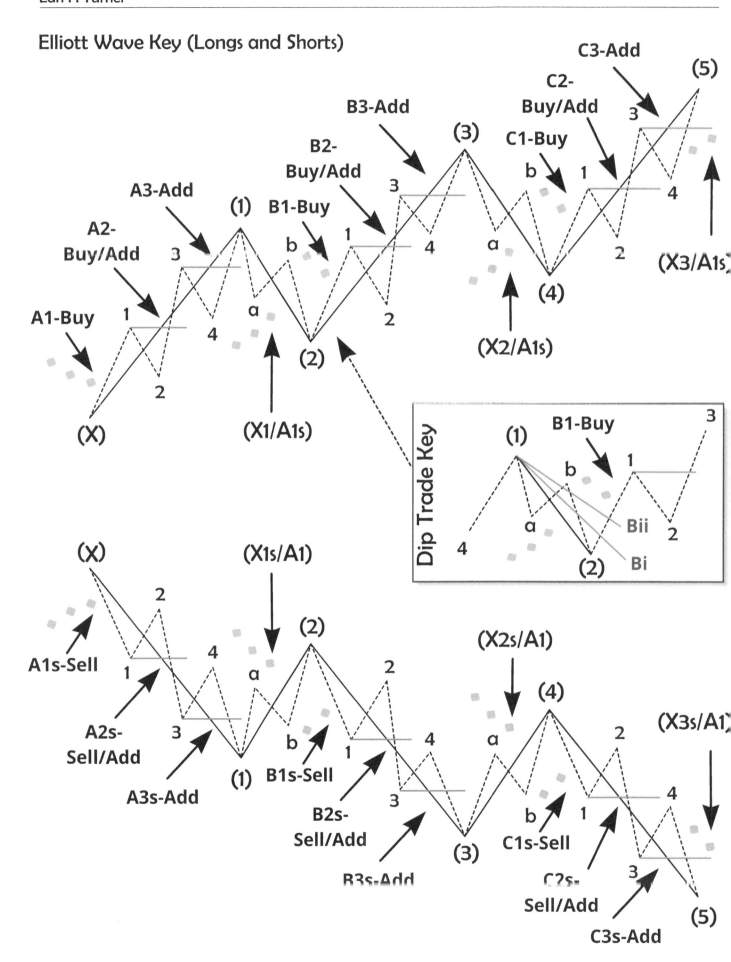

Rule 2

Fibonacci Ruler
Measure Elliott Waves Using Fibonacci

Lan Turner's Crash Course In Trading

Stocks * Futures * Forex

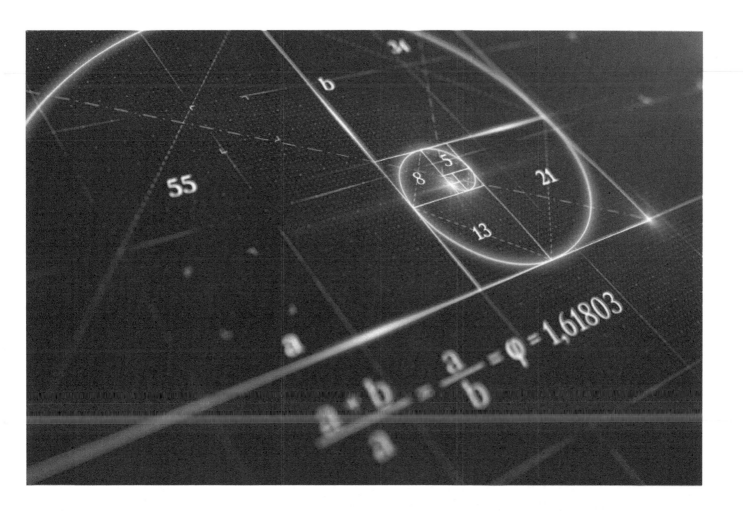

What is the Fibonacci Ruler?

The Fibonacci Ruler is just that, it's a measuring stick designed to measure the different ABCD legs of the Elliott Wave.

The Fibonacci Ruler is a tool used in technical analysis to measure the different drives of an Elliott Wave pattern. It can be used to measure the individual ABCD legs of the wave as well as the full move from top to bottom. The Fibonacci sequence is a well-known concept in the trading world and understanding it can be beneficial for traders.

Fibonacci is such a huge subject, that I couldn't begin to do it justice here, but just recognizing this one concept will help you tremendously.

Why Does Fibonacci Work?

Fibonacci works because people/traders make it work. Think of the market as a big machine, it's only job is to fill orders. The market does not know if when it fills your order whether you experience a gain or a loss, it doesn't know. All the market knows is that you placed an order at a specific price level, along with a bunch of other traders, and it's the job of the market to fill your order; therefore the market prices move to where there are the most orders waiting to be filled; Fibonacci is a reflection of those orders.

In summary, Trading with Fibonacci involves using multiple technical analysis tools based on the Fibonacci sequence to anticipate potential levels of support and resistance in the market to make more informed trading decisions for both entry and exit.

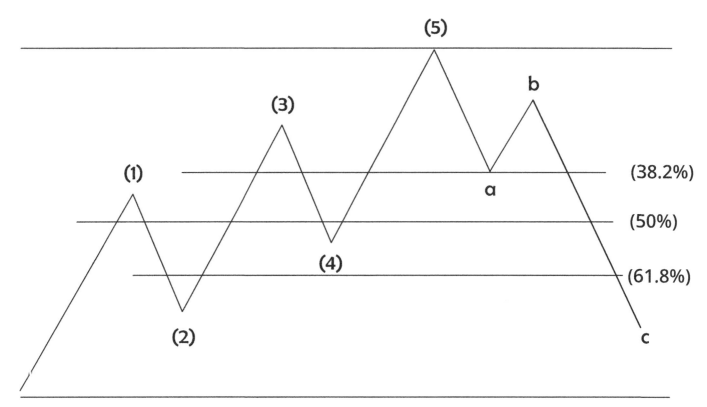

Why Does Fibonacci Work?

Think about a single day's trading action.

1. Morning bell rings. If there's some kind of fundamental catalyst, we see traders, "in the know," start to build positions, which causes the stock to rally on open, or sometimes even pre-market.

2. Once the market opens, more traders pile on, and our stock continues to rise.

3. Now the market is starting to heat up, so more traders pile on, alert systems begin to ring, and our stock starts to climb to the top of popular retail trader's favorite scanner lists.

4. More traders pile on causing a 'feeding frenzy' where more and more traders begin to pile on, and existing traders adding onto their positions.

5. 0% of traders are considered 'position traders,' sometimes called 'swing traders,' meaning they plan to hold their positions overnight for a long(er) term play. Only 20% of traders are day traders who aggressively jump in and out of markets throughout the day.

6. 80% of our traders, who got in on the opening volley of the stock, begin to move their stops to break-even. Lots and lots of stop orders are now starting to accumulate, pile up somewhere in the price range experienced during the first 30 minutes to hour of trading.

7. As market momentum begins to wane, and traders are no longer adding onto or getting into new positions, the market starts to lose momentum and slow down; no more orders up there anymore...

8. Where are all the orders now? What is our market filling machine supposed to do? Fill orders, right? Where are all the orders? Back down there...about half, or 61.8% behind the current price, back down where everyone moved all their stops to break even.

9. So, where does the market go? Back down, to do what? Fill as many orders as it can, which is at approximately 50% to 61.8% off today's highs.

10. You see, it's the previous (mornings) action of the market that determines the retracement levels and counter trends, measured by using the Fibonacci Ruler; we the traders determine where those points will be, by moving our stops to break even.

The levels of Fibonacci at 38.2%, 50%, and 61.8% are commonly used in technical analysis to identify potential levels of support and resistance in the market. These levels are based on the Fibonacci sequence, which is a series of numbers where each number is the sum of the previous two numbers (e.g., 0, 1, 1, 2, 3, 5, 8, 13, 21, etc.).

The Fibonacci levels of 38.2%, 50%, and 61.8% are derived from the Fibonacci sequence and are commonly used to identify potential areas where the market may change direction. For example, if the market is in an uptrend and reaches a resistance level near the 61.8% Fibonacci level, it may be a sign that the market is likely to reverse and head back down. Similarly, if the market is in a downtrend and reaches a support level near the 50% Fibonacci level, it may be a sign that the market is likely to reverse and head back up. These levels are not guaranteed to be accurate, but they can be useful as a way to anticipate potential areas of support and resistance in the market.

Fibonacci Ruler Continued...

The Fibonacci Ruler is most commonly used to measure the pull-back or retracement of the entire morning session move from top to bottom on an intra-day (minute) chart, or, it can be used to measure each individual leg of the Elliott Wave as exampled below.

In this chart, you can see how we've used the Fibonacci ruler to measure the X1, and X2 pull backs, once the market hits support at one of our Fibonacci levels, 38.2, 50, or 61.8, we anticipate a reversal. This is known as the "Fibonacci Sweet Spot."

*The Bulls 'n Bears Cheat Codes calculate the Fib Sweet Spot, and turns the price bars yellow.

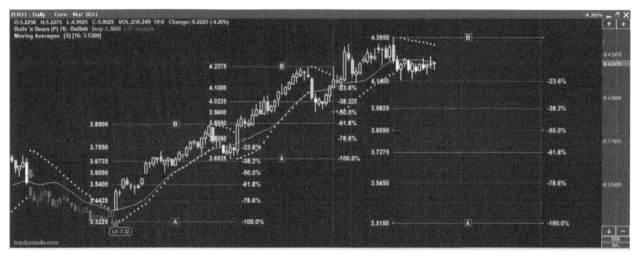

The Fibonacci Ruler is most commonly used on intra-day charts, which show price data for a single trading day at regular intervals (e.g., every minute). When using the Fibonacci Ruler on an intra-day chart, it is typically used to measure the pullback or retracement of the entire morning session move, which is the price movement that occurs during the morning trading hours.

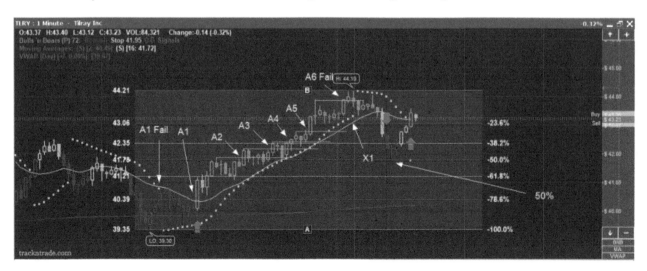

In addition to being used to measure pullbacks or retracements on intra-day charts, the Fibonacci Ruler can also be used to measure each individual leg of the Elliott Wave.

The Fibonacci Bow Tie

Using Fibonacci To calculate projections using extensions. There are two basic patterns within the Elliott Wave formation that we use Fibonacci to help project where prices will be in the future. (Remember, Fibonacci is just a ruler we use to measure each legs of the Elliott Wave pattern; it's based on the Fibonacci scale, rather than the traditional inch.)

Pattern A: Extension   Pattern B: Retracement (Bow Tie)

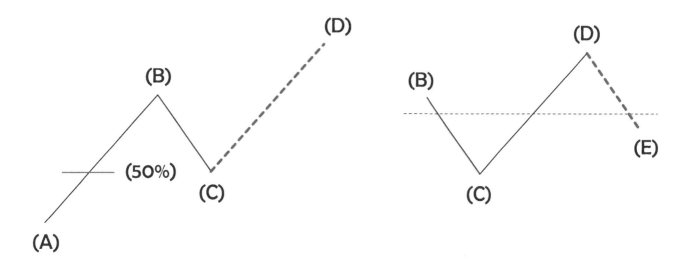

We use Fibonacci with pattern A to help us determine where D will be, and in Pattern B, we use Fibonacci to help determine where E will be.

To use Fibonacci extensions, we first identify a significant low and high point on a price chart. We then draw a Fibonacci retracement grid from the low to the high point and look for potential support and resistance levels at the various Fibonacci levels (e.g., 23.6%, 38.2%, 50%, 61.8%, etc.). We can then use the Fibonacci extensions to project potential levels of support and resistance beyond the initial highs and lows. These extensions are typically drawn from the low point and extend beyond the initial high point.

It's a simple calculation, and your trading software has tools to do this for you.

Pattern A predicts where D will be, in both price and time, by measuring the distance from A to B, waiting for C to present itself (approximately 50% to 61.8% pull back) then project the same time and distance that the market made from A-B to project C-D.

Pattern B predicts where E will be, in both price and time, by measuring the distance from B-C, waiting for D to present itself (approximately 100% to 130.9 extension) then project the same time and distance that the market made from B-C to project D-E.

I like to refer to this as my SWAG (Scientific Wild A$$ Guess) nobody knows where a markets going to be in the future, but we as traders want to be as scientific about our wild-ass-guesses as possible.

Fibonacci

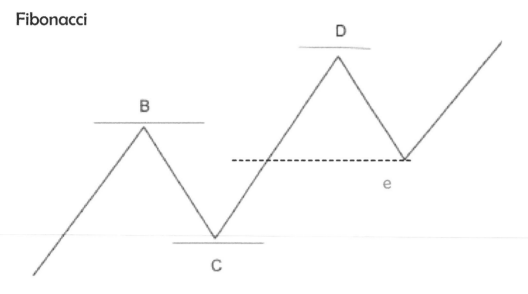

Despite its mathematical roots, the Fibonacci sequence and the various tools that are based on it (such as the Fibonacci retracement and extension levels) have become popular among traders and investors as a way to identify potential levels of support and resistance in financial markets.

How to put Fibonacci to work.

Measure from (C) to (D), which is 100%, and then (E) equals our pull back or retracement level. Just by looking at it, you can see that this level (E) is about 50% pull back between C and D. Pretty simple stuff, right? Now, our in depth studies have proven to us that markets like to pull back to approximately 61.8%, which is our Fibonacci golden mean, or the Golden Ratio as its known, it pulls back to this level, supposedly, more than any other level. Fibonacci extensions are typically used in conjunction with Fibonacci retracement levels, which are horizontal lines that indicate areas where a price trend is likely to experience a temporary reversal.

I believe this happens as a self-fulfilling-prophecy, most traders know this, so they make it happen.

Now, how can this help us? Well, in this industry, we have little mantra's, or rhymes that we like to tell ourselves to help us remember specific trading strategies. One such mantra is, "Buy the Valley's and Sell the Rallies." So, to do that, we need to know where the valley is, and where the rally is...right? Well, that's exactly what Fibonacci and Elliott Wave, teamed up, can help us do. (Side bar here: I also like to use Slow Stochastics to help me identify rally points, but that a topic for later discussion.)

Hopefully, by now, the lights are starting to come on, and you're seeing how this is beneficial. According to our mantra, we would be buyers at the (C) and (E) pull back areas, right around the 50% to 61.8% levels of the Elliott Wave.

Now, the next part of our mantra says, "Sell The Rallies." So, let's sell the rally. How do we know where that is? Well, once again, Fibonacci comes to the rescue. Fibonacci extensions can be a useful tool for traders who are looking to enter or exit positions based on potential levels of support and resistance.

Looking at a Fibonacci scale, we can now project out into the future where we anticipate the next rise in price, or leg of the Elliott Wave. We can accomplish this by measuring the C to D leg, calculating the E leg, then projecting where F will be. Don't worry, the math is all done for you with tools built into your Track 'n Trade software.

Fibonacci

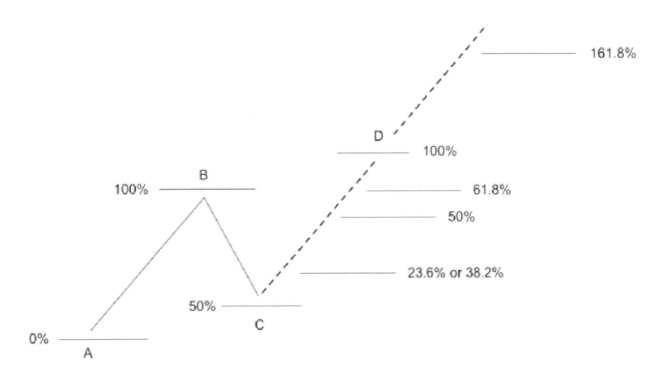

Here's my "super-secret" Fibonacci trading strategy:

1. Wait for the market to pull back to level C. (Buy the Valley)

2. Place a stop ENTRY order at 23.6%, or 38.2% projection level. (Should match up as close as possible with your Bulls 'n Bears Blue Light, A1, B1, C1)

3. Once stop entry order is filled, place stop loss order behind (C) Point. (This is your risk vs. reward ratio, or in other words, the amount of money you would lose if you got stopped out from where you entered.)

4. Place limit orders to exit and take profits at: 50%, 61.8%, 100%, 161.8% (Reward)

5. Trail the market with multiple stop loss orders behind areas of support and resistance, Bulls 'n Bears Blue Light System, and/or PSAR/ATR Stop systems.

NOTE: You'll notice, if you look close at the next few examples and charts, that the Bulls 'n Bears indicator is turned on too (Red, Yellow, Green bars). Look close, shhh, here's a secret insight to the mathematics behind the proprietary Bulls 'n Bears indicator.

The Bulls 'n Bears proprietary indicator is based on Fibonacci/Elliott Wave theory, measuring and projecting, which is what makes the Bulls 'n Bears so powerful, we do all this crazy math and calculations for you, and then turn the price bars the color of the Fibonacci levels, Bullish, Bearish, or Neutral, the Blue Lights represent the waves of the Elliott Wave...all done for you!

Fibonacci extensions can also be used in conjunction with other technical analysis tools, such as trend lines, moving averages, and oscillating indicators such as STO/MACD to provide a more comprehensive view of the market.

The Fibonacci Bow Tie

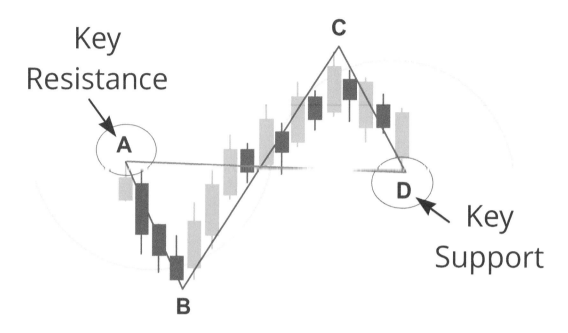

Support and resistance are key concepts in technical analysis that refer to price levels at which a financial asset is likely to experience a temporary reversal in its price trend. When the price of an asset is trending upwards, the levels at which it has previously encountered resistance (i.e., the price was unable to break through this level) may become levels of support (i.e., the price bounces off this level and continues to rise) if the asset is able to break through this resistance level. Conversely, when the price of an asset is trending downwards, the levels at which it has previously encountered support may become levels of resistance if the asset is unable to break through this level and instead bounces off it.

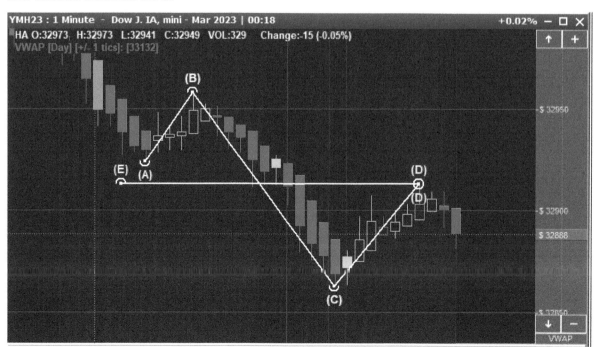

The Fibonacci Projections

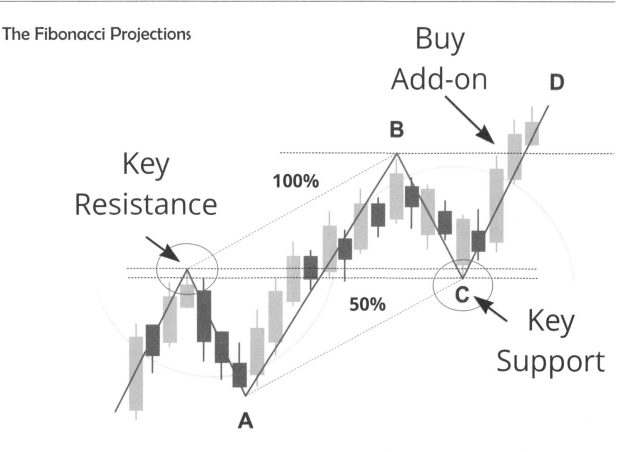

Support and resistance levels can be identified using a variety of technical analysis tools, such as trend lines, moving averages, and Fibonacci retracement and extension levels. These levels can be used by traders as potential entry and exit points for trades, as well as to help identify potential price targets. It is important to note that support and resistance levels are not guaranteed to hold and can be broken through, especially if there is a significant fundamental event (such as a change in economic conditions or company news) that impacts the asset's price.

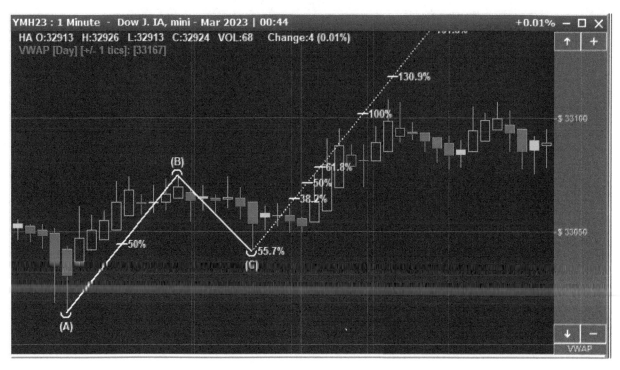

Fibonacci Extensions, and Bow Tie market examples. Extensions and retracements are used to measure and predict (SWAG) each leg of the Elliott Wave pattern.

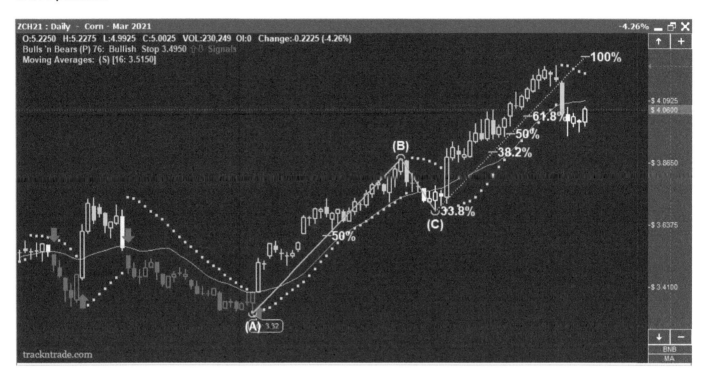

In this example, notice how the Fibonacci Extensions work hand-in-hand with the Bulls 'n Bears Blue Lights, using their breaking points as our areas of support and resistance to project the next Fibonacci leg.

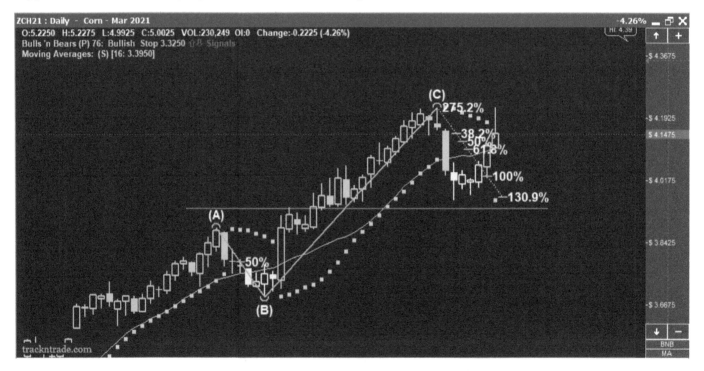

In this example, also take note that the Bulls 'n Bears Blue Lights are the key giveaway (cheat codes) that tell us where to start and end our Fibonacci projections and retracements.

How To Calculate The Fibonacci Cone of Probability; Version 1

Fibonacci ABC-D Extensions can be calculated from multiple A starting points, which will give a price range, or 'Cone of Probability,' for fun, I like to call this the Bermuda Triangle, which is a Fibonacci calculation of where the market is projected to run.

In this example, you can see that we're setting our 1-A and 2-A points where we would generally find the pull-back, or dip trade locations, between the X1, X2, and X3 legs of our count and measure system. (Elliott Wave X, and 2 points.)

Use two separate Fibonacci projection tools to calculate the Cone of Probability. Start the first projection from 1-A, then extend the calculator to the high point, what might be the 3 point of the Elliott Wave, which will be a common point between the two tools. Set the C point at the next pull-back location, which will give us a Fibonacci Projection, 2-D

Use the second Fibonacci Projection tool in the exact same manner as the first, only this time, start 2-A on the next higher pull-back, or counter trend of the advancing wave. Place the next B and C Points on the same common B & C Point as before,
which will produce a variant to the projection.

The Cone of Probability is the difference between the two D points, 1-D & 2-D.

If all things stay equal, we anticipate the market will stay inside the Bermuda Triangle.

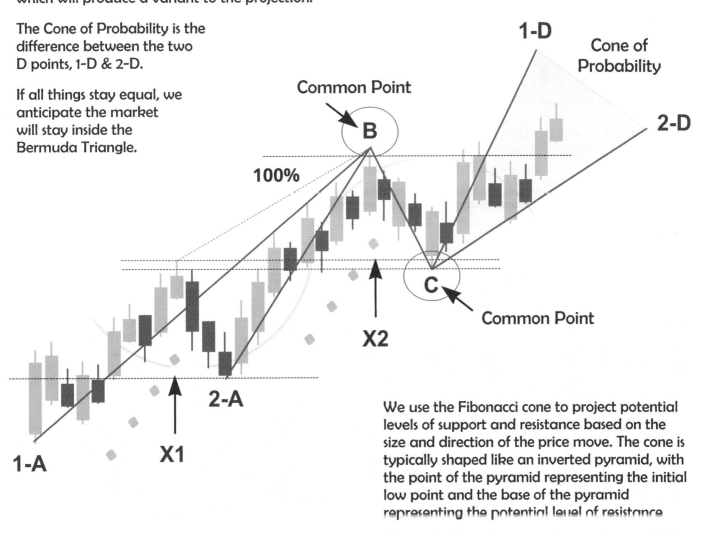

We use the Fibonacci cone to project potential levels of support and resistance based on the size and direction of the price move. The cone is typically shaped like an inverted pyramid, with the point of the pyramid representing the initial low point and the base of the pyramid representing the potential level of resistance

This projection is based on the previous volatility of the trend, with an expectation that the volatility will stay approximately the same throughout the move.

Fibonacci Cone of Probability (The Bermuda Triangle) Version 1

The Fibonacci cone is used to project potential levels of support and resistance in financial markets based on the size and direction of a price move.

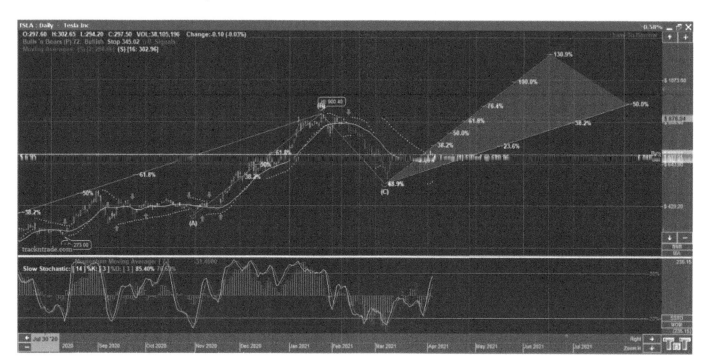

To use the Fibonacci cone, we identify two significant low points, and one high point on a price chart. We then draw two Fibonacci projection tools from the low points to the high point then use the Fibonacci sequence to divide the line into a series of segments, with each segment representing a different percentage of the overall move (e.g., 23.6%, 38.2%, 50%, 61.8%, etc.). We use the Fibonacci cone to project potential levels of support and resistance based on the size and direction of the previous price move. The cone is typically shaped like an inverted pyramid, which is the projected path of the market.

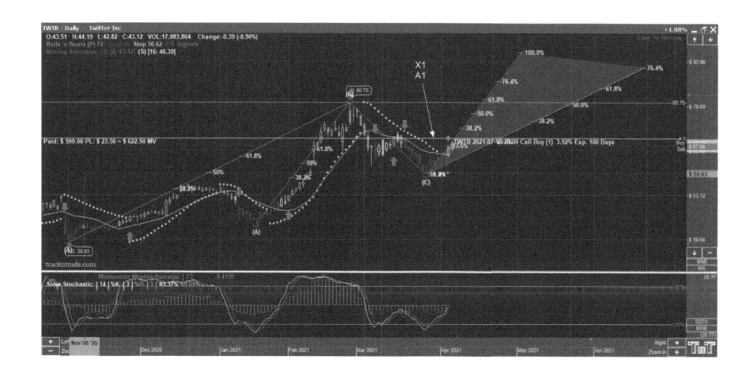

How To Calculate The Fibonacci Cone of Probability; Version 2

The Fibonacci Cone of Probability (The Bermuda Triangle) can be calculated in several ways, this is the second version, and I call this one my, "Don't Ask Too Much of a Market," version.

If you notice, in Version 1 of the Fibonacci Cone projection, we start the A Point at the low of the previous trend, and the B point at the high. That means that our projection, or D point projection is calculating the HIGHEST point of the next leg of the trend, but wait, what about the LOWEST point of the next leg of the trend? Where's that projection?

We need to also project the LOWEST point of the trend, because if we don't we may accidentally put our Stop Loss Order too close to the market, inside the Bermuda Triangle, which will surely get us stopped out prematurely; keep stops below the Bermuda Triangle.

Start by placing our traditional Fibonacci ABC-D projection tool, calculating the Cone of Probability HIGH point. This is done by placing the A point at the trend low, the B point at the trend high, and the C point at the next counter trend low, which projects the top, or high point of the Fibonacci Cone.

Now calculate the Trend Low, start the A point at the same location, trend low, now here's where we change it up, we place the B point beneath the price bars, at the natural trend line. Then place the C point at the same location as before, the bottom of the counter Trend, which creates a Cone of Probability.

The Fibonacci cone of probability,

Defines all that can be and will be.

Its spiraling curves, a beautiful design,

Follow the patterns of nature's own.

It tells us the chances of events to occur,

Helps us see the hidden patterns and strings.

So let us appreciate,

The Fibonacci cone of probability.

-- Author unknown.

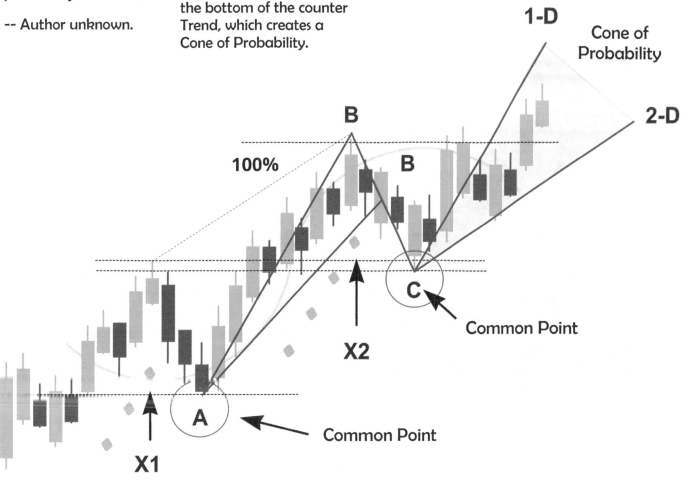

Fibonacci Cone of Probability (The Bermuda Triangle) Version 2

A second method of calculating the Fibonacci Cone of Probability is to use the same starting point along a trend, but two separate rally points. You can see in these examples we're using the same (A) point in the trend, and the high rally point for the first leg of the triangle, but with the second drawing of the Fibonacci projection, we use the same (A) starting point, but then extend the (B) point to a level further down the Fibonacci retracement scale, in this case; the crossover of the Blue Light breaking point.

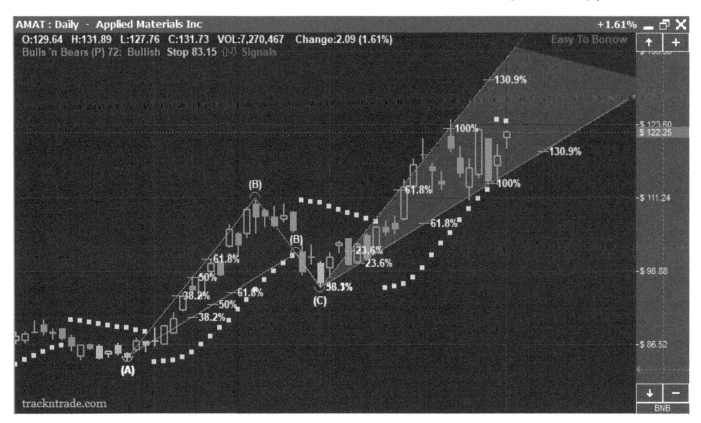

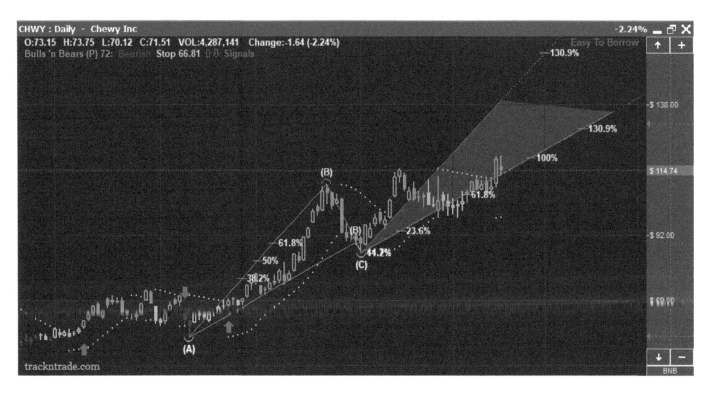

Buy on Fibonacci 61.8 and 78.6 Levels

Fibonacci levels are highly respected by traders and are often excellent places to enter new trades.

In the example below, you can see that the market rallied hard off the initial Bulls 'n Bears Bullish Signal and the crossing of the Blue Lights, which started a new uptrend. However, the market eventually failed to break previous resistance and sellers took this as a sign that the market was overbought, causing the market to tank.

Additional sellers jumped in and started riding the short side back down the Fibonacci Ladder, but they stopped at 78.6%, where they started to cover their short positions, causing the market to rally once again.

As a strategy, you can put limit buy orders at 50%, 61.8%, and 78.6% and catch the market on the way down, dollar cost averaging into a larger position size as the market hits these key levels of support. We place your stop at the 100% level as a final exit if we're wrong.

A more conservative approach would be to put your first buy limit at 61.8% and another at 78.6%, but since the market regularly rebounds off of 50%, you may miss some trades. This is what is known as the Fibonacci Flea Flicker, where you dollar cost average into the market at levels of Fibonacci.

Notice the change in color of the price bars. Bulls 'n Bears uses mathematics and color coding to show where the Fibonacci Sweet Spot is located. Whenever you see yellow bars, this indicates that the market is neutral and at a decision point. These are generally turning points along the trend and should correspond with the breaking of the Blue Lights.

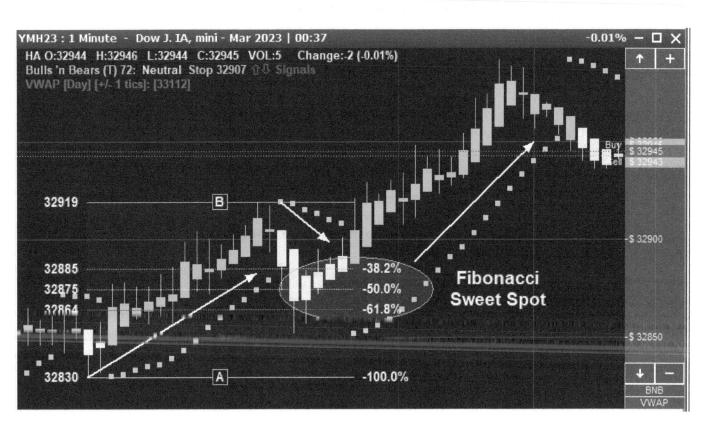

The ZigZag Calculator

What is the ZigZag (Elliott Wave/Fibonacci) Calculator?

The ZigZag calculator has been developed for the purpose of helping traders automatically calculate the Fibonacci Projections and Retracement levels against the prevailing trend.

The tool has many powerful characteristics, but it's primary function is to provide us with the Fibonacci mathematics calculated against the Elliott Wave. The ZigZag indicator is a technical analysis tool that is used to identify significant trends and chart patterns.

One of the key features of the ZigZag indicator is its ability to filter out small price movements and focus on the larger trends. This can be especially useful in markets that are prone to noise or volatility, as it helps to identify the underlying direction of the market.

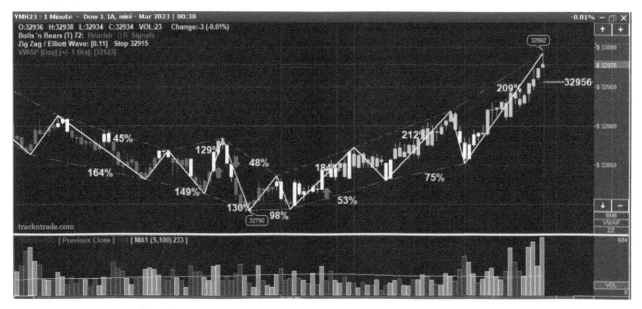

In this example, you can see that the Zig Zag has been "tuned" in to a level that identifies the larger waves of the market. (The indicator has a sensitivity slider, similar to the Bulls 'n Bears tool, that can adjust the calculator to provide you with the metrics you are interested in, whether that's very small micro pivot points, or the overall longer trend, as you see here.

If you look close at the image, you'll see in the center a 41%, this is is how far back against that section of the trend that the market retraced, or pulled back. Also notice above the trend, the 194%, that is how far the market projected higher against the previous trend.

Fibonacci Calculations, retracements and projections are usually always made against the previous trend as the baseline.

The blue arrows are indicating the turning points for the trend, and the horizontal white line on the far right, of this example labeled 246.74, is where the market would have to return to to create a new zig, or zag. (Of course, the white line will advance with each new price bar higher high, but will not decline.) Try using this tool in combination with the Bulls 'n Bears.

Rules 3 & 4

Setups and Triggers
Identifying Setup Patterns & Triggers

Lan Turner's Crash Course In Trading

Stocks * Futures * Forex

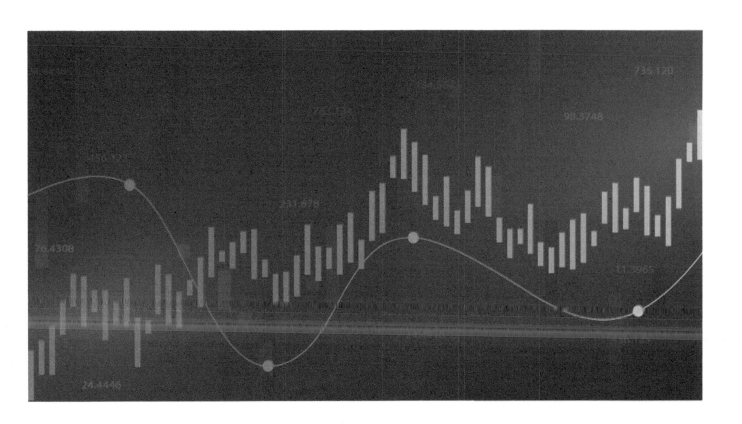

Recurring Price Patterns

What is a Trend Line?

A trend line is the most fundamental of all technical price patterns, setups and triggers. During a bull market, we call it an uptrend, in a bear market, we call it a down trend, and in a neutral market, we call this a sideways trend.

All rules of technical analysis are based upon these three concepts; up, down, sideways. During a bull market we generally draw our trend line beneath price bar lows, (blue) in an bear market we generally draw our trend line above price bar highs, (red) and in a neutral market, we bracket the trend, highlighting market highs and lows (black).

When we draw our trend line beneath price bar lows, we call this support, it's like the markets floor, and when we draw our trend line above price bar highs, we call this resistance, it's like the markets ceiling.

On the next page, you'll see different recurring patterns that the market creates based on price movement through price and time. The breaking of a trend line is called a decision point, it's where the market makes the decision to either continue to rise, or to change direction and fall, or vaisa versa.

As technical traders, we see these decision points as buying and selling opportunities. Support and resistance are key concepts in technical analysis that refer to price levels at which an asset's price tends to find difficulty breaking through. Support refers to a level where an asset's price tends to find support as it falls, and resistance refers to a level where the price tends to find resistance as it rises.

A trend line break, either above resistance or below support, can signal a change in trend and provide a potential opportunity to enter or exit a trade.

What are recurring price patterns?

Recurring price patterns are ways of quantifying price action in the markets. The basis for all recurring price action is the concept of higher highs quantifying an uptrend, and lower highs quantifying a down trend, and when markets either switch from bullish to bearish, or bearish to bullish, they create well known patterns, such as Head and Shoulders, and ABC Tops and Bottoms. These patterns are usually the catylist for our X, X1, X2, and X3 breakouts.

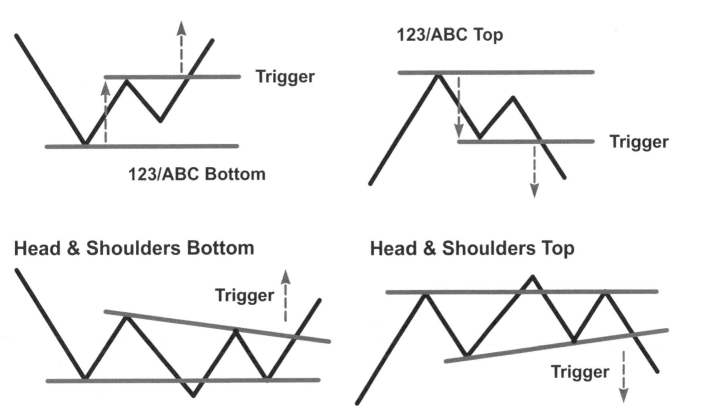

Markets can move in three primary directions: up, down, or sideways. Upward moves are known as uptrends, downward moves are known as downtrends, and sideways moves are known as sideways or horizontal trends.

In the process of making these moves, the market can create a variety of patterns that can provide insight into the underlying trend and potential future direction. These patterns can include reversal patterns, which indicate a potential change in trend, as well as sideways patterns, hesitation patterns, and continuation patterns, which can suggest that the current trend is likely to continue.

Reversal patterns, such as head and shoulders and double tops and bottoms, are characterized by a series of peaks and troughs that indicate a potential trend reversal. Sideways patterns, such as ranges and channels, suggest that the market is in a period of consolidation and that it may be preparing to move in a particular direction. Hesitation patterns, such as flags and pennants, suggest that the market is uncertain and that it may be preparing to make a move in either direction. Continuation patterns, such as wedges and triangles, suggest that the current trend is likely to continue.

Recurring price patterns?

Additional popular patterns with generally strong breakouts are exampled below.

Neutral patterns such as the narrow sideways channel, sometimes referred to as the Darvas Box, look for markets ready to break out the horizontal levels of support and resistance. These patterns are often the catalyst for our A1, A2, and A3 breakouts.

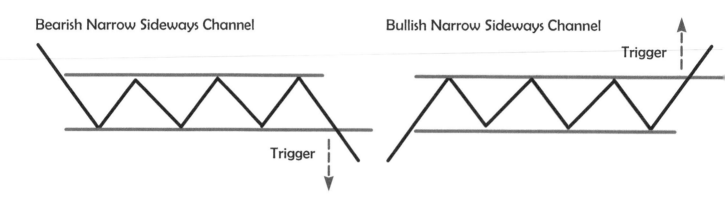

We also see flags and pennants, which are considered continuation formations. These patterns are hugely popular with traders, they are usually well defined within the trend, and generally receive a lot of volume on break-out. Within our count and measure strategy these patterns are generally seen as our A2, A3, B2, B3, and C2, C3 breakouts.

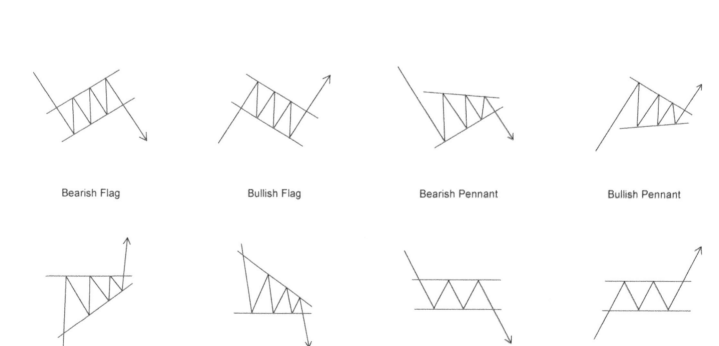

Trading Breakouts; Continuation Formations

What is a "breakout?" What does it mean when we say, "Trade the breakouts?" Of course we want to trade the breakouts, that's when a market runs, right? The big question is, how do we know which breakout to trade? How do we know what is a good breakout vs. a bad breakout, and which breakouts do we take? In this article, we're going to answer these questions.

First, we must define a breakout. As far this article is concerned, we're going to define a breakout as a recurring price pattern that has three points along the trend. (Three times a charm.) We must first have two points along the trend before we can identify point three, or the breakout, which generally occurs at the third point. Here's an example.

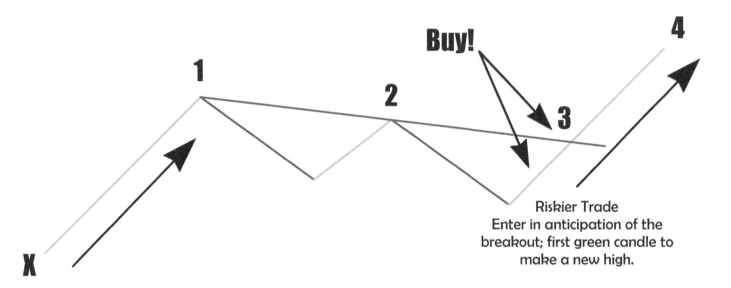

It's important to establish that the market is moving and shakin. We look for these types of trades primarily during the Goldilocks hours of 9:30 AM to 11:00 AM Eastern, and then again during Power Hour, which is 3:00 PM to 4:00 PM Eastern. (Or around fundamental news events.)

We want a market thats been in a strong trend, either up or down. In the example above, this is an up trend, the market's been in a rally, but has hesitated, and started to drive sideways. Many traders jump in prematurely at point two along the trend only to get stopped out. (In a strong market, sometimes the breakout at number two works, and traders are rewarded for their premature entry.) Generally speaking, we want to avoid entering on the number two point because it has a high(er) failure rate.

The best/strongest breakouts occur at the number three point along the trend. Why? Because we must first establish a trend that we can break, and to do that we must have two points for the trend line to be drawn across. In this example, we start drawing our trend line at 1, across 2, and then anticipate the rally and break at number three, as the market price breaks above the natural trend line. This breakout point SHOULD NOT FAIL. If it does, STOP TRADING, don't try to jump in again and again, if the breakout at the number three point is a failure, you're most likely in a weak market. Double check your volume, it's probably too low. On the next several pages you'll see examples of what these setups look like in the real world.

Recurring price patterns, such as reversal patterns, sideways patterns, hesitation patterns, and continuation patterns, are an important aspect of technical analysis and can provide insight into the underlying trend and potential future direction of a financial asset. These patterns can occur within the context of the overall trend, which is defined by the Elliott Wave theory as a series of five waves in the direction of the trend and three waves against it.

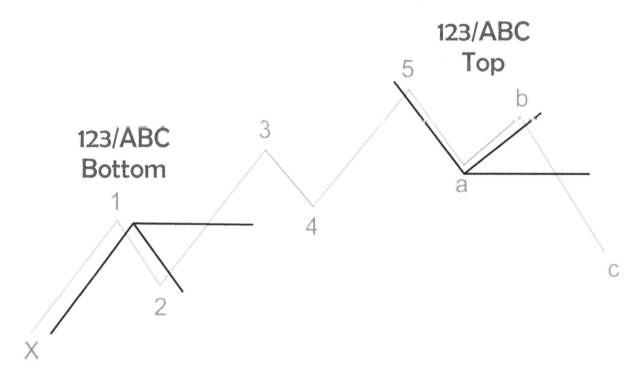

The Elliott Wave theory suggests that financial markets move in a fractal manner, meaning that larger patterns can be composed of smaller patterns, and vice versa. This means that you may see larger Elliott Wave patterns and smaller micro patterns within the overall trend. It's important for traders to consider the larger trend when analyzing price patterns and to confirm signals with other technical indicators to increase the reliability of their analysis.

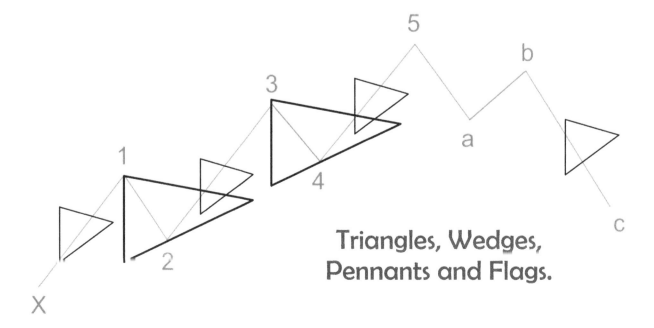

Triangles, Wedges, Pennants and Flags.

Your Primary Day Trade / Scalp Pattern. Why Trade Anything Else? One and Done!

The 1-2-3, or ABCD pattern is the single most powerful recurring price pattern in the financial markets; as a beginning trader, start by just trading this one pattern, and nothing else.

How? The key to trading the ABCD pattern is to only trade from C-D. Yes, that's the key, never try and trade the A-B, wait, and wait, and wait, until you get an ABC pattern, then only trade from C-D. (Anticipate the C-D move to be approximately the same size as the A-B move; Bullish, or Bearish)

The reason most traders lose money is they try to anticipate the move from A-B, so in a weak market, they keep looking for the breakout, jumping on every little one bar burst; Stop Doing That!!!!

Wait for the market to prove it wants to move first, wait for it to create the ABC pattern, then jump on for the ride from C-D with large size; always take profits along the way. (If you don't get a strong A-B move, then DON'T TRADE the upcoming C-D move, which will probably also not be strong either.)

The best times to find this pattern is first thing in the morning, or during Power Hour (The last hour of the day.) This is when we generally see the most volatile markets. In our example below, the first yellow bullish arrow came from a crossover of the Average True Range (ATR), which is our A Point.

We don't jump in on the A point (first break-out), we wait until we get the pull-back, and the second break to the upside, which in this example, is the third yellow arrow. (Second bullish arrow.) Once we get the signal, this is where we back the truck up, take a larger than usual position size, then start liquidating positions along the way; taking profits as they come. (Exit FAST if this pattern fails.)

One advanced strategy would be to dollar cost average into the winning trade, take profits along the way by also adding positions back in. (Exit all but one contract on the first red bar, then trail your stop either one price bar back, or on the dot system to final exit, just in case the market wants to continue.)

By starting with multiple contracts, rather than just one, when you dollar cost average into the winner, and start removing contracts to take profits, you are far less likely to get knocked out of the trade; consider leaving one contract open, with a stop at break-even for the Hail Merry day-long-move.

The most difficult part of trading is to walk away when you're ahead. Don't turn around and give all your profits back to the market in an attempt to get more! Stopping when you're ahead is actually the real secret to trading; most can't do it.

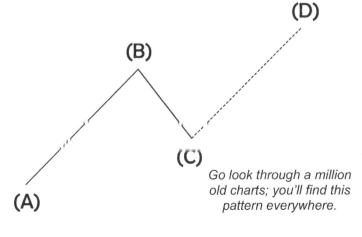

Go look through a million old charts; you'll find this pattern everywhere.

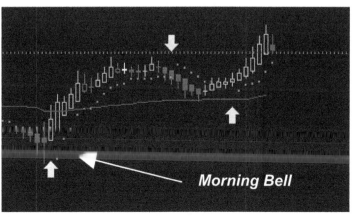

Morning Bell

CONTINUATION PATTERN

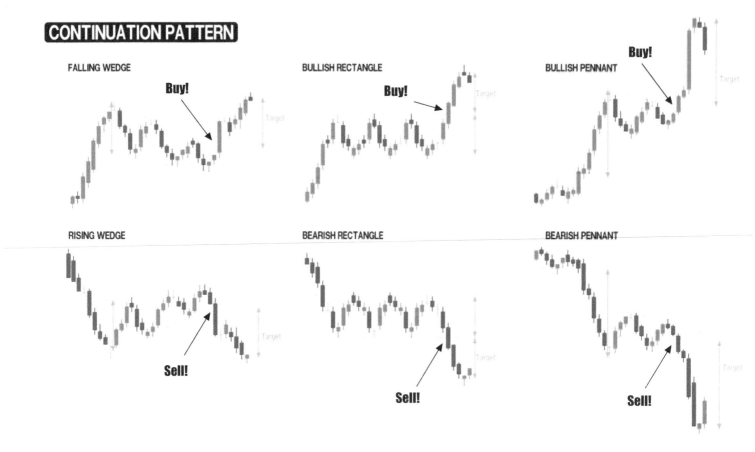

FALLING WEDGE — Buy!

BULLISH RECTANGLE — Buy!

BULLISH PENNANT — Buy!

RISING WEDGE — Sell!

BEARISH RECTANGLE — Sell!

BEARISH PENNANT — Sell!

REVERSAL PATTERN

DOUBLE TOP — Sell!

HEAD AND SHOULDERS — Sell!

RISING WEDGE — Sell!

DOUBLE BOTTOM — Buy!

INVERSE HEAD AND SHOULDERS — Buy!

FALLING WEDGE — Buy!

BILATERAL PATTERN

H.M. Gartley was a stock market technician, Gartley described a number of chart patterns that he believed were useful for identifying potential trading opportunities. These are now known as Gartley patterns. Here's four of his most popular.

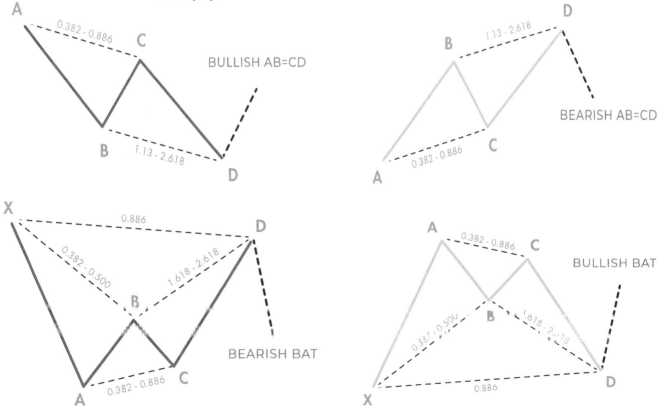

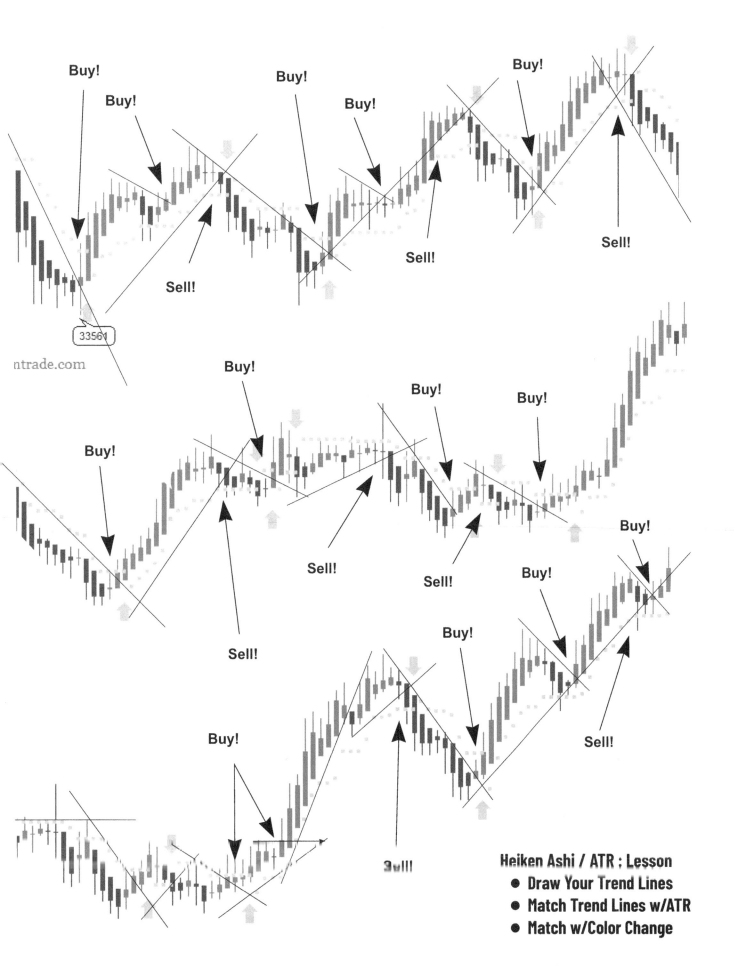

Heiken Ashi / ATR : Lesson
- Draw Your Trend Lines
- Match Trend Lines w/ATR
- Match w/Color Change

Candlestick patterns are a useful tool for traders and investors to analyze price movements and predict future price trends. These patterns are created by the combination of the open, high, low, and close prices for a particular time period, typically a day. The body of the candlestick represents the range between the open and close prices, while the wicks represent the high and low prices for the period.

1. There are several different types of candlestick patterns, each with its own unique characteristics and implications for price movements. Some of the most common and widely recognized candlestick patterns include the following:

2. The hammer and hanging man: These patterns are characterized by a long lower wick and a small body near the top of the candle. They indicate a potential trend reversal, with the hammer pattern signaling a potential uptrend and the hanging man pattern signaling a potential downtrend.

3. The doji: This pattern is characterized by a small body with virtually equal open and close prices. It is often seen as a sign of indecision or a lack of conviction in the market.

4. The engulfing pattern: This pattern is characterized by a large body that completely engulfs the body of the previous candle. It is often seen as a strong reversal signal, with the larger body indicating a change in sentiment and a potential trend reversal.

5. The morning and evening star: These patterns consist of three candles, with the middle candle being a doji. The morning star pattern is seen as a bullish reversal signal, while the evening star pattern is seen as a bearish reversal signal.

Candlestick patterns should be used in conjunction with other technical analysis tools and fundamental analysis in order to make informed trading decisions. It is important to remember that these patterns are not foolproof and that past performance is not necessarily indicative of future results.

In conclusion, candlestick patterns are a useful tool for traders and investors to analyze price movements and predict future trends. By understanding the characteristics and implications of these patterns, traders can make more informed decisions and potentially improve their trading outcomes.

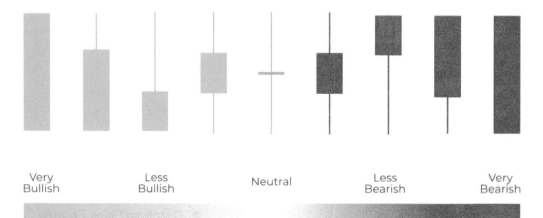

Very Bullish   Less Bullish   Neutral   Less Bearish   Very Bearish

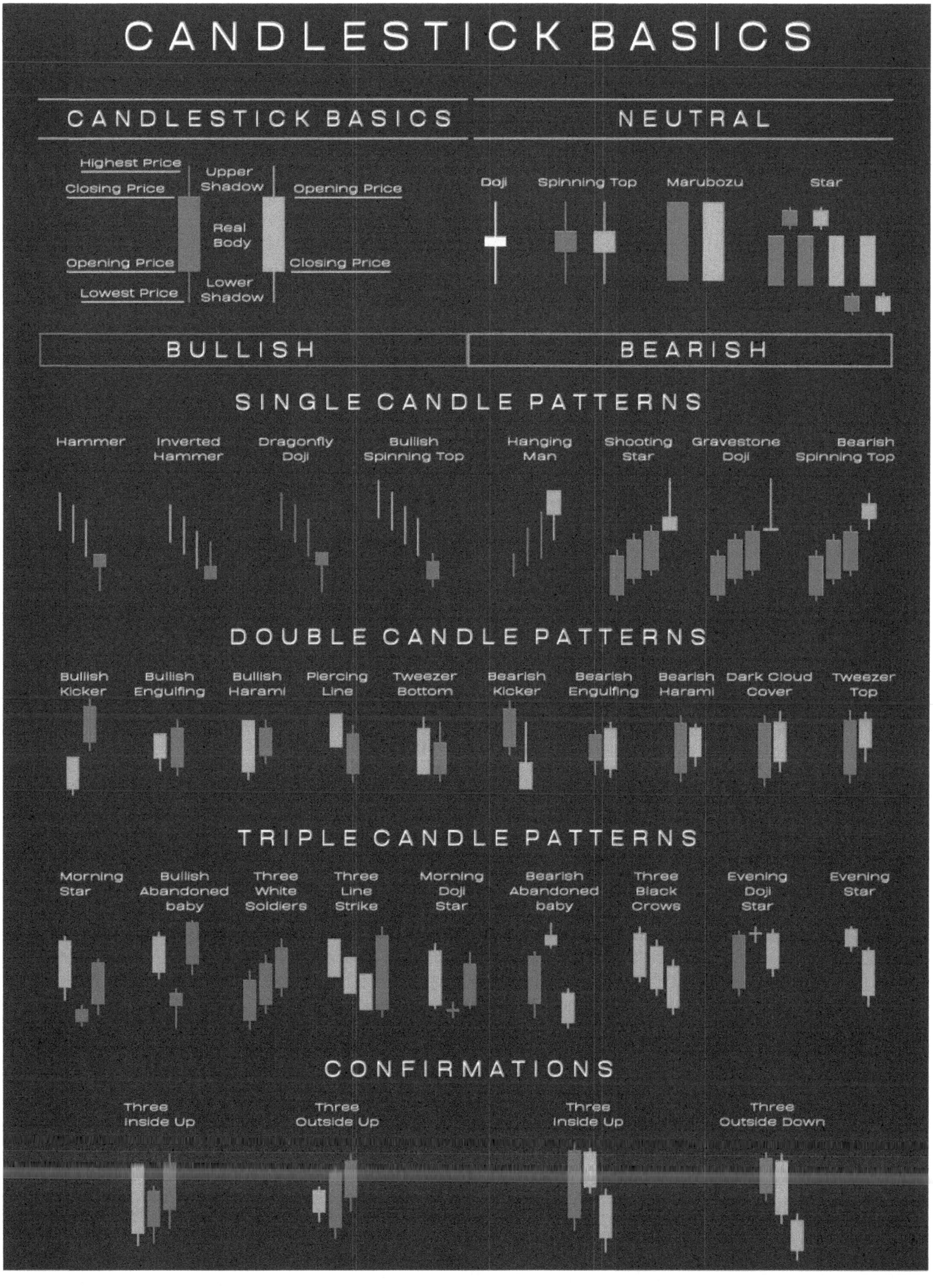

CANDLESTICK BASICS

CANDLESTICK BASICS

Highest Price
Closing Price
Upper Shadow
Opening Price
Real Body
Opening Price
Closing Price
Lowest Price
Lower Shadow

NEUTRAL

Doji   Spinning Top   Marubozu   Star

BULLISH

BEARISH

SINGLE CANDLE PATTERNS

Hammer   Inverted Hammer   Dragonfly Doji   Bullish Spinning Top   Hanging Man   Shooting Star   Gravestone Doji   Bearish Spinning Top

DOUBLE CANDLE PATTERNS

Bullish Kicker   Bullish Engulfing   Bullish Harami   Piercing Line   Tweezer Bottom   Bearish Kicker   Bearish Engulfing   Bearish Harami   Dark Cloud Cover   Tweezer Top

TRIPLE CANDLE PATTERNS

Morning Star   Bullish Abandoned baby   Three White Soldiers   Three Line Strike   Morning Doji Star   Bearish Abandoned baby   Three Black Crows   Evening Doji Star   Evening Star

CONFIRMATIONS

Three inside Up   Three Outside Up   Three inside Up   Three Outside Down

Day Trading Patterns

Day Trading Patterns: Here are four variations of our number one day trading pattern. Remember, just because we're talking day trading here in this document, it doesn't mean these patterns don't work on longer-term time frames. They certainly do. You can even use these same patterns for trading options if you would like. They're universal.

Thrust Bar Resistance Break Out Strategy (Micro Pullbacks):

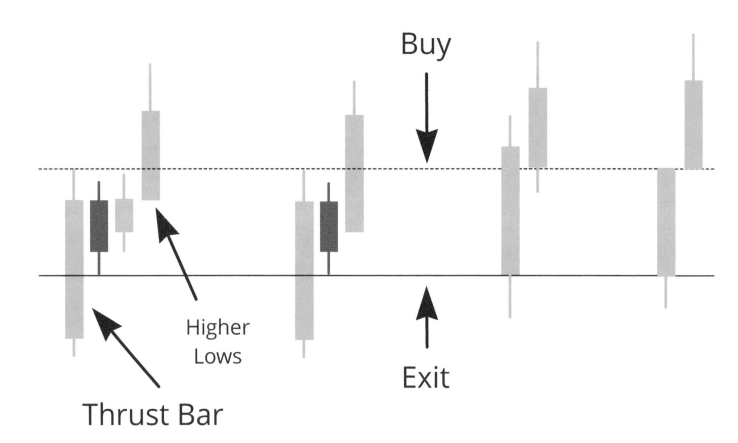

The most important thing to remember about day trading is volume and follow through.

This is commandment number one: If you see this pattern set up and it fails on you, then you are not trading a solid market and should probably step aside and let this market go to other traders. In other words, this pattern should not fail. If it does, stop trading. There are not enough players, buyers (or sellers if you are playing this same pattern to the short side) to make a market.

Trading is not hard if the market is trending. (Which is what all the YouTube channel creators show you.) When there are a lot of participants are moving through the market, this is what causes the market to better respect the rules of technical analysis. It's in low-volume, low-participation markets where we generally lose money because there's not enough players to push the market through the patterns and trends as expected, basically turning the market over to the bots to destroy anyone who's left.

Being able to identify the right time to trade is the key to success or failure. Patterns, setups, triggers, and risk management are all important, but being able to identify a tradable market is key number one.

What's the best way to identify a tradable market? I just told you. If this pattern fails, then stop trading."

Gunning For Stops

It's the market's job to fill orders. Mr. Market does not know when it fills your order if that made you money or not. All it knows is that you've placed an order at a specified price, and it's Mr. Market's job to fill that order if it can. This is often called 'Gunning For Stops,' where traders feel like the market is 'after them,' which it actually is; it's doing its job. It's filling your orders.

The market price action goes to where the most open orders are, filling those orders. (Think of Mr. Market as a gas station attendant. He doesn't care about anything other than filling your tank. He doesn't care about you. It's his job. It's how he gets paid.)

Strategy: It's very common for traders to trail exit/entry open stop orders one price bar behind an advancing/declining market. (Track 'n Trade can do this for you automatically.) Mr. Market's job is to fill those orders. Therefore, watch for Mr. Market to break an advancing/declining trend by a single price bar, after which it will continue in the original direction. (It does this to fill the orders that are trailing the market, usually one price bar back. That's why it's important, once the market has moved past your initial entry, that you do not continue to trail one price bar back to exit.)

- If you're looking to catch a longer trend, switch your trailing stop to trail a mathematical model, such as the Blue Lights, the PSAR, or the ATR.
- Alternatively, use the Heiken Ashi bars, which have a built-in buffer precisely for this purpose. At that point, you can continue to trail one price bar back.

When you see this happen, place your stop entry order above the high bar of the trend bar and capture the market continuation. Look back in history and see how often this happens. The 'Gun Bar' does not even have to necessarily change to red. It just has to break the low/high of the trend."

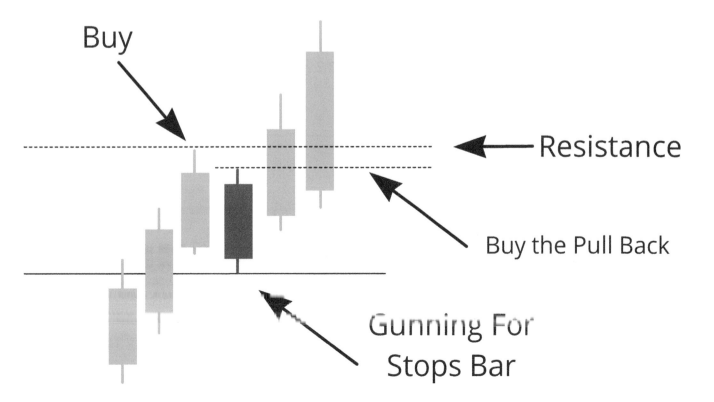

Favorite Trading Patterns:

Trading Pivot Points: This is another favorite pattern, trading the pivot point of a previously failed first green candle to make a new high pattern. Place an open stop order above the failed pivot bar, then wait for the break above (or below if we're playing this pattern short). Again, if this pattern fails, we should probably call it a day and stop trading. In an active market, this pattern should not fail. The key here is to identify the direction of the trend, which is why the thrust bar is important. Don't look at this as a trend reversal strategy. It's not. It's a trend continuation formation. (Watch for the 'Rule of Six,' where the peak of a green rally will be the high of the sixth green bar.)"

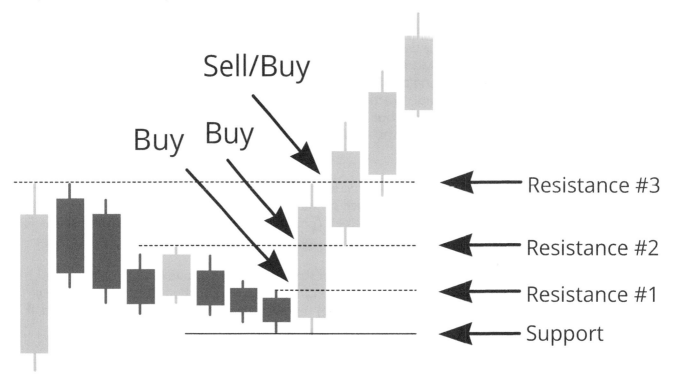

Variation; Bull Flag break out. (Buy the break of a previous high, or the dip, first green candle.) Take profits as the market breaks previous trend high.

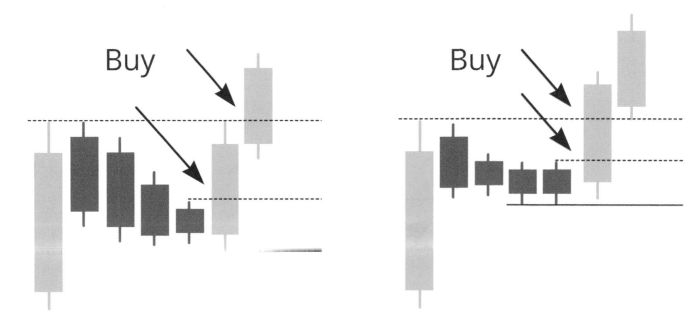

"Flat Top Ninja:

I call this the Flat Top Ninja because this is another favorite of day traders. Again, if you're trading a proper good market, this pattern should not fail. If it does, then consider stopping for the day, or waiting for a warmer market. (When I say 'should not fail,' I mean the market should break and move far enough that you can easily move your stop to break-even without getting stopped out; by trailing one price bar back.)

You will find several variations of the Flat Top Ninja, just like any other pattern. There are several variations. I could draw examples of each, but the drawings themselves would all look basically the same, so here's a list of the variations:

The Flat top is identified by a series of price bars that establish a level of resistance. Of course, if we're looking at the short side of the market, it would be a series of price bars that establish a level of support. (I call these shelves, and just like any other pattern, can be bullish or bearish.)

The easiest way to identify the flat top/bottom is by using the ATR overlay inductor, which identifies flat tops and flat bottoms through a series of sideways dots. (Yellow in this example.)

The whole dollar and half dollar support/resistance levels. Many new traders don't pay enough attention to the whole and half dollar (.00 and .50) price levels, which is a big mistake. Many professional traders, large speculators, and, in particular, computerized systems work off of these half and whole dollar price points. You'll often see Flat Top/Bottom Ninjas playing right off of these levels. Play close attention to whole and half dollars in all aspects of your trading. We use them for target levels, as well as support and resistance levels. Also, as a side note, watch for Fibonacci clusters to occur around the whole and half dollar levels as well."

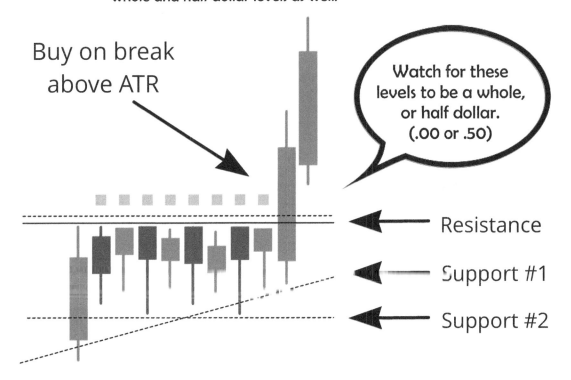

The Fibonacci Bow Tie

I can't stress enough how important the Fibonacci Bow Tie pattern is to our trading. This pattern is the single most powerful recurring price pattern in our entire arsenal. It encompasses the majority of our other patterns, but the key to this pattern is how the market moves through price and time.

Understanding the primary underlying wave pattern that markets make, as they move through price and time is key to our success or failure.

The key here is the rally point to Level A, which establishes our new high, and trend direction (Bullish in this case.) We get the pull back against the trend, as highlighted in a previous pattern chart, then the new rally, first green candle to make a new high, and then a green bar break above the A Point, along with red gun for stop bars as we rally up to Level C.

The key here is the price action from C to D, notice that D is a return to the price Point A, at which point we would begin looking for the market to turn and begin to rally once again, using this level as support. (This pattern is discussed in great detail in our Fibonacci & Elliott Wave Cheat Sheet.)

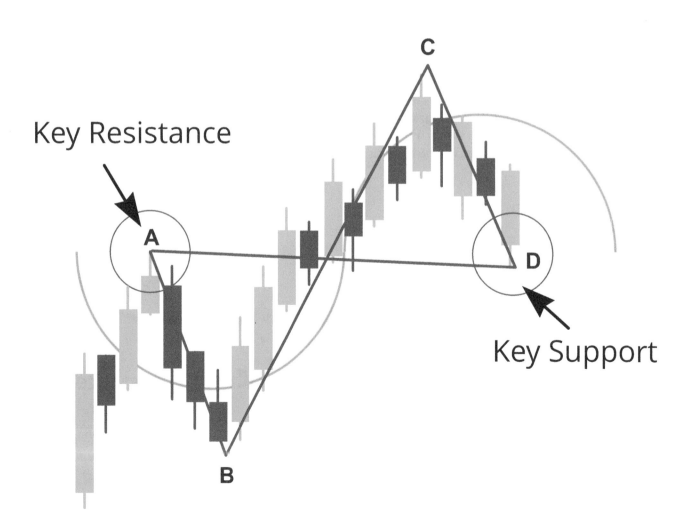

Have you ever heard of a "tell" in poker? It's a slight change in a player's behavior or demeanor that gives a hint about their hand. When professional poker players sit around a table for hours, watching each other closely as they play, they're always on the lookout for these tells.

Well, the same concept applies to day trading. Think of patterns within a trend as the market's "tell." One pattern to watch for is the "Clearing Bar," which is often created by Market Maker bots. If you can identify this pattern, it's like you've uncovered their poker "tell."

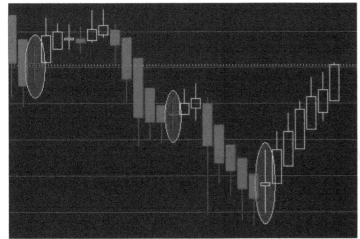

Here's an example of a Clearing Bar pattern: it has long tails at the top and bottom, with a small body (called a Heiken-Ashi). When the market moves through a trend (either bullish or bearish) and retail traders start to lose interest, this creates an area of low volume.

This is where the market makers have the opportunity to "clear the table," pushing the price up and down and taking out all the surrounding stops and limits above and below. Then, the retail traders step back in and choose a new market direction, less hindered by the market maker bots, and a new trend begins.

Here's how to interpret the two-bar pattern that the Clearing Bar creates: in a downtrend, if you get a red Clearing Bar followed by a flat-top red bar, this is generally a continuation formation.

On the other hand, if you get a red Clearing Bar followed by a flat-bottom green bar, this is considered a trend reversal formation. The opposite is true for an uptrend: a green Clearing Bar followed by a flat-bottom green bar is generally a continuation formation, while a green Clearing Bar followed by a flat-top red bar is a trend reversal formation.

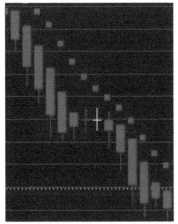

For example, let's say you're in the middle of a strong downtrend and you see two Clearing Bars in a row. The first red bar, after the green one, is a bar of indecision. We don't get the flat-top confirmation bar until the second red bar.

Sometimes, while trading, I see that flat-top red bar as it's building and I jump in, trying to catch the market early. This can be risky, as the bar may still come back and stop me out, ending up as a bar of indecision.

However, sometimes this works out well and I get in a bit earlier with a smaller risk-to-reward ratio. It's a trade-off and you, as the trader, have to decide if jumping in early is a risk you're willing to take. Keep in mind that just because you get a Clearing Bar doesn't mean that a new trend will follow. In weak markets, you'll see a lot of Clearing Bars because that's where the market makers and their bots thrive.

The key is to stay out of weak or sideways markets and wait for a strong multi-bar ABCD pattern before you trade.

On the next page, you'll see examples of more candle patterns, or "tells."

Be mindful of the danger signs.

Flat, narrow channels with a lot of bars that have topping and bottoming tails, with low volume. These are account killers, avoid them like the plague!

> There is a always an exception to every rule. I have a strategy called the Reverse Psychology Trade that you'll learn later in this chapter. This is a strategy where we take advantage of low volume markets and trade the reverse of what we might normally do.

Wait until a market is trending before you take the trade: Avoid chasing the A1 Breakout, take the A2, or B1.

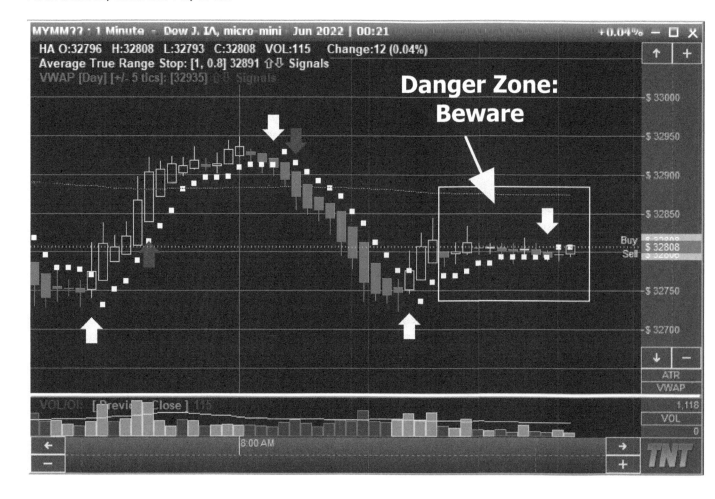

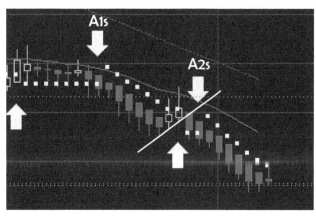

Wait for a market to start to trend, then catch the second leg. We often miss the first breakout of a narrow channel, or the A1; wait for the A2.

In this example, since we're going short, we add the "s" to the symbol, making them A1s and A2s, which stands for Short.

Mathematically Calculated Trend Lines

I call the Blue Lights the "cheat codes" of trading, they're mathematically calculated trend lines. We generally receive one up for every down, or in other words, one bearish counter trend for every bullish trend, or visa-versa, we use them as our guide for drawing trend lines.

You'll often hear me refer to them as, "a long set of dots, (the trend) followed by a short set of dots, (the counter trend)."

We use the counter trend crossover to re-enter the next leg of the trend, or the next set of long dots. We're trend traders, so we don't trade counter trends, but we do use counter trends to identify and enter, or re-enter the prevailing trend, whether that's long or short, it works both directions, bullish, or bearish.

These are the break points between the three Elliott Wave legs. What you see labeled Drive 1, A Drive, Drive 2, B Drive, and Drive 3, or C Drive.

Other mathematical indicators, such as ATR (Average True Range), PSAR (Parabolic Stop & Reverse) can also be used to identify support and resistance trend lines. These indicators use historical data and statistical calculations to identify patterns and trends in the market. By analyzing these patterns and trends, we can make informed decisions about where to draw our support and resistance trend lines.

Here's an example of the Blue Light at work. Notice the long set of dots represent the trend, the short set of dots represents the counter trend. It's the short set of dots where the pull-backs, and the key to the next rally, or leg of our Elliott Wave, and the pivot points, or fractal Elliott Wave points are highlighted, in this example; B2, B3, and B4 as discussed on previous pages, and in previous examples.

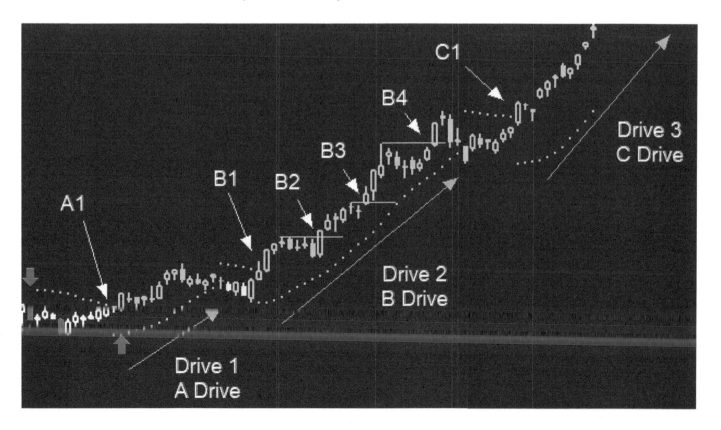

What is a Bull Trap? What is a Bear Trap?

Markets have a tendency to create equal highs and equal lows, if we draw a line beneath the lower levels, this is called support, if we draw a line above the high price points, this is called resistance. The more hits we have along the trend line, the stronger the area of support, or the stronger the area of resistance.

It's common for technical traders to buy on a break above an area of resistance in anticipation of a rising market, and it's common for them to sell on a break below support, in an anticipation of lower prices.

A Bull Trap is when we get a false break-out to the up-side, and a Bear Trap is when we get a false break-out to the down side.

These false break-outs cause traders to jump into the market only to have the market immediately reverse, and stop them out. It's very difficult to know which break-outs are going to be Traps vs. a solid price action move, so most traders will take each break-out, and then protect themselves with a tight stop. (This is exactly what causes the traps in the first place.)

The market is a huge machine, it's job is to fill orders, and when a break-out occurs, it's generally because there are a lot of orders sitting just above resistance, or just below support, causing the market order filling machine to break up to fill those orders. The trap occurs when there are not additional orders that continue to push the market higher, or additional orders below support that pushes the market lower, therefore we get a trap, as the market breaks up, fills all the orders, then falls right back down below support and fills all the stops.

It's common to see these failed break-outs as a catalyst for a market reversal. If the market breaks out, and fails, then it has a high likelihood of a complete reversal. It's often said that a failed pattern is the strongest pattern of all, as the market tips its hand, and shows you it's cards.

These failed breakouts that immediately reverses are often referred to as Wyckoff Springs, as they act as a springboard in the opposite market direction.

Richard D. Wyckoff was an early 20th century stock trader and market analyst who is considered to be one of the pioneers of technical analysis. He is the author of several books on technical analysis, including "Studies in Tape Reading" and "The Day Trader's Bible," and he is known for developing a number of technical tools and techniques that are still in use today.

> Wyckoff was a proponent of the idea that financial markets move in a cyclical manner and that they are influenced by the actions of institutional investors. He believed that by analyzing price and volume data, traders could identify patterns and trends that could be used to make informed trading decisions.

> Wyckoff's work had a significant influence on the development of technical analysis and is still widely studied and applied by traders and investors today.

Wyckoff died in 1934, and is considered to be one of the five titans of technical analysis along with Dow, Gann, Elliott, and Merrill.

The misconception that many traders have is that a single trend line is a level of either support or resistance, and when that line is broken, it becomes the entry or exit trigger.

Although this can be a solid strategy on a short-term basis, we must think of support and resistance as an "area" of support and an "area" of resistance, not a single trend line. This is why we refer to it as, "An area of support and resistance," not necessarily a single price line.

Markets can only do three things, they can go up, they can go down, and they can go sideways. A market has a tendency to go through stages of growth and contraction, we call these price channels, or accumulation and distribution. We also see, what I call, price changes, which is when the market leaves the area of accumulations, aka, a trend, headed for the area of distribution, which is where profit takers exit.

Areas of accumulation and distribution are generally sideways, or non-trending markets, it's only the break-out and move from accumulation to distribution that is the actual market trend.

During the accumulation stage, large institutions are buying and selling the stock, but in the process of doing so, they're actually accumulating more than they're distributing, building up an ever larger and larger position in the market without causing the price to rally.

They do this in an attempt to get the retail trader (you and me) to sell them shares at, what they consider to be, a low bargain price. Once they've accumulated a large position in the market, they "Pump" the gas, which causes a breakout, which is the trigger for retail traders to jump aboard, causing the market to rally giving the large institutions buyers to whom they sell their significantly accumulated holdings to.

As the retail trader is buying, buying, buying on a rising market, the institutions are selling their shares to the buyers. Once all their shares are liquidated, and the institutions have made a killing, the selling stops, and generally, either the bottom falls out of the market, leaving the retail traders holding the bag, or it stops trending, and begins to drift sideways. This is known as the distribution stage.

There are many retail traders who have caught onto this little game the large hedge funds and commercial speculators play, and have been trying to work against the professional firms in an effort to give them a taste of their own medicine, these traders have formed several social media groups they call WallStreet Bets; catching the large institutions in a heavy short position has been their favorite move.

It's often said that support becomes resistance, this carries through to the accumulation and distribution fazes of the markets as well, when we receive a large accumulation faze, where the market moves sideways, and the institutional buying begins, the market generally goes through a process of making higher lows before the final break-out.

Once the market does make its run (trend) to the next distribution price level, many times we don't see a full sell off, the market just begins to trend sideways once again, where a whole new set of share accumulation begins, therefore distribution becomes accumulation.

Once the institutions have gathered enough shares, they hit the gas peddle, which break the market out of the trend, causing the retail feeding frenzy all over again. This process is what creates recurring technical price patterns, such as Elliott Wave ABC, 123, and head and shoulders formations.

"The market does not beat them. They beat themselves, because though they have brains, they cannot sit tight." - Richard D. Wyckoff

In summary, according to the Wyckoff approach, there are three main stages in the development of a trend: the accumulation stage, the markup stage, and the distribution stage.

During the accumulation stage, institutional investors are believed to be buying the asset, driving up demand and pushing the price higher. During the markup stage, the asset's price continues to rise as retail investors join the trend. Finally, during the distribution stage, institutional investors start to sell their positions, leading to a decline in the asset's price.

IWyckoff theory also involves using technical indicators, such as moving averages and oscillators, to confirm trend direction and strength.

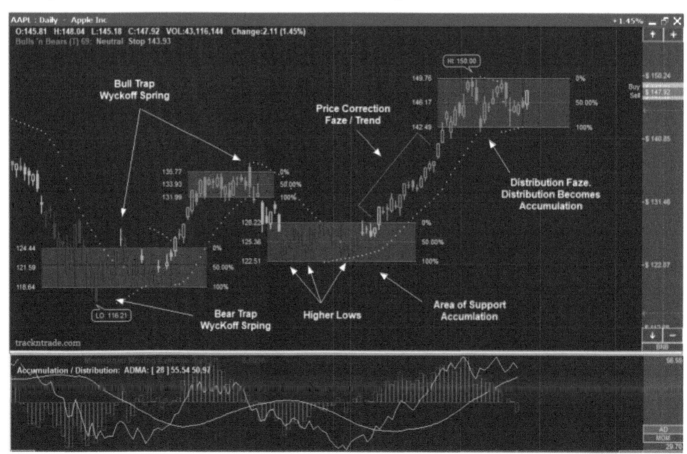

The Wyckoff AD Model

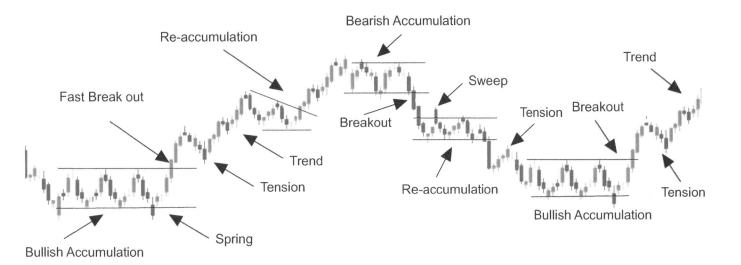

"The successful trader is the man who knows what to do when he
doesn't know what to do."

"Listen to what the market is saying about others, not what
others are saying about the market."

"The greatest losses come from buying speculative stocks when
the market is in a bull swing."

"When you trade, you are not competing against other traders,
but against your own weaknesses."

"The key to success in trading is not predicting what will happen
next, but being prepared for whatever happens next."

"The goal of a successful trader is to make the best trades.
Money is secondary."

"The best trades are those where you have the least risk and the
most potential profit."

"The object of speculation is not to be right all the time, but to
profit by being right more often than wrong."

"The question is not whether you have lost money trading stocks,
but whether you are going to persist in doing so?"

-- Richard D. Wyckoff

Richard D. Wyckoff was a prominent figure in the early 20th century stock market and considered one of the "titans" of technical analysis. He started his career as a stock runner in a New York brokerage firm at the age of 15 and eventually became the head of his own firm. Wyckoff was also the founder and editor of "The Magazine of Wall Street," which had over 200,000 subscribers at its peak. He studied the market activities and campaigns of successful traders, such as JP Morgan and Jesse Livermore, and codified their best practices into a trading methodology, money management, and mental discipline he called the Wyckoff Theory.

Wyckoff was dedicated to educating the public about the "real rules of the game" as played by banks, hedge funds and large speculators. He founded the Stock Market Institute, offering a course that integrated his insights on how he identified large operators' accumulation and distribution of stocks. His theories and approaches to the markets, including guidelines for identifying trade candidates. Wyckoff's method can be applied to any market, including commodities, futures, bonds, and currencies.

Step 1, the first step of the Wyckoff Method involves determining the current position and future trend of the market by analyzing market structure, supply and demand. This helps to decide whether to participate in the market and what positions to take, whether long or short.

Step 2 of the Wyckoff Method involves selecting stocks that are in harmony with the current market trend. In an uptrend, choose stocks that are performing better than the market, while in a downtrend, choose weaker stocks.

Step 3 Involves selecting stocks with a sufficient "cause." The horizontal trading range represents the cause, and the subsequent price movement represents the effect. When taking long positions, choose stocks that are under accumulation or re-accumulation with a sufficient cause to meet your objective.

Step 4 requires determining the readiness of a stock to move. This is done by applying tests for buying or for selling, which help to determine if the market conditions are favorable for entering a trade.

For example, if the stock has been in a prolonged rally, the selling tests are used to determine if there is significant supply entering the market, which may indicate that a short position is warranted. Alternatively, if the stock appears to be in an accumulation phase, the buying tests are used to determine if supply has been successfully absorbed and is ready to move higher.

Step 5 in the Wyckoff Method involves timing your investment decisions with the overall trend in the stock market. This is because the majority of individual stocks tend to follow the direction of the general market. To maximize your chances of success, it's important to protect your position by placing a stop-loss order and adjusting it as necessary until you close the position.

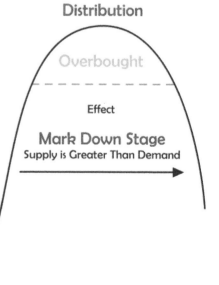

Distribution

Overbought

Effect

Mark Down Stage
Supply is Greater Than Demand

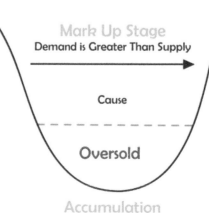

Mark Up Stage
Demand is Greater Than Supply

Cause

Oversold

Accumulation

"...all the fluctuations in the market and in all the various stocks should be studied as if they were the result of one man's operations. Let us call him the Composite Man, who, in theory, sits behind the scenes and manipulates the stocks to your disadvantage if you do not understand the game as he plays it; and to your great profit if you do understand it."

-- Richard D. Wyckoff

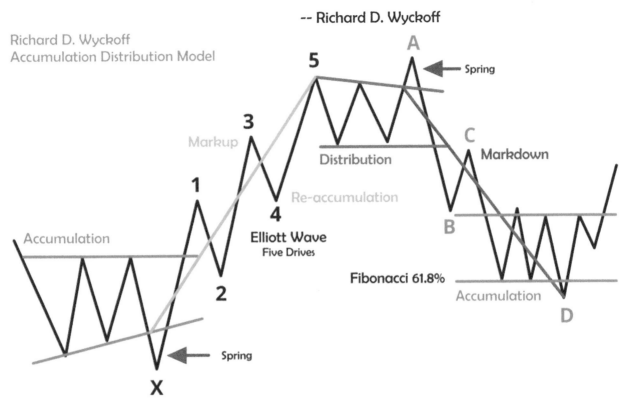

Richard D. Wyckoff
Accumulation Distribution Model

Wyckoff's teachings are based on his observations of the market activities of LARGE PLAYERS, something he called the "Composite Man." According to Wyckoff, the Composite Man carefully plans and executes trades and tries to attract the public to buy shares that THEY, the large players, or Composite Man, has already accumulated.

Wyckoff's teachings are based on the idea that stock prices are primarily influenced by institutional and large investors who manipulate prices for their own personal benefit. (SURPRISE!) To understand this concept, one must study individual charts and look at them from the point of view of the composite man.

Understand, within these markets there is one buyer for every seller, therefore if the retail traders are buying shares, then someone must be selling them; that someone is the Composite Man, or LARGE Players.

Consider, why are they selling while we're buying? The simple answer is, because they've already bought, and are now liquidating to us, the retail market, and collecting their profits.

In the above model, the large players are buying/accumulating during the Accumulation stage, (Narrow Sideways Channel) The small retail speculator is buying during the markup stage, while the large players are selling out their accumulation of shares. The large players call this, "Feeding the ducks." We're the ducks! And they'll continue to feed us as long as they have shares (feed), or until we've had our fill and stop buying/eating. They then reverse the entire process once again, accumulating shares for the short sale during the Distribution stage, then "feed the ducks," through the markdown stage, where the entire process starts over once again.

This is my interpretation of the Wyckoff Theory intertwined with my knowledge and experience of Fibonacci and Elliott Wave. I believe that if we combine these three powerful strategies, we get the best of all three worlds.

A detailed break down of the Richard Wyckoff Model mingled with Elliott Wave and Fibonacci

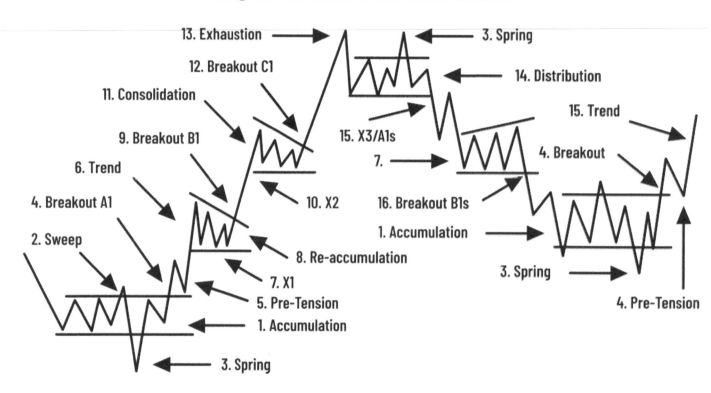

Stage 1: This is the initial stage of accumulation or preliminary support, where substantial buying begins after a prolonged down-move. Volume increases and the price spread widens, signaling that the down-move may be approaching its end. This is generally where most retail trades get chopped up, trying to continually jump on every little rally, looking for the quick "V" recovery reversal, only to get stopped out time and time again. This is where the large players begin accumulating large numbers of shares.

> The process in which the large speculators accumulate their shares without driving the market higher is through a process of manipulation, where they buy, for example, 100 shares, then sell 90, then buy 100 shares, then sell 90, continuing this strategy over a period of weeks or even months. This in effect causes the market to "chop" back and forth, with no definable trend, allowing the large players to continually accumulate shares prior to the rally, or markup stage.

Stage 2: The sweep is a false breakout that occurs during the accumulation stage, and is intended to test the strength of the retail traders resolve; are they ready to start eating? This also serves to stop out a number of traders as they drive the market lower, generally into the Spring.

Stage 3:   The Spring is where the large manipulators drop the market fast and hard, taking out the stops of the retail traders who entered long on the sweep. This is one more way the large players convince retail traders to sell them their shares. This is considered part of the accumulation phase for the large players, a way of misleading the public of market direction. (Another dirty trick they play to take retail money at a bargain.)

> At this point the widening spread and selling pressure usually climaxes as heavy panicky selling by the public is being absorbed by the large players at or near the bottom. Often price will close well off the low reflecting the buying by these large players. Note: Springs or shakeouts usually occur late within the accumulation stage, and allow the big players to make a definitive test of available supply before their markup campaign unfolds.
> If a bottom is to be confirmed, volume and price spread should be significantly diminished as the market approaches support. It's common to have multiple false breakouts after the Spring.

Stage 4:   The Breakout, or what we call the A1 in Elliott Wave theory. The rally occurs as intense selling pressure greatly diminishes. A wave of buying easily pushes prices up; this is further fueled by short covering from those who shorted the Spring. The high of this rally will help define the upper boundary of the accumulation, and the A1 break out. We often miss this breakout, because we've been burned by the Sweep so many times, we don't trust it. I generally recommend that we wait until we receive the A2; a micro pull back, or the Pre-Tension.

Stage 5:   The Pre-Tension, or terminal shakeout is like a spring on steroids. Shakeouts may occur once a price advance has started, with rapid downward movement intended to induce retail traders and investors in long positions to sell their shares to the large players. This is generally a low volume reversal and short lived, as new buyers step in and price starts to rise once again, giving us the coveted Elliott A2 entry.

Stage 6:   This is where new buyers, retail traders enter the market, and the large players begin to "feed the ducks," or start their initial distribution stage of selling off their holdings, and collecting profits.

Stage 7:   is the end of the first Elliott Wave drive, or the X1, this is where price falls back against the trend, generally through the Fibonacci neutral zone into a level of consolidation, often recognized by traders as a triangle, wedge, or flag formation.

Stage 8:   Large players consider this an opportunity to re-accumulate additional shares, as they prepare to "feed the ducks" during the next drive up.

Stage 9:   The breakout of the triangle, or wedge pattern, what we call the B1 or beginning of the second drive of the Elliott Wave.

Stage 10:   The Elliott X2, or second Elliott Wave exit as we move past the Elliott B2, and B3, and our Elliott B Drive comes to an end. The B drive is generally our largest and most profitable range.

Stage 11:   We now anticipate another hesitation in the trend, giving us the second exit point, or X2 of the Elliott Wave. This is a second opportunity for the Large Players to accumulate additional shares for the third drive high.

Stage 12   Our third drive high, or C1 on the Elliott Wave scale. It's usually our weakest drive of all, as retail trader is start getting weary of buying into an over-extended market. Large speculators love retail traders who buy high, and sell low, which is what the Elliott C Wave is all about.

Stage 13:   The exhaustion bar, often seen as a high volume bar at the top, or bottom of a trend, and is indicative of a trend reversal.

Stage 14:   The point of Distribution, which is where the Large Players liquidate any remaining long positions, and begin the process of accumulation once again, only this time for the short sell. Once they've accumulates sufficient short positions, they'll once again run the gamut as previously described, creating Sweeps, Springs, and Breakouts to the downside, scaring retail traders into selling their positions as the Large Players buy them back, once again profiting from falling prices.

Despite his efforts to educate the public on these practices, Wyckoff's method's are still not widely followed among individual traders. However, with practice, you can learn to align yourself with the strategies of the "smart money" and avoid being caught on the wrong side of the market. Proficiency in Wyckoff analysis requires dedication, but the benefits are well worth the effort.

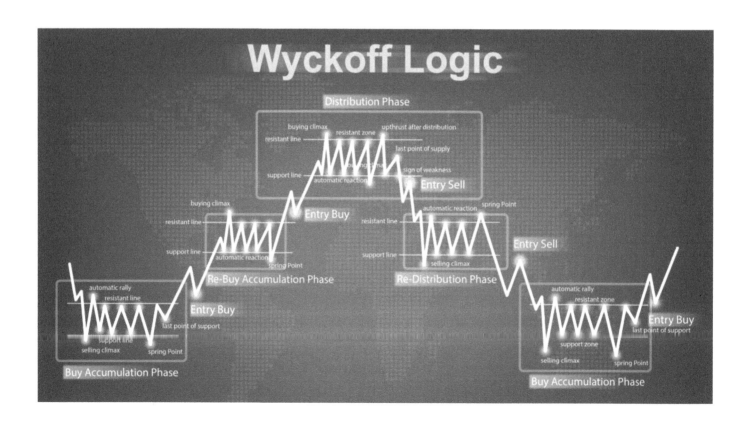

Dr. Jekyll & Mr. Hyde

Wyckoff tells us that we should think of the market as "us against them," and when he says them, he means the large banks, hedge funds and large speculators; the guys in the know, "the smart money," the insiders. We, the small retail speculators are the one's who trade against the large insiders; their profits come from our pockets. (And, visa versa.)

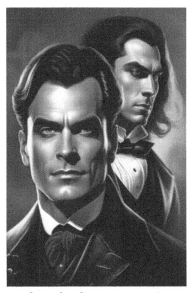

Wyckoff tells us, when trading, we should think of all the banks, large specs, and hedge funds as if they're one entity, something he calls the Composite Man. I like to think of the Composite Man as Dr. Jekyll and Mr. Hyde.

Mr. Hyde hates us, he's Dr. Jekyll's evil alter ego, who wants to take all our money without remorse. Dr. Jekyll, on the other hand, is the well-respected and intelligent trader who wants to help us make money. Therefore, I call this strategy Dr. Jekyll & Mr. Hyde.

When we trade, it's common knowledge small traders like to enter markets on a break above a previous high. Therefore, Mr. Hyde likes to pop the market, and get all of us retail traders to enter, only to reverse the position and stop us out, taking all our money.

On the other hand, Dr. Jekyll sees Mr. Hyde perform this act of hostility, steps in, and tries to help us make back our money by pushing markets higher once again. Here's the strategy.

Markets have a tendency to ride through narrow channels, and then break out. In this example we're only going to discuss the bullish side, but the bearish side works just the same.

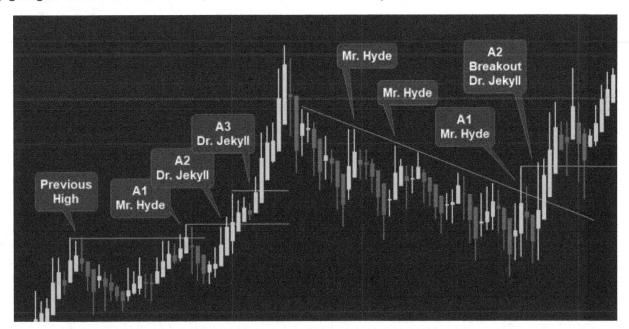

1. Never take the first breakout, what we call the A1, you've heard me say it time and time again, never chase the A1, wait for the A2. Here's the setup and the trigger.
2. Follow the down-trend, identifying each A1, or first breakout back to the upside. (This is Mr. Hyde, trying to get all the small retail traders to jump in on the first move.) This gives Mr. Hyde the opportunity to drop the market back down, where he buys up cheaper positions; your stops.
3. Dr. Jekyll then jumps in and runs the market higher, usually on the second breakout, or the A2, where Mr. Hyde profits from our miss fortune.

Review the next four charts, and see if you can identify the accumulation, re-accumulation, and distribution zones, the markup stages and mark down stages, the Springs, and Shakeouts. I've overlaid the Track 'n Trade Red, Yellow, and Green, Bulls 'n Bears color coding system to help you with this task.

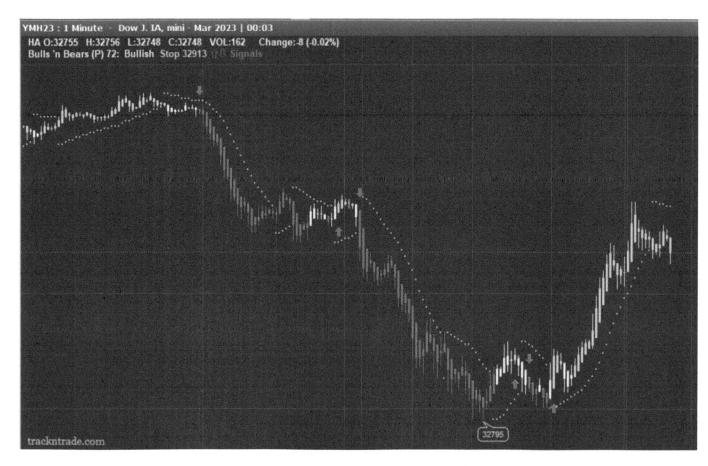

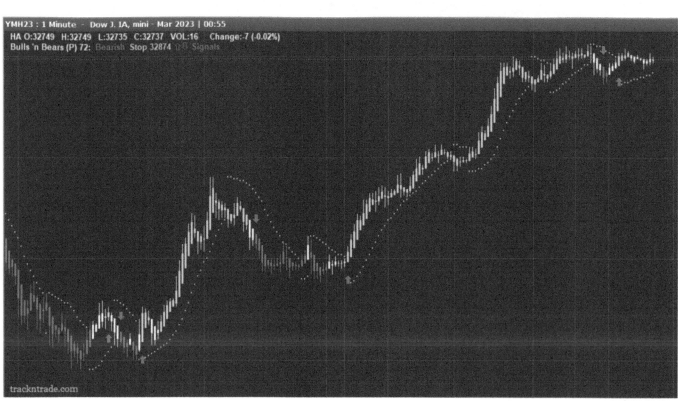

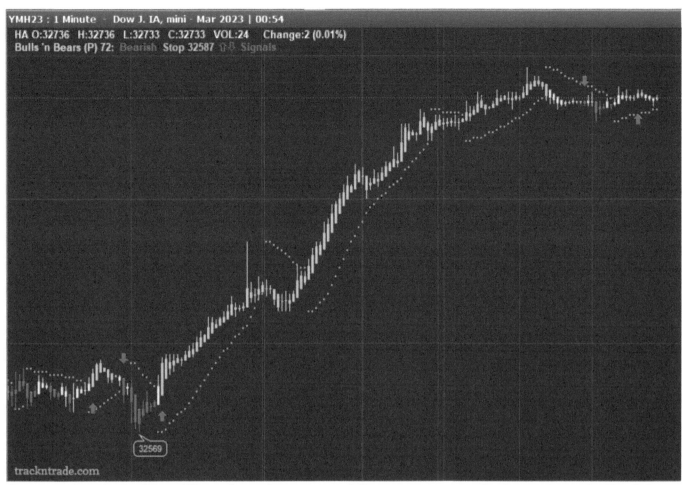

Can you identify the Elliott Wave three drive pattern? (Imagine trying to do that without the Track 'n Trade Red Light, Green Light, Elliott Wave System Plug-in.)

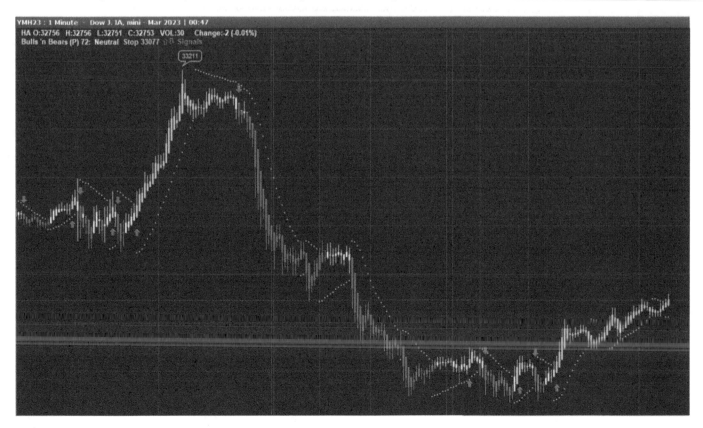

What is Laddering?

You've heard me say it time and time again, when scalping, day trading, or even long(er) term swing trading, it's important not to sit on losers, but that said, we can also work to have a more robust stop strategy as well.

Stop-loss orders are a vital tool for managing risk in day trading. By setting a stop loss, you can limit your potential losses on a trade if the market moves against you. This is important because it allows you to manage your risk and avoid significant losses that could potentially wipe out your trading account.

> However, simply using a single-stop loss order can be risky. You may get stopped out prematurely only to see the market take off in your initial direction.
> When trading with multiple contracts or shares, you can provide more staying power and create a more robust trading strategy by breaking your stop-loss orders across multiple price levels.

This technique is known as "laddering." Instead of using a single-stop loss order at a specific price level, you can place multiple stop loss orders at different levels. For example, place your first stop-loss order one price bar back, then consider placing additional stops on mathematical models, such as ATR, Blue Light, or PSAR. (Make sure you have equal stops for the number of shares or contracts you're trading.) You could even place stops at specific percentages below your entry price at progressively lower levels.

> This strategy provides several benefits. First, it allows you to manage your risk more effectively by providing multiple levels of protection. Second, it can help you avoid being stopped out of a trade prematurely if the market experiences a temporary dip. Finally, by laddering your stop-loss orders, you can gain a more robust trading system less likely to be affected by market volatility.

In summary, laddering stop orders is an essential technique for day traders who want to manage risk and increase the robustness of their trading system; Laddering can be used both for entering a trade, as well as exiting. Ladder in, and/or Ladder out.

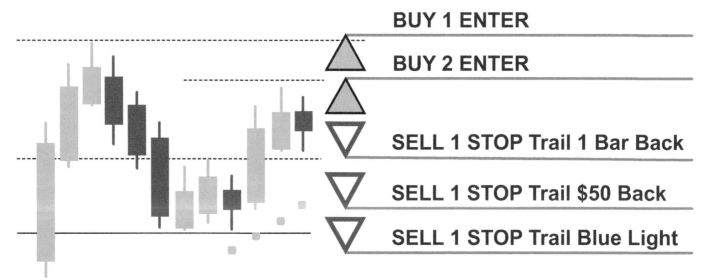

BUY 1 ENTER

BUY 2 ENTER

SELL 1 STOP Trail 1 Bar Back

SELL 1 STOP Trail $50 Back

SELL 1 STOP Trail Blue Light

In this trading example, we're seeing the market from two points of view. On the left hand side is a two minute chart time frame, and the same market on the right hand side is from a one minute time frame. Notice how the patterns are similar, but we get more granularity (chop) on the right hand chart.

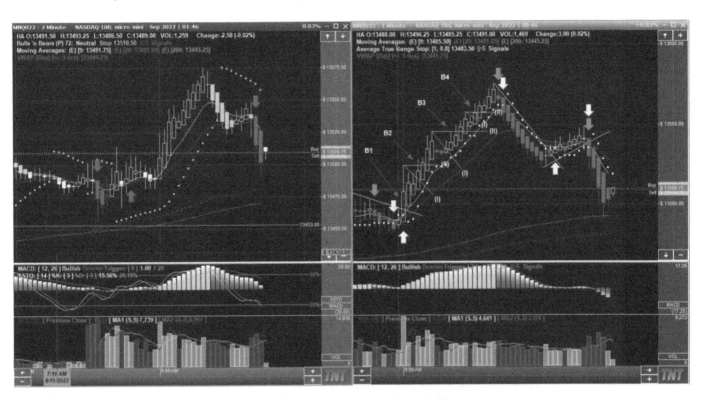

My favorite strategy is to Scalp 'n Trail, which means enter the market with multiple contracts on the break of the accumulations stage, capture some quick profits, scalping to cover expenses and then trail to exit with the remaining contracts. If the market moves far enough, I'll trail on both the one minute chart and the two minute chart, giving my strategy a more robust exit. (This is covered in greater detail in future chapters.) I did want to point it out here in this section as it's part of our overall trading strategy.

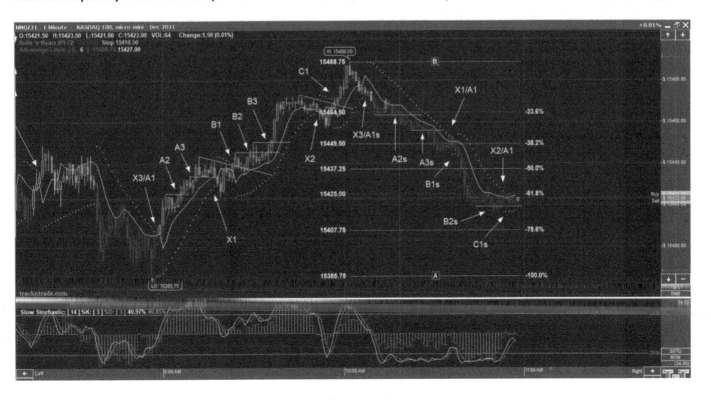

The Impossible Burger

While working at the Chicago Board of Trade, one of my mentors, Larry, used to always say, "I can give you the setups, projections, entry and exit points, and teach you all the strategies of a master trader, but I can't make the market trend."

As trend traders, we need a trending market to profit, and the key to our success is knowing, or at least having a good idea, of when that might happen. In my experience, the best way to determine when a market is going to trend is to pay close attention to two primary factors: our economic calendar and the time of day.

The economic calendar is our most important tool when it comes to determining when a market is going to trend. Government and institutional reports that are released to the public are a primary driving factor in the anticipation of an actively trending market. (My favorite calendar is online at: DailyFX.com/Calendar).

Generally, in the few hours before an important economic calendar report, we often see a market go through what I call the Impossible Burger pattern, as shown below.

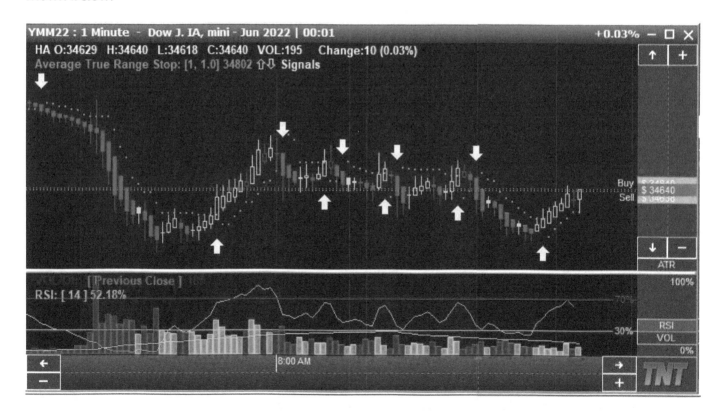

You can see that right after the morning bell, the market fell hard, recovered, then went completely sideways while waiting for the economic news release. If you're trading after the retracement stage and get caught whipping back and forth through the sideways channel, this is where most traders blow up their trading account. Knowing when to stop trading and not take a position is more important than knowing when to take a trade.

Study these patterns, look back through historical charts, and learn to identify their key giveaway points – when they usually begin, how long they usually last, and where they usually end (see my three times a charm pattern).

One key indicator for this type of pattern is the RSI or CCI, as these two indicators show inactive markets as the trigger line travels horizontally between the two outer thresholds.

The second key giveaway is volume – watch volume as it falls and travels below the 50-period moving average. When anticipating a breakout of this pattern, we'll look for the Three Times a Charm pattern and watch for an increase in volume as the CCI indicator breaks to the long or short side thresholds, and a short position if the RSI breaks below the lower threshold, which may seem counterintuitive.

The Pop 'n Drop strategy

The Pop 'n Drop refers to a situation in which a trader enters a position and the market immediately drops back against them. This can sometimes result in the trader being stopped out, particularly if they are trading large size and holding their stops close, or using the Break-Out or Bail-Out strategy, which is common in day trading. However, it is common for the market to then turn around and rebound, making new highs and continuing in the trend.

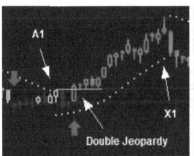
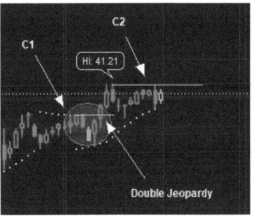

To capitalize on this pattern, traders can use the Double Jeopardy strategy, which involves placing a new order at the same exact entry price as before. This trade generally comes with a high probability of resulting in a winning trade as the market breaks and runs higher once again.

Examples of the Double Jeopardy trade can be seen in the provided charts, where the market initially drops back against the trader's position (A1 & C1) but then rallies and crosses the initial entry point for a successful long run.

However, it is worth noting that the Double Jeopardy setup can sometimes fail, as seen in the third example. In these cases, the market may continue to drop and the trader gets "slapped twice" for taking the same trade.

Bullish, vs. Bearish.

It is well known that markets tend to fall faster than they rise. This phenomenon can be observed by looking at historical charts across various markets, including Stocks, Futures, and Forex.

It is also worth noting that financial markets tend to be more volatile in the short term than in the long term. This means that prices can fluctuate more dramatically over the course of a few days or weeks than they do over the course of several years. As a result, it is not uncommon for markets to experience more rapid declines over shorter periods of time.

One reason for this is trader psychology. When traders enter a market, they often accumulate positions slowly, and some traders may even build large and unstable positions through an upside down pyramid structure. This can create fear in the market and cause traders to bail out of their positions quickly to avoid potential losses.

> Additionally, traders are often more likely to sell short or take profit from falling markets rather than entering long positions, especially when shares are available to short and the trader has a non-retirement margin account that allows for short positions. It is important to carefully analyze market conditions and consider these factors when making trading decisions.

Short Squeeze:

A short squeeze is a phenomenon that occurs when a heavily shorted stock or other asset suddenly experiences a significant price increase. This can happen for a variety of reasons, such as a positive earnings report, a change in market conditions, or increased demand for the asset.

When the price of a heavily shorted asset begins to rise, short sellers may panic and rush to cover their positions by buying the asset. This influx of buying can further drive up the price of the asset, leading to even more panic among short sellers and a self-reinforcing cycle. A short squeeze can result in significant losses for short sellers and profits for long buyers.

Long Squeeze:

Also known as a "short squeeze in reverse," occurs when the price of a heavily longed asset suddenly experiences a significant price decrease.

A Long Squeeze can happen for a variety of reasons, such as a negative earnings report, a change in market conditions, or decreased demand for the asset. When the price of a heavily longed asset begins to fall, long buyers may panic and rush to sell their positions to cut their losses. This influx of selling can further drive down the price of the asset, leading to even more panic among long buyers and a self-reinforcing cycle.

A long squeeze can result in significant losses for long buyers and profits for short sellers. It is important for traders to be aware of the potential for a long and/or short squeeze and to carefully manage their positions to mitigate the risk of significant losses.

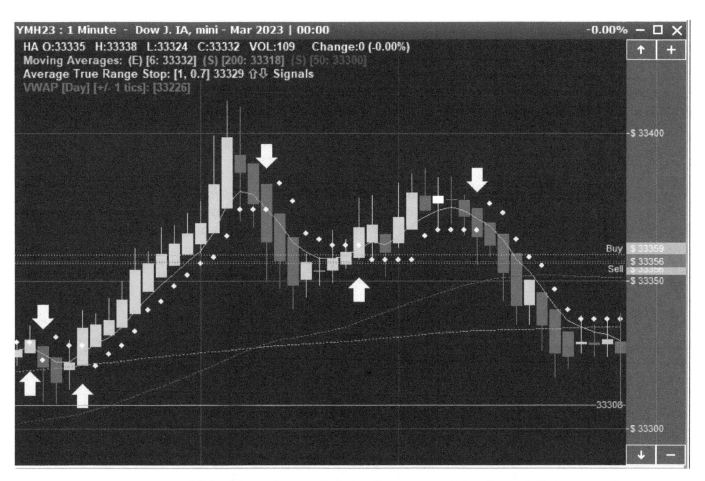

In this chart the market slowly rose over time through the accumulation stage, as traders gradually bought and accumulated positions. However. Due to a negative market event or shift in market conditions, the price of the asset suddenly began to fall dramatically. This led to panic among long buyers, who rushed to sell their positions in an effort to cut their losses.

In this example, it took only five red price bars (five minutes) for the market to lose 50% of the value it gained over a period of 15 green price bars (15 minutes).

The market attempted to rebound as buyers stepped in and short sellers covered their positions, but this was unsuccessful. As a result, the market fell hard again losing all of the gains it had made earlier.

The formation of lower highs, or the 1-2-3 top formation, was a strong indication that the market was ready to fall once again. It is important for traders to pay attention to these types of patterns when analyzing market conditions.

The influx of selling further drove down the price of the asset, resulting in a long squeeze. The market fell significantly, resulting in significant losses for long buyers and profits for short sellers.

This illustrates the importance of carefully managing positions and being aware of the potential for a long squeeze, and how quickly a market can reverse course. Its these reversals that we as day traders and scalpers love to take advantage of.

Catching a Falling Knife (CAFK)

Predicting market tops and bottoms is like trying to catch a greased pig - it's a slippery and challenging task that can lead to a lot of frustration (and potentially some financial losses). Many traders have tried and failed to catch the absolute bottom of a trend, and it's no surprise - nobody has a crystal ball that can tell them exactly when a market will stop falling. That's why it's so important to use a count and measure strategy to assess the probabilities of a potential reversal.

Instead of trying to time the bottom perfectly, a better strategy is to wait for the market to give us some clear signs that it's ready to turn around. A head and shoulders pattern or a 123/abc bottom formation can be good indicators that the trend is shifting. Once we see one of these patterns forming, we can feel more confident that the market has actually turned the corner and is entering a new uptrend.

> If you do decide to try and catch that falling knife, be sure to approach it with caution. Consider only taking the Elliott Wave X1/A1, X2/A1, or even X3/A1 patterns.

Don't try to grab it with both hands - start with small test positions and see how the market responds. That way, you can minimize your risk if things don't go as planned. After all, we don't want to end up with a bruised ego (and a lighter wallet) from trying to catch a falling knife.

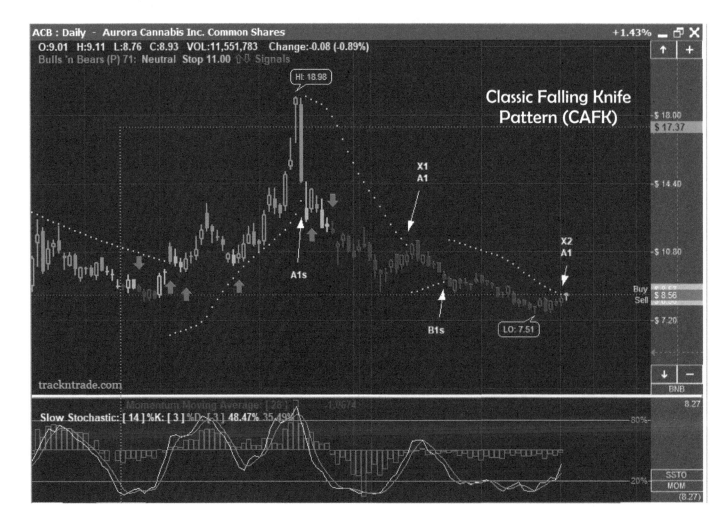

What About Indicators?

Everyone seems to believe that if they can just find that one magic mathematical indicator, they'll be rich beyond their wildest dreams. People are constantly looking for the holy grail of indicators, jumping from one indicator to another, or worse yet, adding a half dozen indicators on their chart all at the same time. Let me just say right now, there is no such thing as the holy grail of indicators.

1. Indicators are designed for one purpose: to help you locate the best entry and exit points on your chart. Throughout this document, we've already helped define where those optimal points are: A1, B1, and C1, or A2, B2, or C2, X1, X2, etc.

2. So, what we're really doing is trying to find an indicator that can, with a high degree of reliability, help us identify A1, A2, A3, B1, B2, B3, C1, C2, C3, and X1, X2, and X3 points on a chart. Isn't that our ultimate goal? (The correct answer is "yes, it is.")

3. The problem with most traders is that they're not even aware that that's what they're looking for. Without the fundamental knowledge of how to count and measure a chart, these individuals (I hesitate to even call them traders) are blindly wandering around in a dark room, wondering why their RSI indicator just gave them a buy or sell arrow.

4. Simply put, indicators have been designed to help you identify the points within the count and measure system that we've already been discussing. They attempt to identify the turning points for each new A1, B1, and C1, and then they try to help identify the pivot points along the trend: the A2, A3, B2, B3, C2, and C3 points.

5. Until you realize that's what those indicators are primarily attempting to do, you'll sit there and stare at the chart, wondering why those damn MACD, RSI, or Stochastics indicators keep telling you to sell all the way up an obvious uptrend. (Hint: they're trying to highlight the pivot points.)

Once you actually learn how to read a chart, and how to count and measure each wave of the patterns yourself, using two simple tools (Bulls 'n Bears and the Blue Light Systems), you can throw the other indicators out the window. (That said, I do like Stochastics and Momentum for their convergence and divergence, along with their overbought and oversold capabilities. I don't often use their buy/sell arrows.)

On the next page, we'll take a look at a couple examples of what I consider to be the "best" indicators. They usually do a fairly good job of pointing out the A1, B1, C1, X1, X2, and X3 entry and exit points. Sometimes, they can even help point out the A2, A3, B2, B3, and the C2 and C3 pivot points.

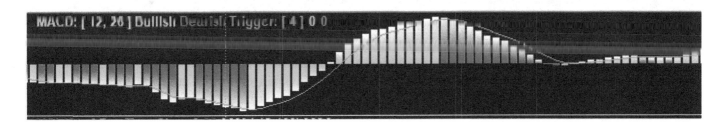

MACD: [12, 26] Bullish Bearish Trigger: [4] 0 0

Trading Signals and Setups

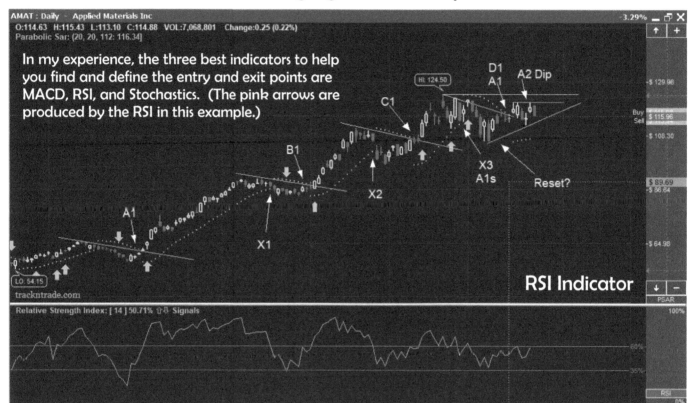

In my experience, the three best indicators to help you find and define the entry and exit points are MACD, RSI, and Stochastics. (The pink arrows are produced by the RSI in this example.)

The RSI is a technical indicator that helps traders understand how strong or weak an asset's price action is by comparing the size of its recent gains and losses.

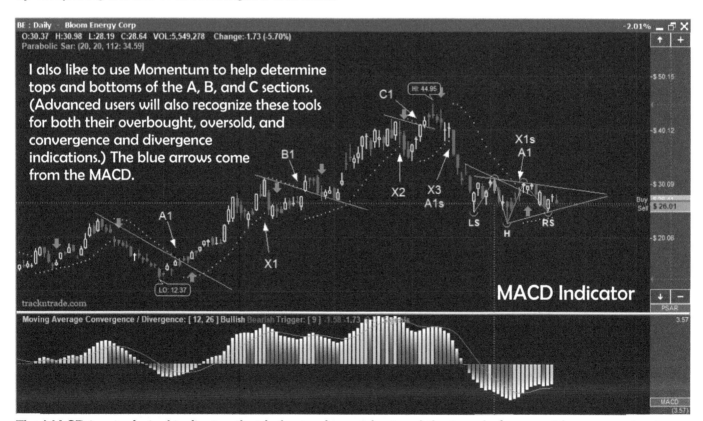

I also like to use Momentum to help determine tops and bottoms of the A, B, and C sections. (Advanced users will also recognize these tools for both their overbought, oversold, and convergence and divergence indications.) The blue arrows come from the MACD.

The MACD is a technical indicator that helps traders understand the trend of an asset by comparing two moving averages of its price and identifying changes in the direction of the trend.

Technical indicators like the Stochastics and RSI are known for their ability to show when a market is overbought or oversold. When a market is moving sideways with a bunch of ups and downs, these indicators can often predict the turning points. This is because the market is kind of balanced and not clearly trending up or down.

Both the Stochastics and RSI have a fixed scale, usually from zero to one hundred. As long as the market stays within this range, these indicators can be accurate at predicting tops and bottoms. But if the market moves beyond these boundaries and starts trending, these indicators might not work as well. This is called the Stochastics push, when the market goes beyond the limits of the indicator.

Many traders will wait for the Push to occur, (either bullish or bearish), and take that as an indication that the market is getting ready to trend. The Stochastics and RSI are basically the same thing, with the Stochastics having a wider scaling function. If you put these two indicators on top of each other, they're almost identical. It's important for traders to understand the limitations of these indicators and to use them with other analysis techniques to get a full understanding of the market.

These indicators can be useful for identifying potential turning points in a sideways market, but are much less reliable when the market is trending strongly, where they give a lot of false signals.

It's important to consider the overall market context and use both fundamental and technical analysis when making trading decisions. In short, the Stochastics and RSI can help show when a market is overbought or oversold, but it's important to understand their limitations and use them with other analysis techniques.

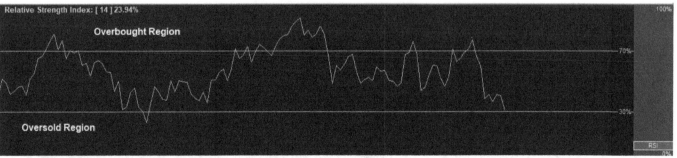

The Relative Strength Index (RSI) was developed by J. Welles Wilder Jr., a technical analyst and author, and was introduced in his 1978 book "New Concepts in Technical Trading Systems."

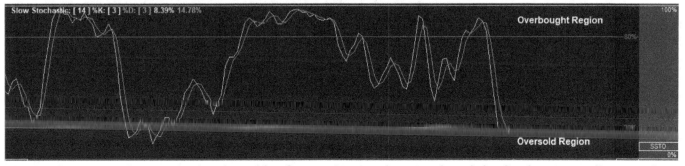

The Stochastics oscillator was developed by George Lane, who introduced the Stochastics oscillator in the 1950s as a way to identify overbought and oversold conditions in the market.

One of the most powerful features of oscillating indicators is the concept of convergence and divergence. Convergence is when the indicator is showing higher highs at the same time that the price chart is also showing higher highs. Divergence is when the price chart is showing higher highs but the indicator is showing lower highs.

My top picks for spotting convergence and divergence are the Momentum and MACD indicators. But you can also use the RSI and Stochastics to identify these patterns.

When a market starts to lose steam, you'll see the indicator stop rising and start showing lower highs while the price chart keeps going up. Or, if the price chart is showing lower lows, you might see the indicator showing higher lows. This is usually a good sign that the market is about to change direction.

It's important to note that convergence and divergence can occur in both uptrends and downtrends. For example, if you see divergence in an uptrend, it could be a sign that the market is about to reverse and start trending downward. On the other hand, if you see convergence in a downtrend, it could indicate that the market is about to turn and start trending upwards.

To use convergence and divergence to your advantage, it's important to pay attention to the overall trend of the market and look for signs that the trend is about to change. This can help you identify potential trades and make better informed decisions about when to enter or exit a position.

It's also worth noting that convergence and divergence are not always reliable indicators and should be used in conjunction with other technical analysis tools and techniques. As with any trading strategy, it's important to do your own research and use risk management techniques to minimize potential losses.

I'm not going to dwell on indicators. This book is more about learning and understanding market price action than it is how to implement mathematical modeling.

In my opinion, if you know and understand price action, you have little use for oscillating indicators.

Indicators, again, in my opinion, are the lazy man's way of trying to understand price action.

Using indicators is like a crutch you lean on when you haven't invested the time to learn price action.

Indicators were designed to tell you the turning points of price action.

If you learn price action, again, you have little need for indicators.

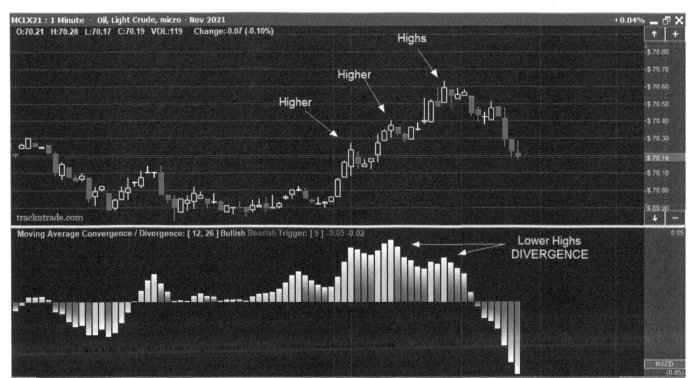

The Moving Average Convergence Divergence (MACD) indicator was developed by Gerald Appel, and introduced in 1979.

Follow the Leader

Trading requires concentration and skill, so most traders will focus all their efforts and attention on a single chart at a time, particularly when day trading.

Trying to do too much at once can be a mistake. Overloading oneself with too many tasks can cause a trader to "get behind the market," leading to mistakes and missed opportunities.

To manage multiple markets more efficiently, traders can use tools like auto-trailing stops, OCO (One-Cancels-Other), and OTO (One-Triggers-Other), which are types of order management tools that can significantly reduce workload and allow traders to trade more than one market at a time.

It's important to note that not all markets are active at the same time, where trades might work out, therefore while you concentrate your efforts into one market, it's possible to miss opportunities in other markets.

Traders who are looking to manage their workload and keep an eye on multiple markets at once can benefit from using a trading platform like Track 'n Trade, which offers a multi-chart mode feature, allowing traders to view multiple charts simultaneously.

One strategy that can be effective when using this feature is to watch the movements of all four major indexes at once. By paying attention to which market is leading the others, traders can potentially trade the followers, as they often follow the leader.

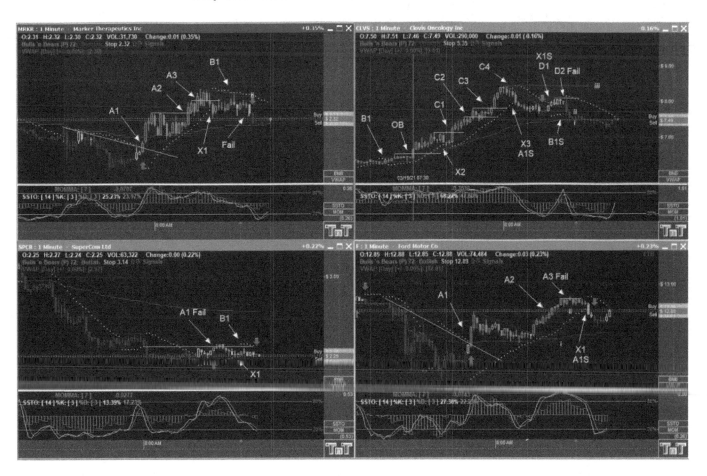

Trading Multiple Time Frames (Day Traders)

If Elliott Waves are fractal, then that would mean Fibonacci is also fractal. That would also mean recurring price patterns are fractal, therefore that would mean our entire trading strategy is fractal, right? Fractal, of course, means that we can trade this strategy on any time frame, or even multiple time frames simultaneously.

> In this example, you can see that we're trading four different time frames at the same time, counting and measuring each one as we go. 1 Min, 5 Min, 15 Min, and Daily.

> Always make sure to take the long(er) term time frames into consideration. I like to start at the high(er) time frame, identify my entry point, then move down to shorter-term time frames for execution; this is called the Top Down approach.

For example, if I'm day trading on a one minute chart, my long-term chart might be a five minute, or even a two minute chart. Referencing long(er) term charts in an effort to define the long(er) term trend is a prudent way of entering markets with a much higher degree of directional accuracy.

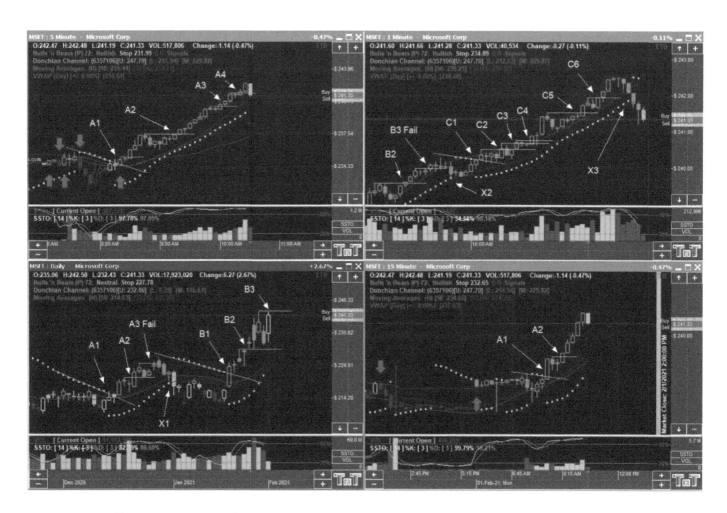

Trading on different chart time frames can allow you to take advantage of both short-term and long-term market movements, and can help you make more informed trading decisions by providing a more comprehensive view of the market.

Trading Multiple Time Frames (Active Investor)

Not everyone wants to be a day trader, many traders manage their funds from a long(er) point of view, as an active investor, keeping and holding positions for the long-term.

When managing my "personal hedge fund," for me, I like to use a 15 minute chart, a Daily Chart, a Weekly Chart, and a Monthly chart. Again, Always make sure to take the long(er) term time frames into consideration.

> I like to start at the high(er) time frame, identify my long term projections, drop down to a lower time frame to establish my entry and risk levels, then move down to shortest-term time frames for execution; this is called the Top Down approach.

When trading options, with a long(er) term horizon pay-off, such as LEAPS, we'll often manage our positions, once established, from the Weekly chart, which eliminates a lot of the 'chop' or 'choppiness' experienced on lower time frame charts.

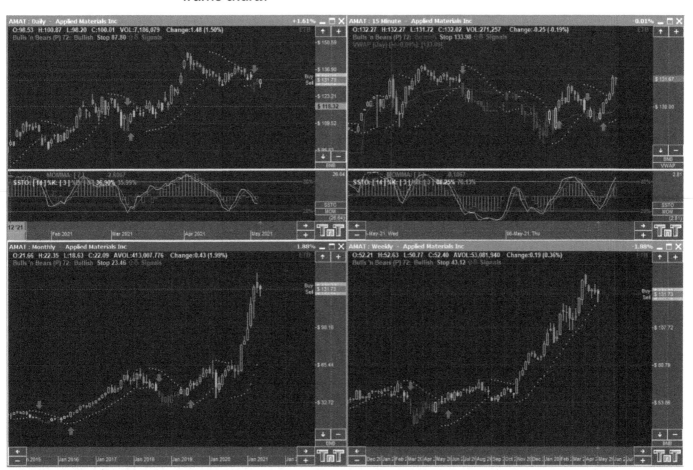

One of the advantages of using long-term charts in trading is that they provide a big picture view of the markets. By looking at longer time frames, such as daily or weekly charts, traders can get a better understanding of the overall trend of the market and identify key levels of support and resistance.

This can help us make more informed decisions about when to enter and exit trades and can also help them to manage risk more effectively.

Rule 5

Follow Through to Exit
How To Exit, When Right, and When Wrong

Lan Turner's Crash Course In Trading

Stocks * Futures * Forex

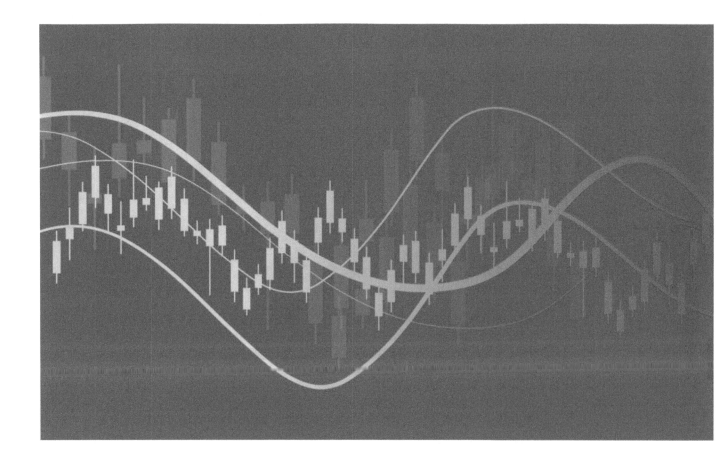

Rule 5

How to get out of the market?

Stop Loss Strategies. "Getting into a market is easy, consistently getting out with a profit takes a master trader with real skill." -- Lan Turner

If I'm wrong, when do I exit?

Break-out or bail out. "Trading is not about making money, trading is about not losing money, and until you realize that most important point, you'll never find success in trading." -- Lan Turner

Stop orders are a risk management tool used to automatically close out a position when a certain price level is reached. These orders are typically used to minimize potential losses by setting a predetermined point at which to exit a trade.

Guidelines:

1. Never enter the market with a market order; always use an entry stop, or limit. A market order is an emotional order, and generally not well thought through.

2. Once your order is triggered, place your Stop Loss Order one price bar behind the trigger/active bar. We never risk more than one price bars value on initial entry.

    We want to see an immediate pop, rally, and continuation of the trend. If you don't, then the market is weak, and the trigger point you chose was not a good one; no other traders saw it and joined in with you for the new trend; get out, wait for the next opportunity. (Don't jump in an out, and never hold onto losers.)

If I'm right, when do I exit?

1. Trail behind the low of the previous active price bar, one price bar back to break even, wipe the sweat off your brow and exit the trade in five years! ;-)

2. Continuously trail one price bar back until exit. <u>Don't jump to break even too soon,</u> let the market dictate, don't make decisions based on the active bar.

3. Break stops apart, trail one stop one price bar back until break even, trail one stop on the Blue Light, trail another stop on the PSAR, trail another stop on the ATR, trail another stop two price bars back, etc.

4. Trail any variation of trailing stops that tickles your fancy. People often ask, which is better? Nobody knows until after-the-fact, that's why we do multiples.

Limit orders can also be used to take profits by selling a Limit to sell at a higher price than the current market price. While Limit orders can be a useful tool for managing risk, it's important to carefully consider the placement of these orders as they can also limit potential profits.

What is the Bid / Ask Spread?

Every time you enter the market, you are entering through an auction process. If you've ever visited a cattle, or art auction, where the auctioneer is rattling on prices so fast that you almost can't even tell what he's saying, then you understand the process of an auction.

There is the bid price, which is the price the buyer is offering, and there is the ask price, the price that the seller is requesting. When you enter the market, you enter at the ask price, and you exit at the bid price; the difference between these two numbers is called the spread.

The spread can, in some markets, especially options, get very wide, and very expensive. (Generally speaking, the higher the volume, the tighter the spread, which is why we like trading markets with lots of volume, which results in tighter bid/ask spreads, and less 'slippage,' which is the term we use for the amount of money between the bid and the ask.

In an attempt to reduce confusion, Track 'n Trade developers have renamed the Bid/Ask spread lines to Buy/Sell lines. This makes it easier to know which side of the spread you'll be entering, and/or exiting on. If you buy the market, your order will execute on the buy line, if you sell, your order will be executed on the sell line. (When labeled Bid/Ask, many traders get confused.)

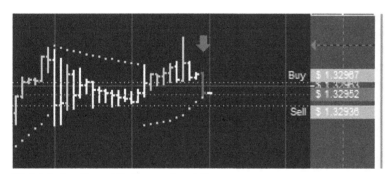

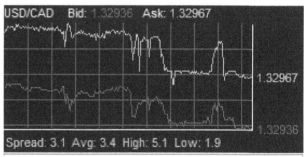

Bid / Ask : Buy / Sell on-chart lines.   Bid / Ask spread calculated in Forex

Different types of orders.

The Market Order is probably the single most popular order type there is, if you want to buy a stock, you simply click the button in your software that says buy, and generally speaking, that button will be a Market Order.

A market order fills your request at the first available price, as quickly as possible. (You are not guaranteed a specific price, you're just filled at the first available price.) I don't recommend traders enter the market using Market orders, since they're emotional orders, usually not well thought out.

- When day trading, I'll sometimes use the Market order as a quick way of taking profits along the trend, reducing our holdings incrementally as markets move in our favor. (Never say never)

The Stop Order is my favorite order type, it's the most universally used order of all the orders. In my methodology, 90% of all entry and exit's are based on Stop Orders.

it's an order that specifies a price level that the market must pass through to become filled, it's like a price trigger, and can be used for both entry as well as exit.

Buy Stops are placed above the market, and sell Stops are placed below the market. When the market moves through the price specified, the order is triggered, becoming a market order, therefore a stop order is subject to slippage.

The most common use of the stop order is for exit. A trader will continually move, or trail, their stop up behind levels of support or resistance looking to lock in profit as a market rises in price; better known as stop loss orders.

I like to trail an open stop order for entry on the Blue Lights, the TnT software can automatically trail a rising/falling market with the intent to enter the market (or exit) when the indicator 'intercepts' price.

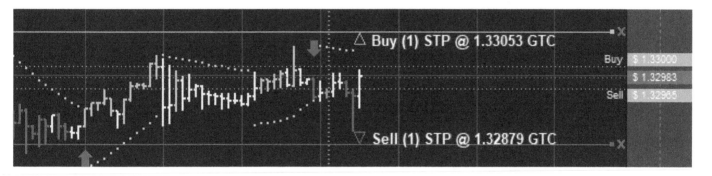

Limit Orders; when placing a limit order you are guaranteed by the exchange to receive the specified price or better. If the exchange is unable to give you the price requested, your order will not get filled, therefore there is no slippage when trading with Limit orders.

When placing a limit order, you must place the buy limit below the current market price, and the sell limit above the current market price. Limit orders are most commonly used for taking profits when a specified price is reached.

My favorite use scenarios for the use of Limit orders is to take profits at various locations as a market rallies/falls and hits target price levels, and when trading the revers psychology trading strategy (See strategies section.)

Intercept and Contingency Orders

Stop orders are our most powerful weapon. Within the Track 'n Trade platform, we have the ability to setup auto trailing stops based on various strategies, including price bars back, which trail behind levels of support, percentages, dollars back, tics back, or on any number of mathematical models such as the Blue Light, the PSAR, or the ATR. These are called contingency & intercept orders, and we use them for both entry as well as exiting the market.

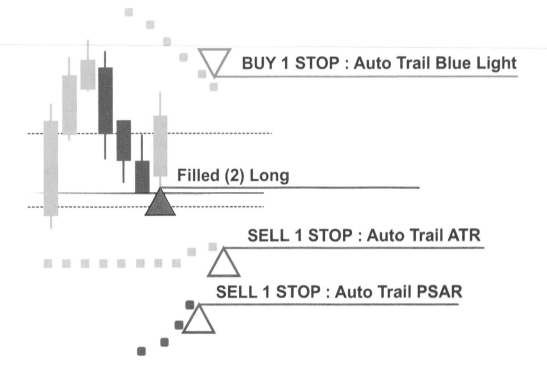

BUY 1 STOP : Auto Trail Blue Light

Filled (2) Long

SELL 1 STOP : Auto Trail ATR

SELL 1 STOP : Auto Trail PSAR

OCO (One Cancels Other) and OTO (One Triggers Other) are advanced order types that allow Stops and Limit orders to trigger or cancel each other.

Within the Track 'n Trade platform, these (Q-OCO) order buttons can be pre-programmed for a complete one click trading strategy; trigger-entry, auto-exit, and auto-cancel un-filled orders, all with a single click of the mouse. Many of our trading strategies (see strategies section) implement the use of OCO/OTO order tools, which makes trading fast, fast, and simple.

Stop Loss Strategies

Moving stops to break-even is an art, not a science. Break out or bail out; one popular method is to count three bars, if the market has not broken out in your favor within three bars, then exit the trade.

My Rule: As long as the price bars continually cross over your entry (strike) price, remain in the trade; as soon as you get a complete OHLC bar that prints below your entry strike, exit the trade.

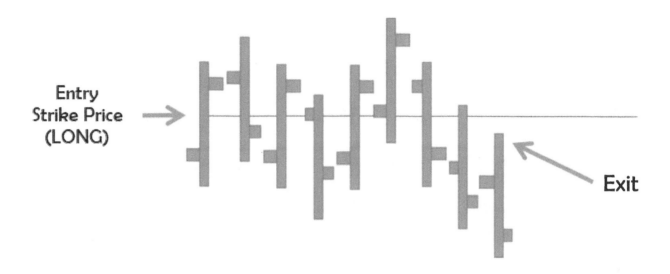

Entry
Strike Price
(LONG)

Exit

One you get a complete OHLC bar that prints above your entry (strike) price, begin to move your stop to break-even behind levels of support. Be patient, sometimes it takes several bars before the market begins to trend once it breaks your trigger point.

There are several different types of stop loss orders, including basic stop loss orders, trailing stop loss orders, and adjusted stop loss orders. Each type of stop loss order has its own specific characteristics and can be used in different market situations.

Entry
Strike Price
(LONG)

Move Stop
To Break-Even

Stop Loss Strategies

Where to drop initial stop orders, then trail stops on red lights, blue lights, or split between.

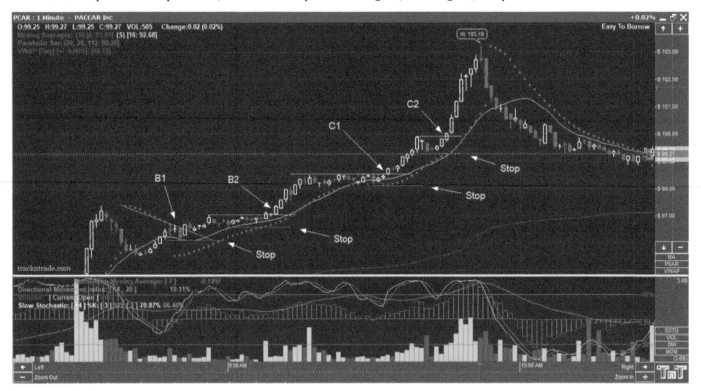

Stop loss orders are a useful risk management tool, as they allow you to set predetermined levels at which your positions will be closed. This can help to ensure that losses are kept to a minimum, even if the market moves against what you expect.

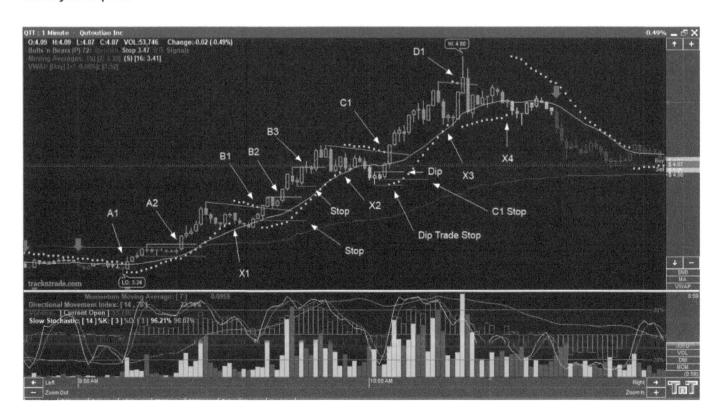

Multi-Order Exit Strategy

As the old saying goes, "There are multiple ways to skin a cat," and the same goes for exiting a market; there are multiple strategies designed to exit a profitable trade in an attempt to maximize our profit potential, here are three strategies for your consideration.

1.   Continually trail behind the Blue Light System, or any combination of mathematically calculated trailing stop systems. (See next page.)

2.   Continually trail behind levels of support and/or resistance, use a combination of support and resistance levels along with mathematically trailing stops locations, to achieve the best of both worlds.

3.   Trail to break-even, stop trailing, wait for exit signal from your favorite indicator (See example below.)

Had we entered on A1, or possibly B1, and continued to trail the Blue Light, we would have been taken out of the trade several times throughout the trend.

That said, had we simply entered on A1, brought out stop to break-even, and waited for the Red Exit Arrow from our Bulls 'n Bears indicator we would have caught the entire down trend from start to finish.

This does not mean we should buy on every buy signal and sell on every sell signal, we still want to be mindful of our A1, B1 and C1 Entries, and protect our entries with stop orders. (This is food for thought, markets are dynamic, therefore each new trade usually ends up being a combination of strategies.)

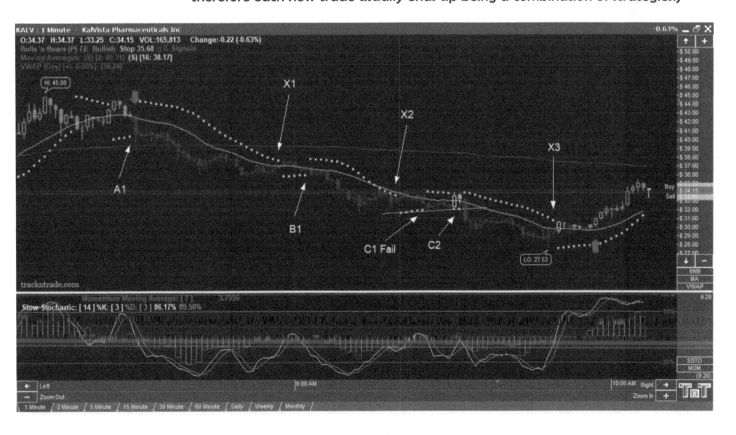

Advanced, Multi-Leg Stop Loss Strategies

You've heard me say, "cut your losers short, let your winners run!" You've also heard me say, "Take profits along the way." So how do we do both? How do we get the best of both worlds?

In this chart example, we see three different mathematically calculated trailing stop systems all running simultaneously, The Red Light (PSAR), the Blue Light (Bulls 'n Bears), and the Yellow Light (ATR, Average True Range.)

> I think it goes without saying, that you can trail on any system that you want, you can trail on the Red Lights, the Yellow Lights, or the Blue Lights, or you can break your stops apart and trail on any combination thereof, or just wait for exit arrow. There are advantages and disadvantages to each system, depending on how you setup the system in the first place.

I think of it like the three bears, the red light are Baby Bear, it's very short/small trends, jumps you in and out of the market more quickly, the Yellow Lights are Papa Bear, which attempts to keep you in the market for as long as possible, less whipsaw, whereas the Blue Light is Momma Bear, my favorite, which is in between the other two, and takes the middle road; not too aggressive, but not too lackadaisical.

Trader's ask me all the time, which is better, Red, Blue, or Yellow? I always say, "I don't know until after the fact, so that's why we often-times use all three simultaneously."

Once you enter the a trade with multiple contracts, one of my favorite strategies is to attach an auto-trailing stop to each of the three mathematical models, and let the market determine when we exit.

If you get stopped out, take profits, with the red light, consider reentering the trade with the next red light signal, playing each system independently but all at the same time, creating a very robust strategy

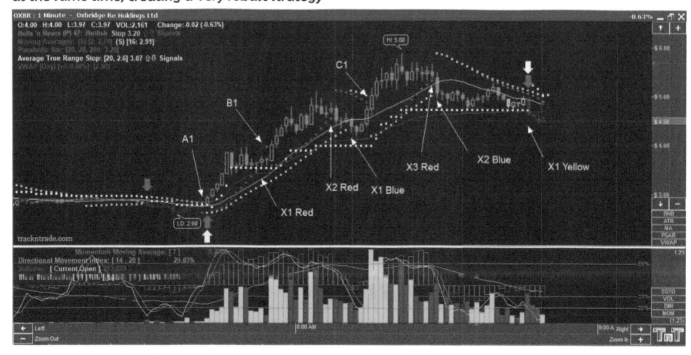

Fear & Greed. Trading Brave, or Scared?

> "Trader's are generally brave when they should be scared, and
> scared when they should be brave." -- Lan Turner

Generally speaking, when a trader starts to make money, and the market finally moves in their favor, traders have a tendency to start to get scared, scared their going to lose the small winner they're experiencing.

Most traders have a tendency to jump in and out of markets randomly, on each single bar rally, looking for a new break out. These patterns have a very high failure rate, so when they finally catch a small winner, they're scared it's going to fail once again, so they quickly jump out with a very small winner.

On the other hand, when this same trader is in a losing trade, he has a tendency to hang on to his winner. He has patience for his losers, but not for his winners. He's brave through the losers, telling himself, "Hold on! It WILL come back!" But scared during his winners.

Trading scared when you're winning, and brave when your losing is generally caused by over trading, and not having a solid trading plan. Traders who quickly jump on every one bar rally, or trade from a point of anxiousness generally find themselves in this reverse camp of being brave when they should be scared, and scared when they should be brave.

When you're in a trade, and it's making money, this is the time you should be brave, and run your risk management strategies for letting your winners run. When you're in a losing trade, this is when you should be scared, and be looking for a graceful exit quickly and decisively, before you get your ass handed to you by the market.

> Not all profitable trades can be huge winners with long-lasting trends; most great trades are small three to five-bar rallies, where price moves to test previous areas of support or resistance.

We've been taught to stay in for the big win; let your winners run! The flip side of this issue is that traders refuse to take profits along the way as price hits key areas of support and resistance. Where markets have a tendency to reverses which results in it hitting our trailing stops, frequently turning winners into losers or very small winners at best.

This is a common occurrence when trading, which stems from the two most powerful emotions in the market: fear and greed. Traders often believe they can ride the wave of success, causing them to hold onto their winning positions for too long, hoping for maximum profits. But, because markets are unpredictable, the price can suddenly drop, leaving the trader with a significant loss.

This is why having a sound risk management strategy is critical. This strategy should involve taking profits at predetermined key support and resistance levels and cutting losses if the market moves against you; learn to balance your fear and greed.

Risk Management

Maximizing Returns Minimizing Risk

Lan Turner's Crash Course In Trading

Stocks * Futures * Forex

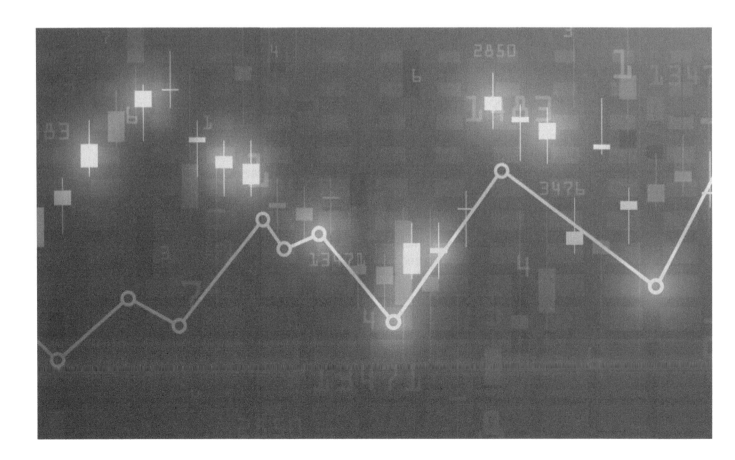

Risk management is a crucial part of trading and investing. It's all about identifying and assessing the potential risks in your portfolio and taking steps to minimize or mitigate those risks. Good risk management can help you maximize your returns, minimize potential losses, and achieve your financial goals.

One way to manage risk is through diversification. This means investing in a variety of asset classes and securities rather than putting all your eggs in one basket. Diversification helps spread out your risk, so that if one investment doesn't pan out, it won't have a huge impact on your overall portfolio.

Stop-loss orders are an important tool for risk management. Setting predetermined levels at which you'll sell an asset if it drops in value, in order to minimize potential losses. By establishing clear exit points for investments that aren't performing as expected, stop-loss orders help you manage risk.

But risk management isn't just for traders and investors — it's a concept that's applicable to all areas of life. Have you ever heard the saying "the house always wins" in gambling? That's because casinos have mastered the art of risk management. They understand the odds of each game and set the rules in their favor to minimize their risk of loss. As a result, they're able to make a profit even when the majority of players don't.

If you want something, you must declare it!

1. Understand and set realistic goals.

2. Define how much money you want to make, then do the math to figure what it will take to achieve your goal.

3. Don't have unrealistic expectations.

Fixed Risk Investment Strategy #1; Fixed Percentage; 1% to 5%. (Beginner)

1. At 5%, of a $10,000 account, you would invest in any one trade $500.

   b. At 1%, of a $10,000 account, you would invest in any one trade $100.

Fixed investment position sizing helps control risk; good for beginners.

Position Sizing Strategies #2; Breakout or Bailout. (Advanced)

1. 75%-100% of your account into a single position; tight stop.

   a. Advantage: If the trade moves as expected, large returns.

   b. Disadvantage: Missed opportunities on other markets.

   c. Stop Exit Risk Percentage; 1% to 5%.

      i. At a 5% stop risk, you could lose 20 times in a row before blowing up your account.

      ii. At 1% stop risk, you could lose 100 times in a row before blowing up your account.

Risk vs. Reward Ratios, The 1% Rule

The 1% rule is a principle in trading and investing that suggests you should never risk more than 1% of your account on any given trade. This means that if you have a $10,000 account, you should never risk more than $100 on a single trade. The idea behind the 1% rule is to protect your capital and minimize the potential for large losses.

By following the 1% rule, you can reduce the impact of any one trade on your overall portfolio. This can help you manage your risk and stay in the game even if you have a string of losing trades.

If we work from a simple 2:1 Risk vs. Reward Ratio, we can do some simple math to figure out how much money we can make, and still be wrong most of the time.

Let's first do some math. Let's say we have a $30,000 account, how many times can I trade and lose in a row before I blow up my account?

- Risk 1%, or $300, would be 100 trades

- Risk 3%, or $900, would be 33 trades

- Risk 5%, or $1,500, would be 20 trades

If we risk just 1% of our account, ($300 per trade) and we're wrong 100% of the time, we could make 100 trades before blowing up our account.

Now, let's say we're not wrong 100% of the time, let's say we're only wrong 50% of the time. In this scenario, a 50% winning ratio, with a 2:1 winning percentage, trading 100 times would produce the following results.

- If we win 50% of the time, we would make $600.00 each trade ($30,000)

- If we lose 50% we would lose $300.00 each trade ($15,000)

- If we made 100 trades, losing 50%, we would still profit $15,000

Now, the question is, how many times could we lose, and still be profitable?

- If we win 33% of the time, we would make $600 each ($19,800)

- If we lost 67% of the time, we would lose $300 each ($20,100)

- In this 2:1 Risk vs. Reward model, we would still make, $600 in profit.

Strategy: Don't put all your eggs in one basket. Let's say you decide to risk 1%, or $300 per trade, if you spread that across multiple opportunities, you could raise the odds of catching a rising star exponentially.

For example, you could risk all $300 on a single stock, or you could risk $100 on three stocks, or you could risk $50 on six stocks. This is how you built yourself a larger and larger portfolio over time.

Position Sizing

Position sizing is all about how much of your account you use for each trade. It's a way to manage risk by controlling how much of your money is on the line with any given trade. By figuring out the right position size for each trade, you can trade with a comfortable level of risk and maximize your returns over the long term.

There are a few things to consider when determining your position size, like the size of your account, your risk tolerance, and your overall trading strategy. By taking these factors into account, you can decide how much to invest in each trade and build a diversified portfolio that aligns with your goals and risk tolerance.

Position sizing isn't just about risk management though. It can also help you optimize your returns by allowing you to take advantage of good trades without overexposing your account. Calculating your risk vs. reward ratio is always the first step before placing any trade. Calculating our reward is trickier than calculating our risk, risk is a simple and easy process described here; we cover calculating reward potential in our Fibonacci Projection section of this manual.

Whenever you enter the market, make sure the very next move you make is to set your stop loss order, determine the risk you are willing to take, based on your calculated reward. (We call this our risk vs. reward ratio.)

If you get in, and you are wrong, how much money are you willing to give up to the market to find that out? Once that number is hit, get out!

Strategy:

If the move/loss the market must make to prove to you that it is not going to go in your favor is too much money for your taste, then trade smaller positions size.

Here's how to do that...

Step 1:   Determine your entry point.

Step 2:   Determine where your stop loss order is going to go. (Where you are going to get out if you are wrong.)

Step 3:   Determine the amount of money you would be willing to lose if your wrong if the market hits your stop. (1%, 3%, or 5% of your account balance depending on your confidence level; consider Elliott probabilities as your guide.)

Step 4:   Calculate, then buy the number of shares that would result in the amount of money you would be willing to lose if you are wrong and your stop loss order gets hit; that is the number of shares you should trade.

Always calculate for the worst and hope for the best; the closer the stop, the more shares, the further out the stop, the fewer the shares. (Find that sweet spot where it works best for you and your risk tolerance.)

Risk Management

Regardless of your account size, find the right position size that matches your trading style. If you risk too little your account won't grow, if you risk too much, your account can be destroyed with just a few bad trades; set trading limits!

Rule #1: Set your daily profit goal.

- o Beginner, $20 - $100

- o Intermediate, $500 - $1,000

- o Advanced, $3,000 +

Rule #2: Set daily max loss; your first loss is usually your smallest loss.

- o Beginner, $50

- o Intermediate, $500

- o Advanced, $1,500

Rule #3: Number of Losing Trades. (Three strikes your out!)

- o Three losing trades in a row. (Don't over trade!)

- o If you only have three shots at it, you're more likely to only take the very best of the best trades.

Rule #4: Final Exit

- o You hit your daily profit goal.

- o You hit your daily stop loss.

- o You give back half your profits.

Scale Up, Then Scale Out as the Day Progresses

1. Start with small(er) position sizes; build a cushion.

2. Once you've built a cushion, take large(r) position sizes.

3. Once you've reached daily profit/loss target, stop trading.

4. If you continue, then stop trading when you start losing.

5. Only dollar cost average up, not down, don't pyramid, only pillar.

6. Keep total average position behind your trailing stop.

7. Be systematic about adding-on.on't spend all profits on new shares.

8. Take profits along the way.

Traders can take a lesson from Poker players.

1. You don't have to play every hand. (Qualify each and every signal.)

2. Bet small when you get a decent hand/signal. (A3, B3, C3)

3. Bet big when you get a fantastic hand/signal. (A1, B1, C1)

4. Don't expect to recover all your losses in a single hand/trade.

5. Don't trade your P&L, trade the setups, trade the hand your dealt.

6. Never risk more than 10% of your purse on any single hand.

7. Walk away when you're ahead. (Set daily profit goal.)

8. top when you hit your daily max loss. (Set daily max loss.)

9. Losers stay and play, winners walk away.

10. Cards/Markets run cold more than they run hot.

11. When we've got the houses/markets money, that's when we kick it up!

Size Matters

Sizing up and sizing down refer to adjusting the number of shares or contracts you trade in order to manage risk and optimize returns. When you size up, you increase the number of shares or contracts you trade, which can potentially increase your profits if the trade is successful. However, it can also increase your risk if the trade goes against you.

On the other hand, sizing down means decreasing the number of shares or contracts you trade. This can reduce your risk, but it can also limit your potential profits. Sizing down is often used as a risk management strategy, particularly in volatile markets or when trading with a small account.

In the following spreadsheet example, you see the answer to the biggest question I always receive; "What does it take to make a thousand dollars a day?"

> Every new trader thinks, if they can just make a thousand dollars a day, they'll be set for life! This table outlines, using a $5.00 stock, how many shares, down the left column, vs. how far the market would have to move, across the top row, to achieve the desired result.

In the beginning, we start with small share size, (lower risk) and look for long(er) moves in the market, but as we progress in skill, we soon begin to increase share size, and achieve the same results with small(er) market moves

SIZE MATTERS - STOCK MARKET
* Calculations do not represent the difference in the spread, entry vs. exit.

Share Size $ 5.00		Size of Move $ 0.05	$ 0.10	$ 0.20	$ 0.25	$ 0.50	$ 0.75	$ 1.00
Share Qty	Investment							
50	$ 250.00	$ 12.50	$ 25.00	$ 50.00	$ 62.50	$ 125.00	$ 187.50	$ 250.00
75	$ 375.00	$ 18.75	$ 37.50	$ 75.00	$ 93.75	$ 187.50	$ 281.25	$ 375.00
100	$ 500.00	$ 25.00	$ 50.00	$ 100.00	$ 125.00	$ 250.00	$ 375.00	$ 500.00
125	$ 625.00	$ 31.25	$ 62.50	$ 125.00	$ 156.25	$ 312.50	$ 468.75	$ 625.00
150	$ 750.00	$ 37.50	$ 75.00	$ 150.00	$ 187.50	$ 375.00	$ 562.50	$ 750.00
175	$ 875.00	$ 43.75	$ 87.50	$ 175.00	$ 218.75	$ 437.50	$ 656.25	$ 875.00
200	$ 1,000.00	$ 50.00	$ 100.00	$ 200.00	$ 250.00	$ 500.00	$ 750.00	$ 1,000.00
300	$ 1,500.00	$ 75.00	$ 150.00	$ 300.00	$ 375.00	$ 750.00	$ 1,125.00	$ 1,500.00
400	$ 2,000.00	$ 100.00	$ 200.00	$ 400.00	$ 500.00	$ 1,000.00	$ 1,500.00	$ 2,000.00
500	$ 2,500.00	$ 125.00	$ 250.00	$ 500.00	$ 625.00	$ 1,250.00	$ 1,875.00	$ 2,500.00
600	$ 3,000.00	$ 150.00	$ 300.00	$ 600.00	$ 750.00	$ 1,500.00	$ 2,250.00	$ 3,000.00
700	$ 3,500.00	$ 175.00	$ 350.00	$ 700.00	$ 875.00	$ 1,750.00	$ 2,625.00	$ 3,500.00
800	$ 4,000.00	$ 200.00	$ 400.00	$ 800.00	$ 1,000.00	$ 2,000.00	$ 3,000.00	$ 4,000.00
900	$ 4,500.00	$ 225.00	$ 450.00	$ 900.00	$ 1,125.00	$ 2,250.00	$ 3,375.00	$ 4,500.00
1,000	$ 5,000.00	$ 250.00	$ 500.00	$ 1,000.00	$ 1,250.00	$ 2,500.00	$ 3,750.00	$ 5,000.00
1,500	$ 7,500.00	$ 375.00	$ 750.00	$ 1,500.00	$ 1,875.00	$ 3,750.00	$ 5,625.00	$ 7,500.00
2,000	$ 10,000.00	$ 500.00	$ 1,000.00	$ 2,000.00	$ 2,500.00	$ 5,000.00	$ 7,500.00	$ 10,000.00
2,500	$ 12,500.00	$ 625.00	$ 1,250.00	$ 2,500.00	$ 3,125.00	$ 6,250.00	$ 9,375.00	$ 12,500.00
3,000	$ 15,000.00	$ 750.00	$ 1,500.00	$ 3,000.00	$ 3,750.00	$ 7,500.00	$ 11,250.00	$ 15,000.00
3,500	$ 17,500.00	$ 875.00	$ 1,750.00	$ 3,500.00	$ 4,375.00	$ 8,750.00	$ 13,125.00	$ 17,500.00
4,000	$ 20,000.00	$ 1,000.00	$ 2,000.00	$ 4,000.00	$ 5,000.00	$ 10,000.00	$ 15,000.00	$ 20,000.00
4,500	$ 22,500.00	$ 1,125.00	$ 2,250.00	$ 4,500.00	$ 5,625.00	$ 11,250.00	$ 16,875.00	$ 22,500.00
5,000	$ 25,000.00	$ 1,250.00	$ 2,500.00	$ 5,000.00	$ 6,250.00	$ 12,500.00	$ 18,750.00	$ 25,000.00
6,000	$ 30,000.00	$ 1,500.00	$ 3,000.00	$ 6,000.00	$ 7,500.00	$ 15,000.00	$ 22,500.00	$ 30,000.00
7,000	$ 35,000.00	$ 1,750.00	$ 3,500.00	$ 7,000.00	$ 8,750.00	$ 17,500.00	$ 26,250.00	$ 35,000.00
8,000	$ 40,000.00	$ 2,000.00	$ 4,000.00	$ 8,000.00	$ 10,000.00	$ 20,000.00	$ 30,000.00	$ 40,000.00
9,000	$ 45,000.00	$ 2,250.00	$ 4,500.00	$ 9,000.00	$ 11,250.00	$ 22,500.00	$ 33,750.00	$ 45,000.00
10,000	$ 50,000.00	$ 2,500.00	$ 5,000.00	$ 10,000.00	$ 12,500.00	$ 25,000.00	$ 37,500.00	$ 50,000.00

Size Matters Futures vs Forex

One key difference between sizing trades in futures and Forex is the concept of leverage. In Forex, traders often use leverage to trade larger positions with a smaller amount of capital. For example, a Forex broker may offer a leverage ratio of 50:1, which means a trader can trade a position worth $50,000 with only $1,000 of their own capital. This can magnify both profits and losses; use leverage responsibly and manage risk carefully.

SIZE MATTERS - eMINI S&P 500

* Calculations do not represent commissions, fees, and spread.

Contracts Qty	Full Point 1.00 $ 50.00 (Day Margin)	Size of Move $ 0.25	$ 0.50	$ 1.00	$ 1.50	$ 2.00	$ 3.00	$ 5.00
1	$ 500.00	$ 12.50	$ 25.00	$ 50.00	$ 75.00	$ 100.00	$ 150.00	$ 250.00
2	$ 1,000.00	$ 25.00	$ 50.00	$ 100.00	$ 150.00	$ 200.00	$ 300.00	$ 500.00
3	$ 1,500.00	$ 37.50	$ 75.00	$ 150.00	$ 225.00	$ 300.00	$ 450.00	$ 750.00
4	$ 2,000.00	$ 50.00	$ 100.00	$ 200.00	$ 300.00	$ 400.00	$ 600.00	$ 1,000.00
5	$ 2,500.00	$ 62.50	$ 125.00	$ 250.00	$ 375.00	$ 500.00	$ 750.00	$ 1,250.00
6	$ 3,000.00	$ 75.00	$ 150.00	$ 300.00	$ 450.00	$ 600.00	$ 900.00	$ 1,500.00
7	$ 3,500.00	$ 87.50	$ 175.00	$ 350.00	$ 525.00	$ 700.00	$ 1,050.00	$ 1,750.00
8	$ 4,000.00	$ 100.00	$ 200.00	$ 400.00	$ 600.00	$ 800.00	$ 1,200.00	$ 2,000.00
9	$ 4,500.00	$ 112.50	$ 225.00	$ 450.00	$ 675.00	$ 900.00	$ 1,350.00	$ 2,250.00
10	$ 5,000.00	$ 125.00	$ 250.00	$ 500.00	$ 750.00	$ 1,000.00	$ 1,500.00	$ 2,500.00
12	$ 6,000.00	$ 150.00	$ 300.00	$ 600.00	$ 900.00	$ 1,200.00	$ 1,800.00	$ 3,000.00
14	$ 7,000.00	$ 175.00	$ 350.00	$ 700.00	$ 1,050.00	$ 1,400.00	$ 2,100.00	$ 3,500.00
16	$ 8,000.00	$ 200.00	$ 400.00	$ 800.00	$ 1,200.00	$ 1,600.00	$ 2,400.00	$ 4,000.00
18	$ 9,000.00	$ 225.00	$ 450.00	$ 900.00	$ 1,350.00	$ 1,800.00	$ 2,700.00	$ 4,500.00
20	$ 10,000.00	$ 250.00	$ 500.00	$ 1,000.00	$ 1,500.00	$ 2,000.00	$ 3,000.00	$ 5,000.00

SIZE MATTERS - FOREX EUR/USD (Mini Account)

* Calculations do not represent the difference in the spread, entry vs. exit.

Lots Qty	One Pip $ 10.00 (Day Margin)	Size of Move $ 0.0025	$ 0.0050	$ 0.0100	$ 0.0125	$ 0.0150	$ 0.0175	$ 0.0200
1	$ 280.00	$ 25.00	$ 50.00	$ 100.00	$ 125.00	$ 150.00	$ 175.00	$ 200.00
2	$ 560.00	$ 50.00	$ 100.00	$ 200.00	$ 250.00	$ 300.00	$ 350.00	$ 400.00
3	$ 840.00	$ 75.00	$ 150.00	$ 300.00	$ 375.00	$ 450.00	$ 525.00	$ 600.00
4	$ 1,120.00	$ 100.00	$ 200.00	$ 400.00	$ 500.00	$ 600.00	$ 700.00	$ 800.00
5	$ 1,400.00	$ 125.00	$ 250.00	$ 500.00	$ 625.00	$ 750.00	$ 875.00	$ 1,000.00
6	$ 1,680.00	$ 150.00	$ 300.00	$ 600.00	$ 750.00	$ 900.00	$ 1,050.00	$ 1,200.00
7	$ 1,960.00	$ 175.00	$ 350.00	$ 700.00	$ 875.00	$ 1,050.00	$ 1,225.00	$ 1,400.00
8	$ 2,240.00	$ 200.00	$ 400.00	$ 800.00	$ 1,000.00	$ 1,200.00	$ 1,400.00	$ 1,600.00
9	$ 2,520.00	$ 225.00	$ 450.00	$ 900.00	$ 1,125.00	$ 1,350.00	$ 1,575.00	$ 1,800.00
10	$ 2,800.00	$ 250.00	$ 500.00	$ 1,000.00	$ 1,250.00	$ 1,500.00	$ 1,750.00	$ 2,000.00
12	$ 3,360.00	$ 300.00	$ 600.00	$ 1,200.00	$ 1,500.00	$ 1,800.00	$ 2,100.00	$ 2,400.00
14	$ 3,920.00	$ 350.00	$ 700.00	$ 1,400.00	$ 1,750.00	$ 2,100.00	$ 2,450.00	$ 2,800.00
16	$ 4,480.00	$ 400.00	$ 800.00	$ 1,600.00	$ 2,000.00	$ 2,400.00	$ 2,800.00	$ 3,200.00
18	$ 5,040.00	$ 450.00	$ 900.00	$ 1,800.00	$ 2,250.00	$ 2,700.00	$ 3,150.00	$ 3,600.00
20	$ 5,600.00	$ 500.00	$ 1,000.00	$ 2,000.00	$ 2,500.00	$ 3,000.00	$ 3,500.00	$ 4,000.00
25	$ 7,000.00	$ 625.00	$ 1,250.00	$ 2,500.00	$ 3,125.00	$ 3,750.00	$ 4,375.00	$ 5,000.00

There are two common methods for factoring your trade size.

Traders who trade starting with a small amount and add onto their position as the market moves in their favor are using a strategy called pyramiding. This involves adding to a winning position by using the profits from the trade to increase the size of the position. Pyramiding can be a useful way to maximize profits and accelerate the growth of a trading account, but it also carries additional risk because it involves adding to a position that is already in the market.

On the other hand, traders who start with a small position and take off positions as the market moves in their favor are using a strategy called scaling out. This involves closing out part of a winning position at different price levels as the trade moves in your favor. Scaling out can help traders capture profits and reduce risk, but it also means that you may miss out on potential additional profits if the market continues to move in your favor.

Many traders will say, for example, I'm going to start my initial entry with 100 shares at A1, then increase my holdings by adding 50 more shares at A2, then add 25 shares as markets move in my favor at A3.

Other traders will use a dollar size amount, for example, I'm going to start with a $1,000 investment at A1, then add $500 at A2, then add $250 at A3.

> Either method is acceptable, it will depend on what makes the most sense in your mind, and will depend on account size, and share price calculations.

In this example, you can see two comparison tables of the exact same trades, with different share quantity, and the resulting profit and loss, and investment amount required.

SIZE MATTERS - STOCK MARKET SIZING COMPARISON
Simulated day trading a small account vs. a larg(er) account, size and profit/loss comparison.

Symbol	Name	Entry	Quantity	Rate	Cost Basis	Exit	Rate	Gain
OLB	The OLB Group Inc	Bought	100	$ 16.00	$ 1,600.00	Sold	$ 15.35	$ (65.00)
OLB	The OLB Group Inc	Bought	100	$ 13.36	$ 1,336.00	Sold	$ 15.11	$ 175.00
OLB	The OLB Group Inc	Bought	50	$ 13.36	$ 668.00	Sold	$ 13.78	$ 21.00
OLB	The OLB Group Inc	Bought	200	$ 14.50	$ 2,900.00	Sold	$ 14.08	$ (84.00)
OLB	The OLB Group Inc	Bought	100	$ 14.30	$ 1,430.00	Sold	$ 14.23	$ (7.00)
OLB	The OLB Group Inc	Bought	200	$ 13.89	$ 2,778.00	Sold	$ 14.21	$ 64.00
								$ 104.00

Symbol	Name	Entry	Quantity	Rate	Cost Basis	Exit	Rate	Gain
OLB	The OLB Group Inc	Bought	1000	$ 16.00	$ 16,000.00	Sold	$ 15.35	$ (650.00)
OLB	The OLB Group Inc	Bought	1000	$ 13.36	$ 13,360.00	Sold	$ 15.11	$ 1,750.00
OLB	The OLB Group Inc	Bought	500	$ 13.36	$ 6,680.00	Sold	$ 13.78	$ 210.00
OLB	The OLB Group Inc	Bought	2000	$ 14.50	$ 29,000.00	Sold	$ 14.08	$ (840.00)
OLB	The OLB Group Inc	Bought	1000	$ 14.30	$ 14,300.00	Sold	$ 14.23	$ (70.00)
OLB	The OLB Group Inc	Bought	2000	$ 13.89	$ 27,780.00	Sold	$ 14.21	$ 640.00
								$ 1,040.00

What does a winning traders portfolio look like?

New traders easily get frustrated when it comes to trading, because "it looks so easy!"

"Look! If I would have bought there, and sold there, I would have been rich!"
- Said by every trader ever.

While it may be easy to identify the patterns that led to successful trades after the fact, predicting these patterns before they happen is much more challenging. Many people believe that they have a unique ability to succeed in trading, but the reality is that it is difficult for everyone.

The best way to improve your ability to trade in the future is to analyze past market trends and practice identifying recurring patterns as they occur. This requires a significant amount of time spent studying charts and patterns, which is a necessary investment in your development as a trader. Just like pilots need to log a certain amount of "butt in the seat" time to become proficient, traders need to put in the work to hone their skills.

That said, there's nothing more satisfying than mastering a skill that other's find difficult. Anything that's worth doing in life is going to be difficult to achieve, and even more difficult to maintain. There's going to always be someone gunning for you. Admit it, commit yourself, study, and practice, don't take this light heartedly; I can promise you, the guy who's on the other side of your trade is taking this very seriously.

Here's what a winning trader's stages of portfolio growth, profits and losses looks like:

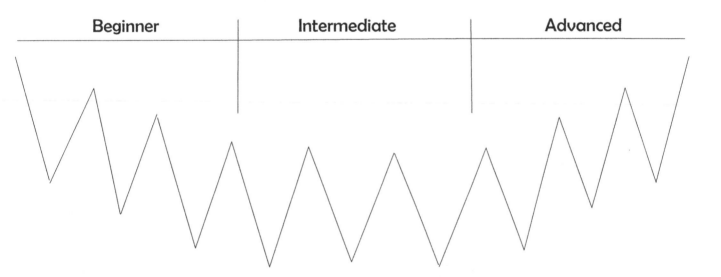

The fallacy is that advanced traders don't take losses, they do, they just have smaller, and fewer losses than they did when they were beginners and intermediate traders.

Most traders, 80% in fact, never make it past the intermediate stage of trading, they have successes, they feel the thrill of victory, but they can't get past the agony of defeat. The difference between an intermediate trader, and advanced is so slight, it's almost unrecognizable.

Many would be great traders get 90% there, and then give up, because they think, for some reason, that they're supposed to now be winning every trade, every day; they have unrealistic expectations.

I'm here to tell you, sorry, that's never going to happen. Every single day is a struggle, even the "Top Gun" traders have losing streaks, and big losing days, everyone must fight the revenge trade virus, every day.

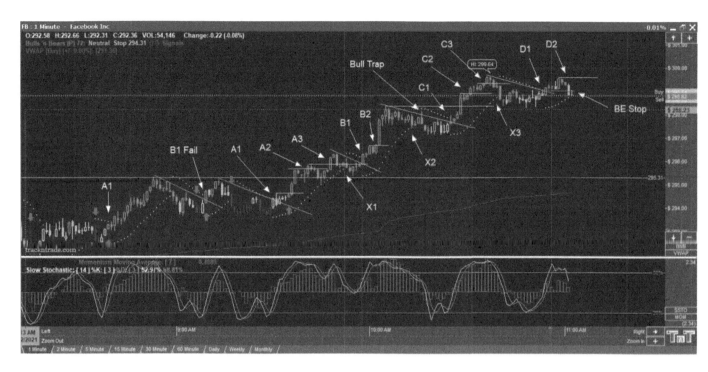

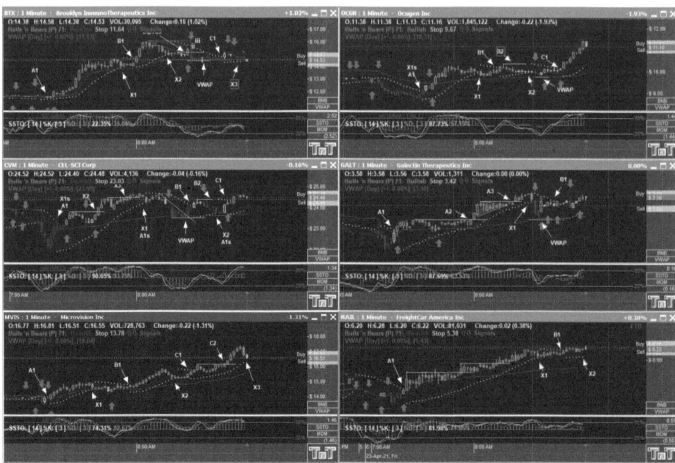

Trading the stock market on multiple charts simultaneously, also known as multi-timeframe trading, can be a useful strategies. By looking at different time frames, we can identify both short-term and long-term trends, and make more informed decisions about when to enter and exit trades. However, it's important to note that this strategy can be time-consuming and may require specialized software (Track 'n Trade) to manage multiple charts effectively.

Learn to have patience

"Investing is not a game where the guy with the 160 IQ beats the guy with the 130 IQ. Once you have ordinary intelligence, what you need is the temperament to control the urges that get other people into trouble."

-- Warren Buffet

When entering the world of trading, the single most important characteristic you can bring with you is not intellect, but temperament, or patience. Here's what Warren Buffet had to say about Temperament and trading.

Men are born, or bread with one single "talent" that both helps and hinders their trading ability, that being a level of high temperament. Men have a tendency to shoot first, and ask questions later. This has served them well in the world of survival, and can be a benefit when trading, being willing to take quick action, which is often necessary.

That said, it can also get them into trouble. When trading, men can take a lesson from woman, who have a more tempered-temperament, and seem to be a bit more methodical about their decisions. In an industry dominated by men, because of temperament, woman do very well in this realm as well.

Cathy Woods is a rock star in the world of finance. As a stock-picker and founder of a $60 billion dollar hedge fund, (ARK Trading) Cathy Woods has made a name for herself in the financial industry, not only because she's brilliant, but because she has the proper temperament; patience.

As a trader, we need to get comfortable with being uncomfortable. Slow down, try to have fun, and refrain from trading during irritating life events.

In summary, as a trader, it's important to be able to not only read charts, technicals, and fundamentals, it's actually more important to have the temperament to make the trade, establish the position, and make wise calculated decisions along the way.

Learn to read your own bodies mind and emotions, learn to recognize when you're getting anxious, and when it's time to take a break; step away from the computer, run around the block, do some push ups, before settling back in for the next trade. Never trade out of FOMO (Fear of missing out.)

There will always be another trading opportunity; you'll never catch them all, or all of them. Check your emotions at the door when the trading begins, and remember, if you're a woman, this is where you can shine in this industry.

Images by Lexica

Automated Trading

Creating & Trading With Bots

Lan Turner's Crash Course In Trading

Stocks * Futures * Forex

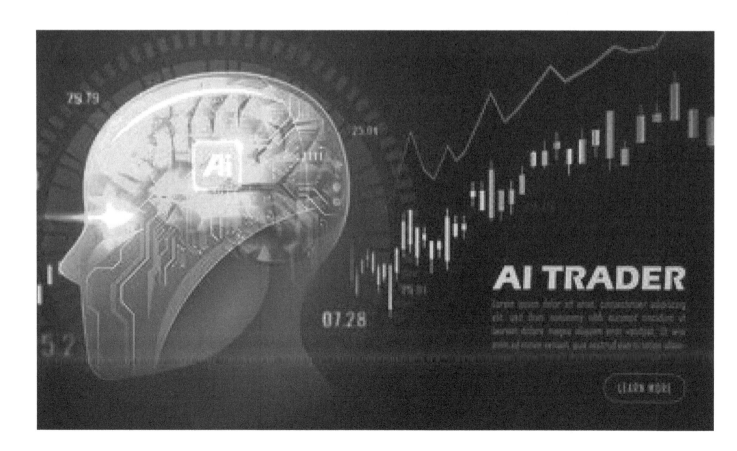

Trading Against The Bots.

Every trade you take in the financial markets is offset by a computer, or "bot." When you make a trade a computer takes the other side of your position, then offsets that position to another trader as quickly as it can, profiting from the bid/ask spread.

Why? Why does the market do this? Liquidity. The exchanges want to give traders a "good experience," by filling your orders in a timely manner. These 'bots" or liquidity computers are known as 'market makers.' Market makers are special firms registered by the exchanges to take the other side of your trade. These bots use algorithms to analyze market data and make decisions on buying and selling based on predetermined criteria. The use of trading bots allows market makers to quickly and efficiently make trades, providing liquidity to the market and helping to ensure the smooth function of the financial markets.

There are other types of trading "bots" as well, many retail traders, as well as large institutions trade the financial markets using computerized trading systems. There are every type of trading bot you can imagine, bots that trade very, very small moves, scalping bots. There are bots that trade long(er) term trends throughout the day, we call these day trading bots, and of course there are bots that look for even long(er) time frames, swing trading, or position trading bots.

> I received a comment from one of our students who said: "Trading bots are changing the landscape entirely to the point no one will be able to make any money trading ever again."

The thing you need to realize about all these bots, is that they are doing basically the same thing we've been teaching you to do, only they've automated the process; taking trades at opportune times, just like you as a retail trader might do. Does this mean they're going to make the markets worthless, so nobody can ever have a winning trade again? No, of course not, we've been trading against bots for years already, and if you look back at a chart from the 1950's, and compare it to the chart of today, they look exactly the same. Markets can only do three things, they can go up, down, or sideways.

Trading momentum, or the trend, is going to always be, whether you're an individual retail trader, an institutional trader, a large speculator, or a trading bot, their's only one way to truly make money in these markets; buy low, and sell high. Just because somebody, or some company programs the computer to buy when the market breaks a new high, or if you do it manually yourself, the result is the same. Bots, still need to place stop loss orders and calculate where to exit if the trade doesn't work out just like you as a retail traders would do.

In fact, with the advent and introduction of computerized trading systems, I've noticed it's actually become easier to predict market moves. You see, computer's don't lose their patience, and they don't preempt the trade, or enter early (or late) in anticipation of a breakout. Computers are disciplined, they've been programmed to only take the trade at predefined mathematical points along the trend. If you've been well trained, you know where those points are, and can easily identify them beforehand. Go look at thousands of historical charts, you'll see where markets break and trend.

The rules of technical analysis work, in large part, because of the bots. They've been programmed to buy and sell on technical setups and trigger points, not fundamental news and information, and they do it religiously. You as a retail trader just have to pinpoint where these trading bots have their calculated entries and exits, then join in on the gravy train, letting the bots push your profits higher.

If you want to automate your own trading, Track 'n Trade has this capability, without the need to be a programmer. You can create automated OCO/OTO bots that will completely mechanize your trading strategy with a single click of the mouse. Track 'n Trade also has a fully capable Autopilot, an auto trading plug-in that allows you to systematize your entire trading strategy. If that's something you want to do, visit the Track 'n Trade website for details on their Autopilot Plug-in.

What is high frequency, algorithmic trading? Have you ever played a game of chess against the computer? If so, who won? The question must be asked, in today's stock market, aren't we all just playing chess against the computer? Is it even possible to win at this point?

Retail traders, guys like you and me, we do have one 'ace up our sleeve.' What's that you say? Other retail traders! As traders, you and I are actually allies, not enemies. Our enemy is the bot, the computer algorithmic traders that are out to take our money. If retail traders band together, we can beat the bots. In this article, I'm going to explain how (it all sounds like a futuristic war game movie, doesn't it, but

this is no longer science fiction, it's now reality). There are many kinds of bots, or algo trading systems, but I'm going to break them down into three primary categories: Market Maker Bots, Institutional Bots, Retail Trading Bots.

Market Maker Bots: What is a market maker bot? A market maker is a company that's registered with the exchange as a trading institution whose sole purpose is to create liquidity for retail traders. In other words, their charter is to take the other side of any trade we might want to make, so we have the ease of entry and exit into and out of whichever markets we want.

If you've ever traded penny stocks, you know that sometimes it takes minutes, or even hours, to get your order filled. That's because there are no market makers. Market maker bots are designed to take the other side of your trade, then hold that position for as little time as possible, offsetting it to someone else as quickly as they can. For providing this service, market maker bots get to make the difference between the bid and the ask.

Let's say you want to buy the eMini Russell 2000, and the difference between the bid and the ask is .10, or ten cents. This means if you wanted to enter and immediately exit, and if the market didn't move a single cent, you would get in at the ask and exit at the bid, therefore losing .10, or ten cents. That's what's known as the bid/ask spread. (In Track 'n Trade, we call them the buy/sell lines, which helps make it a bit easier to understand where you are buying and where you are selling, and at what price.) As traders, we like to trade markets with tight bid/ask spreads.

So, if we sacrifice the difference between the bid and the ask, who gets that money? The market maker. Since you bought at the ask and sold at the bid, that means the market maker sold at the ask and bought at the bid, profiting .10, or ten cents, which is his compensation for providing liquidity to the market.

Sounds like free money, doesn't it? Not necessarily. What if the market moves like crazy and the market maker can't offset his position? He's at risk of taking a big loss. This is where retail traders can beat the bots, and why it's so imperative that you and I, as retail traders, all trade at the same time when everyone else is trading, during high volume times. This is what generally produces nicely trending markets.

"Advantages & Disadvantages of Algorithmic Trading?

It would seem like being a market maker would be a great trading job to have, all I have to do is sell at the ask and immediately buy at the bid and the money comes rolling in, right? Hold on, Jack, not so fast. Rarely do market makers get paid by the exchange to provide liquidity. I've seen it done, but for the most part, a market maker is responsible for using their own trading techniques and strategies to gain profits. And there's usually not just one market maker; usually, there are a number of them, and they're all competing with each other for your business. It's this plethora of market makers that causes very tight bid-ask spreads.

The more market makers there are in any given market, the tighter the spreads will be, as they are continually competing against each other for an ever smaller and smaller cut of the pie. And since market makers, nowadays, are all algorithmically programmed, it's bot against bot.

When you start to experience FOMO (fear of missing out) or if your inner Incredible Hulk, your aggressive trading monster, starts to rear its ugly head and you start jumping in and out of the market randomly, multiple times during very small time frames, such as making multiple entries and exits within a single minute bar, you are now competing against the bots. You are fighting at ground level against algorithmic computers; trust me when I say, this rarely turns out well for most individual retail traders. Ask me how I know.

The best way to avoid being smacked up side the head by an algo bot is to stay out of their sandbox in the first place. Don't get down in the dirt with them, don't try to compete on their level, don't chase after their pennies. They don't like to share. I know it's tempting, you want to cut your losers short, but just like a bad haircut, there is a thing called cutting it too close.

Rather than fighting with the bots for every single penny, be more strategic about your entries. Only take the very best trade setups and signals in the hottest markets during the hottest time of day. The bots love it when you over trade, when you continually jump in and out of the market during low volume times. We call that 'feeding the bots.' Don't do that!

How to beat the market maker bid-ask spread bots? Only take very calculated trades based on high-quality technical setups when there are lots of your pals (retail traders) jumping on the same signals, with everyone making a concerted effort to trend the market. All of us working together like a small army can move the market. That's why we say, 'The trend is your friend,' because trends are not market maker bot-driven. Trends are driven by your other trading buddies, as well as institutional bots, which we'll talk about next."

It's Nothing Personal

I always hear traders say things like, "They came after my stop, they gunned me down, they gunned my order, that damn market, they can see my orders, and they come after me!"

It's true, they can see your orders, and yes, they do come after you, that's all true, but really, it's nothing personal.

First and foremost, bots have no feelings, they don't care, they've been programmed to do one thing, and one thing only, and that's maximize profits, while filling as many orders as they possibly can.

A bot does not know if you make money, or lose money when they fill your orders, all they know is that your order is inside their order filling parameters, they're going to fill your order; if anything, the bot "feels" like it's doing you a favor.

The key here is, if you want the bot to fill your order, put it close to the market, where the bot can reach it, and he will, if you don't want the bot to fill your order, put it away from the current market price, where it's outside the bots parameters, and it won't fill your order; learning where those parameters are is part of gaining experience as a trader, we call this support & resistance, and it takes practice.

As a retail trader, you need to start thinking like other retail traders, this is why we call it boot camp, so you can join our army, so when we're on the move, you can join us; that's what technical analysis is.

When we teach you technical setups, like wedges, triangles, head and shoulders formations, Elliott Wave Patterns, Fibonacci numbers, we're giving you the army field book, we're trying to teach you when we're all going to join together as an army and try and beat the bots.

A wedge break-out pattern isn't just some funny thing Lan Turner made up so he can sell books, it's the retail army field book for retail traders on how and when to join the army in an attempt to beat the bots; we need you to come and attack the bots with us, all at the same time, so we can drive the market higher, or lower, and outrun the bots; the more retail traders we can teach these signals to, the stronger our army.

You also need to start thinking like a bot, where are they hiding? The bots are the enemy, they're behind every bush, tree, rock and hole, how are they going to try and take us out? This is today's game of trading. The hard part of this war is that they have our field guide too. Now, let's talk about the institutional bot.

I'm not going to spend a lot of time entertaining the concept of institutional bots, because I've covered this in great detail in the section titled: Wyckoff Theory. I'll summarize it in this single paragraph, and then you can go back and research my Wyckoff accumulation and distribution cheat sheet for additional details.

Large banks and hedge funds are very secretive about their accumulation and distribution of market shares or contracts. The last thing they want is for other traders to know they're accumulating massive positions in a particular market, so they use bots to perform this action, clandestinely buying and selling shares, causing the markets to go sideways, all the while continually collecting ever larger and larger positions.

Once they have all the contracts, or shares they want, they 'pop' the market, luring in the retail traders, so we'll start the buying frenzy; buyers need sellers, if we're buying, who's selling? The institutional bots, liquidating their positions. Institutional bots can, in some ways, be considered retail trader friendlies.

Large Speculator Bots & Algo Systems

The third category of bots and algo trading that I want to talk about is the retail trading bots and algos implemented by large speculators.

Now, let's get something clear, when I say retail bots, I'm not just talking about you and me, small speculators, I'm also talking about large speculators, banks and hedge funds. Any one person, business, or entity who profits from buying low and selling high through the process of actively trading.

In the futures industry, we have three classifications of traders, we call this the commitment of traders, and it's a federal government report that tracks the trading activity of these three groups. Oh, you thought your trades weren't being tracked by the government? Sorry to burst your bubble, surprise!

 We have commercial traders, large speculators, and small speculators. Large speculators, and small speculators, in my opinion, are of the same basic class, because we both are doing the same thing, we're both in the business of profiting from buying low and selling high, while commercial entities are generally in the business of hedging physical assets, while taking and or making delivery of the commodity futures.

Large speculators and their bots. I want to talk about large speculators who fall into the category just under the institutional bots. These speculators are not large enough to manipulate markets in the same fashion as institutional bots, and therefore actually have to trade in a similar manner to us small speculators, through the use of setups strategy, and momentum, rather than through market manipulation.

These large speculators use a lot of the same strategies that we employ, support and resistance, momentum, Fibonacci and Elliott Wave. The difference is that they have large staffs of programmers, and systems designers who try to program many different aspects of this type of behavior, trying to take advantages of the same types of high probability trading setups that we small speculators trade.

These large speculator bots, in my opinion, are like our generals, they are the big players that we want to mimic, and follow, they have the strength and the volume to move markets, so when they enter, then so should we, and when they exit, so should we; we want to ride their coattails.

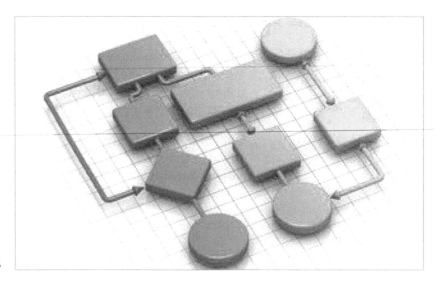

Since these firms, and their bots are very mathematically driven, you're going to find that they enter and exit markets based on mathematical modeling, and this is why many great indicators work so well, such as the Bulls 'n Bears, the Blue Light System, Parabolic PSAR, and ATR. These mathematical models work well, because they don't try to predict market breakouts, they simply report when the market does break out.

Large speculators use a technique known as Monte Carlo back testing to curve fit their trading strategies to the recent market action, and to common repeating patterns. Basically, Monte Carlo back testing is a process of mathematically calculating probabilities, through the simulation of placing millions of trades, which determines the current best settings for a specific mathematical model, or indicator. Monte Carlo traders then trade forward using those settings, and will continue to do so until the Monte Carlo modeling recommendations change, at which point they update their settings and then continue trading once again, using the new findings. This is a continual process of back testing, updating, back testing, and updating.

Next, let's talk about small speculators, and their algo trading strategies and bots.

Small Speculators Retail Trading Bots & Autopilot Systems

The subcategory of small retail speculators and their self programmed, or purchased bots.

Most retail traders are not also computer programmers, so they need tools that don't require them to write code; most retail traders also don't want to spend the resources to continually hire freelance programmers to change their algos every time they have a new idea.

It's for this reason that trading platforms such as Track 'n Trade Live, which have the ability to create bots without the need to program are so popular.

Some other trading platforms sell you other peoples pre-programmed trading bots. Of course, why would someone sell you something for $99 if it was so good, they good make millions trading it rather than selling it, which is the Achilles' heel of these types of EA or pre-packaged, pre-programmed for the masses bots. In my experience, nobody really ever finds long-term success using them.

As a retail trader, you need the ability to be flexible, and having your trading system hidden behind a black box blinder is no way to find long-term success.

In comes the Track 'n Trade Autopilot and OCO programmable buttons. I say programmable, but you don't need any coding language skills to use and modify these systems and tools, they've been designed with complete user autonomy in mind, allowing you to program your bots through a simple If-Then series of selections from a graphical user interface.

This Track 'n Trade implementation allows small retail traders to design systems and update them with a simple click of the mouse, which frees you from relying on black box systems, from having to learn to write coded language, or from having to hire an outside consultant or programmer.

With these tools, an individual trader has almost as much power to create multiple trading systems with historical Monte Carlo back testing capabilities as what many of the large firms employ. You can create your own strategies for trending markets, for accumulation models, or for stagnating markets, and then you can decide when to execute your own personal bot; the right bot at the right time.

Market execution is usually the downfall of many small speculators, they know what they want to do, they've been classically trained, they've studied the patterns, and they've learned the strategies, basically, they know how to trade. Where they fall short is execution. Executing the trading strategy is difficult in two ways, first, it's time consumingly boring to sit and wait for the one right moment, and face it, humans only have a finite amount of patience before they start trading out of boredom, which is a sure fire way to give up your holdings to someone else.

Turning your trading strategy over to the bot solves many of these issues. One problem small speculators experience when bot trading, is the Monte Carlo scenario of executing enough trades for the slight mathematical advantage to work in our favor. We, as small speculators don't execute that many trades, therefore we can't rely on statistical advantages of probability mathematical modeling to work in our favor over a period of time, therefore, we need to be more precise in our execution.

The best retail traders choose when to turn the bot on and off, rather than running it 24/7, Monte Carlo style.

OCO, OTO, and Autopilot Systems

In Track 'n Trade, we have multiple bots, we have OCO bots, we have OTO bots, and we have the Autopilot system, which is a complete bot building module, with Monte Carlo back testing capabilities. We also have, currently under development, another advanced bot, internally we call the Magic Stick; currently in beta. (Feel free to contact our friends at the Track 'n Trade headquarters and ask for a peek at this advanced beta-bot if you're so inclined.)

In this quick summary, I'm going to outline some of my favorite bot strategies, hopefully you can use this guide as a primer for building your own bots.

I want to start off by talking about the Track 'n Trade OCO, (one cancels other) and OTO (one triggers other) order buttons, these buttons are what I call 'mini-bots.' They're automated strategies that you can quickly implement with a single click of the mouse. (If you're not trading with bots, start with these.)

All you have to do is "program" (no coding required) the mini bot to perform a specific task, then to execute your bot, simply click the mouse at the appropriate time, and the computer will enter, manage and exit a complete single trading scenario, all automated. It's one of my most favorite methods of bot trading.

The Track 'n Trade OCO and OTO bot buttons are amazing, you can create an almost endless number of different individual bots, and execute them at the drop of a hat. (See my hook, line, and sinker strategies.)

The Track 'n Trade Autopilot is more of what you might see institutional traders use, where it continually monitors the market for specific events, setups or patterns, then executes your trading strategy for you, time and time again. The Autopilot system has Monte Carlo historical back testing style capabilities, where you can test your trading strategy against historical data, as mentioned previously in this article.

Again, I will say, as small speculators, we don't generally trade Monte Carlo style strategies, we use the Autopilot more as a rifle, rather than a shotgun, setting up our Autopilot to monitor the market, and execute our trading strategy during short durations or through specific trading time frames, or news events.

Again, most traders know what they want to do, they know how they want to execute their trades, but they don't have the time or patience to sit for hours on end watching and waiting for their specific setup, it's for this purpose the Autopilot was created, it can sit for hours, without getting bored, and wait for the perfect setup before executing your trade for you, and that's the true power of the Track 'n Trade Autopilot.

I have four basic strategies I employ when "programming" (no coding required) my Autopilot:

1. Swing trading strategies; where I look for markets that are swinging through high and low trends.
2. Trend trading strategies; where the Autopilot determines the trend, then only executes trades in the direction of the prevailing trend.
3. Scalping strategies; where I program the Autopilot to capture small bursts, or moves in the markets.
4. Long-term portfolio building strategies, where I use the Autopilot to enter long-term position trades.

I call these micro-pullbacks spider webs, we'll cover these in greater detail in other sections of the book.

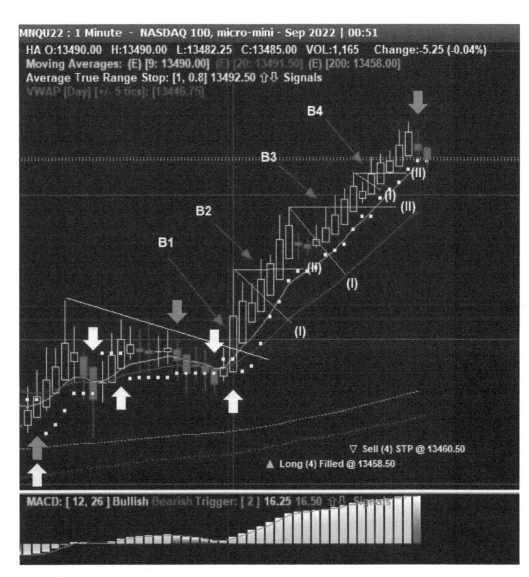

Buying on a dip, also known as buying a micro pullback, is a strategy that involves buying at a lower price after a small decline in value. This strategy is based on the idea that a temporary decrease in price may present a buying opportunity, as the trend is likely to continue upward. However, it's important to note that this strategy requires good timing. It's also important to have a clear exit plan in case the trend doesn't recover.

Day Trading & Scalping Strategies Using Automation Bots

Now that you understand the fundamentals of the three primary categories of trading bots, and how they operate, let's take a look at several chart examples that can help us better understand how to apply this knowledge to our trading endeavors.

As small speculators, our number one primary concern is the Market Maker bots. These bastards are the guys that kill us, destroy our accounts, and who continually knock us out of our trades.

By better understanding Market Makers, we can use this information in our bot trading battle.

In this chart example, I want to highlight for you what's happening, where the bots are, what they're thinking, what you and I as traders are thinking, why we get knocked out, and where we get into the trade.

A: This is our initial entry into this trade, we sell (go short) on a break below the trailing yellow dots, which triggers a yellow arrow.

B: This is our initial stop placement, where we attach the trailing order to the yellow dots, trail to break even.

C: Once we're at break even, we have many choices. I like to begin trailing one (1) Heiken-Ashi price bars back for exit, while trailing the yellow ATR dots for a reversal long entry, which in this example happens at C.

D: Once long at C, then D is our initial trailing stop location, attached to the yellow dots for auto-trail to exit, or trail one bar back.

E: Here's where the trouble lies. This is where the Market Maker bots get you.

Because everyone enters the market at C, and set their stops at D, then moved their stops up to break even at C; now, there are a lot of orders sitting at break even at the C price level, and this is why the Market Makers dropped back down with those two red bars at F, taking out all those stops.

Once the Market Makers completed this setback to F, buyers stepped in and pushed the market higher once again, creating a new buy opportunity at G, (red to green) with a one bar back trailing stop to exit at H.

The question is, how do we avoid getting stopped out at F? We do exactly what you're thinking right now.

1. We could skip the initial entry at C, and wait for the first pull back before entering in the first place, but then we risk missing the trade all together, since that never happened in the A-B-C example.

2. We don't bring our stop up so quickly, but then we risk getting stopped out with a much larger loss.

3. We trail one bar back, take the minimum size hit, then re-enter on red to green.

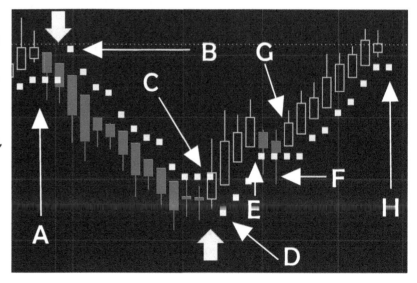

Honor the Arrow

Scalping with the Hook, Line & Sinker strategy is a type of trading that involves taking advantage of small price movements to make quick profits. This high-frequency trading strategy consists of holding market positions for a brief period, usually seconds or minutes, unlike other strategies, where we might be looking for a longer-term trade, holding for hours. With the Hook, Line & Sinker, we're trying to make multiple small profits rather than a few large ones.

The Hook, Line, and Sinker strategy is a counter-trend entry strategy, meaning that it goes against the current market trend. This can be a contrarian approach, as it goes against the general market sentiment. However, it's important to remember that the Hook, Line, and Sinker strategy also incorporates the Average True Range (ATR) indicator.

The ATR indicator measures the volatility of a market by calculating the average range between the high and low prices over a certain period. It can be used to identify whether a market is trending or consolidating. The ATR indicator generates buy and sell signals, which I like to consider when trading the Hook, Line, and Sinker strategy.

When using the Hook, Line, and Sinker strategy, traders should only take positions that align with the buy and sell signals generated by the ATR indicator. For example, suppose the ATR generates a buy signal. In that case, optimally, traders should only use the Hook, Line, and Sinker to take long positions, waiting for a counter-trend pullback against the prevailing long trend. If it generates a sell signal, traders should only take short positions. This helps ensure that we're only taking positions with a higher probability of success, catching the micro-pullbacks of the prevailing ATR trend.

The Hook, Line, and Sinker strategy can be very effective in generating quick profits or even catching a micro-pullback for the long(er) term play. However, it's important to remember that scalping is a high-risk trading strategy that requires discipline, skill, and timing. Always use proper money management techniques, such as setting stop-loss orders, to help manage the risks associated with scalping.

In summary, the Hook, Line, and Sinker scalping strategy is a contrarian approach to trading. (In many cases, you're doing precisely the opposite of everyone else.) The strategy is based on the fact that 80% of traders lose money and continually get stopped out with a loss. Therefore, we're going to do just the reverse and get "stopped out" with a profit. We need to "Honor the Arrow" of the ATR indicator because sometimes, 20% of the time, traders actually make money, which would result in a loss for the contrarian trader.

Art work by: Lexica.art. The Consummate Bull; a self portrait.

Trading Strategies

Trading Strategies

Lan Turner's Crash Course In Trading

Stocks * Futures * Forex

The SKEW: Are you scared yet?

How do you know if the big banks and hedge funds are trading scared? Wouldn't it be nice to know if all the big boys are scared, or not?

Check out the SKEW (Not available in Track 'n Trade demo) What's the SKEW? The SKEW is a measure of the implied volatility of out-of-the-money options in the S&P 500 index options market. It is calculated by the Chicago Board Options Exchange (CBOE) and is also known as the CBOE Skew Index or simply the Skew.

The Skew is used by traders as a gauge of market risk and investor sentiment, with a high Skew indicating a higher perceived likelihood of market declines. The SKEW is the CBOE Index of Put options, or in other words, how many Put options are being purchased on the Chicago Board of Options Exchange.

Why do big banks and hedge funds buy Put options? Because they're afraid of a market reversal, this is how they hedge their portfolios. Buying a Put option is a way of profiting when the market falls, therefore, if you're heavy long the market, as most investing funds are, they purchase Put options as insurance against a falling market.

If we set our SKEW chart up to act like an overbought, and oversold indicator, something like what you might see on RSI, or Stochastics, with our threshold levels set at 140 and 125, then we can see when the big hedge funds are heavily buying Put options as insurance. (Set your SKEW chart to tic style Close.)

When the SKEW is above 140, the big banks are scared of a reversal, when it's below 125, they're not scared.

Why trading is NOT gambling

As a registered 'person' with the NFA, and the CFTC, there are guidelines of things we are and are not allowed to say, things like;

- "You'll be rich, rich, rich beyond your wildest dreams if you come and trade with me!"

- "I've made millions trading options!" (Unless it's true of course.)

- "If you buy my trading course, you'll be able to buy yourself this amazing Lamborghini!"

- "Come and fly in my private jet when you learn to trade like me!"

For obvious reasons, as a member of the NFA, and a registered person, we're not allowed to say things like that. If you see people talking like this on the Internet, then you know they are not regulated entities, and frankly I wouldn't trust those people any further than I could pick them up and throw them across the room.

We also have guidelines of things we're not supposed to associate with trading, and one of those things is Las Vegas style gambling; so the question must be asked, why?

Through the eyes of the regulators, and the investing community, trading is not gambling because when we gamble, if we're wrong, we lose our entire bet.

> For example, if you place $1,000 on black at the roulette table, and the color comes up red, you lose the entire $1,000, no questions asked. Boo hew for you!

> But, when we trade, and we buy $1,000 shares of Microsoft, if the market falls, and we're wrong, we're able to get back out of the market without losing the entire $1,000, usually, it's very rare that a stock goes to zero, and that's why trading is not considered gambling.

I know it seems like a fine line, but it's a very important fine line.

When trading, if you diversify, and you put a small "bet," or investment into 20 different stocks, you don't generally experience one big winner, and 19 total losers like we see in the game of roulette, therefore we have choices not afforded to us when gambling.

When buying a Call option we have unlimited profit potential, while enjoying limited risk. The maximum amount we can lose is the premium we paid for the option, yet there is no limit to our profit potential. When buying a Put, we profit when the market falls, and our profit is only limited if the stock falls to zero, while our loss is capped at the premium paid.

> Cut your losers short, let your winners run; trading is not an all or nothing venture, let the winners pay for the losers.

> *So, then why can't I win at trading?* Here's the two primary reasons why traders never win at trading.

Reason 1: Because they're trading in a demo account, you'll never make money trading in the demo. The demo account is only to learn the strategies and the software features, once that's been accomplished, which should only take a couple

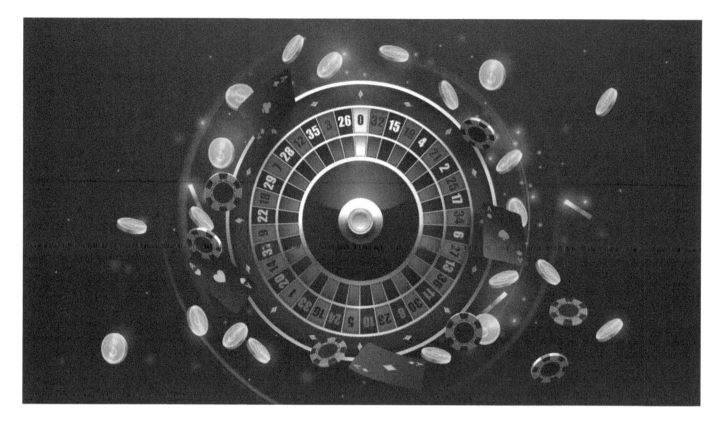

months, then you should no longer trade in a demo account. (It just teaches you bad habits after that.)

Reason 2: Actually, you probably are winning at trading, you just don't realize it. Las Vegas has trained us to think like a loser, which is what they want. When we go to Vegas, we tell ourselves, I'm going to stop gambling when I've lost $xxx amount of money, which is why you generally always lose when you go to Vegas, because you don't stop gambling until you've achieved your goal of losing $xxx amount.

It's the same with trading. Don't think like a loser, think like a winner; stop trading when you're ahead, not when you're behind. Stay disciplined, it can be tempting to continue trading, don't squander your profits, follow your Risk Management rules.

In summary

Trading and gambling may seem similar in that both involve taking risks in an attempt to achieve financial gain. However, there are some key differences between the two. One major difference is that traders do not generally lose their entire investment, whereas gamblers often stand to lose their entire bet. This is because trading typically involves a more calculated approach to risk, with traders using strategies such as risk management and stop-loss orders to mitigate the potential for significant losses. In contrast, gambling often involves taking a more reckless approach to risk, with gamblers relying on luck rather than a well-thought-out plan.

Another difference between trading and gambling is that traders can use a wide range of tools and resources to inform their decisions, such as technical analysis, fundamental analysis, and economic indicators. Gamblers, on the other hand, often rely on pure luck or superstition to guide their bets. Additionally, traders can use leverage to increase their potential profits, while gamblers do not have this option.

Overall, while there are some similarities between trading and gambling, trading involves a more structured and disciplined approach to risk and decision-making, which can ultimately increase the chances of success.

What is paper trading?

Paper trading is what we do when we want to first, learn how to trade, second, practice a new piece of software, or third, test a new trading theory or strategy.

Simulated or paper trading, also known as demo trading, is a way for traders to practice and test strategies without using real money. There are several advantages to this type of trading. First, it allows traders to try out different trading platforms and software without any financial risk. This can be especially useful for new traders who are still learning the ropes and figuring out what works best for them. Second, it allows traders to test out new strategies and theories without the pressure of real money on the line. This can be a good way for traders to gain confidence and fine-tune their approach before moving on to live trading.

However, there are also some disadvantages to simulated or paper trading. One disadvantage is that it does not accurately reflect the real-life conditions of live trading. This means that traders may not get a true sense of how they would perform under real market conditions, and they may not be prepared for the psychological and emotional challenges of live trading. Another disadvantage is that simulated or paper trading can create a false sense of security, leading traders to take on more risk than they would in a live trading environment. It is important for traders to be aware of these limitations and to take steps to bridge the gap between simulated and live trading

I'm sure there are other reasons for paper trading, but trading in a demo account, or paper trading, is a useful tool for a number of different reasons and purposes.

The one problem I see with paper trading, is that people end up getting lost in the world of trading their demo accounts and never venture out to trade real money.

This generally happens for several reasons, first, and the most common in my experience after working with lots of new traders, is that they jump into the market prematurely, they're not quite ready, so they lose a bunch of money, they get scared, figure they better go back to paper trading, where they sit for the next five years, never really gaining the courage to trade real money once again.

This happens for any number of reasons, usually because they have no plan, so they just start gambling in the market, jumping on every little thing that seems to be rising, buying high, and selling low, trading way too large of size, and so on. To be a successful trader you need a plan, which is what this book is all about, and is why I titled it, "A Trader's Secret on How To Gain Discipline & Courage Through Knowledge & Strategy."

Once you've mastered the process of counting and measuring, setups, triggers, and follow through, and you've pretty much figured out how to operate the software platform you've chosen, (Track 'n Trade) then it's time to start trading real money.

We like to tell people to start with 10's and 20's, that's kind of a thing in the industry, a new trader should always start trading with 10's and 20's. What does that mean? Well, it' means you start trading with such small share size, quantity 10 shares, or small dollar size, $20, that your risk is very limited, and not all that painful; that's all you should risk in the beginning.

If you can't be profitable trading 10's and 20's, then you should not be ramping it up and trying to trade with larger share size

Once you master the strategy, and you're making money with 10's and 20's, then you'll naturally start knowing when it's time to ramp it up to 1000's and 2000's. (Not all at once mind you, it should be a slow and natural transition up the scale.)

What Are Pattern Day Trading Rules?

"I'm from the government, and I'm here to help!"

In my opinion, anytime regulators get involved, it seems things just get worse, and again, in my opinion, that's exactly what's happened with Pattern Day Trading Rules; stupid rules designed to help.

If you have less than $25,000 in your stock margin account, you are subject to pattern day trading rules. NOTE, these rules only apply to the stock market, and NOT to the Futures or Forex markets; there are no pattern day trading rules in the futures market, which is why many small speculators gravitate to that market in the beginning, then never leave. (Visit my website CommodityTradingSchool.com to learn more about trading Futures.

Here are the margin account Pattern Day Trader (PDT) key rules.

- You are a "day trader" if you buy and sell, or short then buy back the same stock on the same day. Just purchasing a stock, without selling it back within the same day is not considered pattern day trading.

- You are subject to the pattern day trader (PDT) rules, if you execute four or more "day trades" within a five day period, within the same account.

  o For example, if you enter the market, then place a stop loss order, and your stop loss order gets triggered on the same day, you are a Pattern Day Trader. So, the message here is not to place stop orders once you enter the trade until the next day. (In my opinion, this is the most asinine rule of all, forcing small traders to possibly sit through large losses if the market turns against them.)

The way I avoid this rule, when trading with a small account below $25K, is to place my entry orders just prior to the close, this way, my stop orders won't get executed until the following day. (I have an alarm on my cell phone that fires off 30-minutes prior to the market close, this allows me time to get back to my computer and make my trades.)

Cash account rules are also subject to PDT rules as well, but not quite as stringent.

Cash accounts can engage in certain day trades, but only as long as your trades don't "free ride," which means you can't buy a stock with unsettled funds, which usually takes one to two days to clear, depending on your brokerage firm. (Don't sell a stock, then use that money to buy something else for two days.)

If you break the pattern day trading rules, your account will be suspended for a period of 90-days; "No more trading for you!" it's like being put in the penalty box for bad behavior!

Unfortunately, once you've been tagged as a pattern day trader, your account will remain flagged, and forever more regarded, by your broker, as a pattern day trading account even if you don't day trade any longer.

You CAN call your broker to have your account recoded at any time. If in doubt, always, CALL!

What is Revenge Trading?

Revenge trading is a mental disorder, it's like a virus, that infects our brains the minute we open a real money trading account.

Revenge trading is something that happens to every single trader. I'm of the opinion that it's always there, raging in the background, as soon as we start to take losses, this virus begins to awaken in us, and this is what causes our inner Incredible Hulk to bust out.

When a trader begins to lose money, it's kinda like what happens to the Incredible Hulk when he gets mad.

Our inner Hulk begins to rage inside, and we start to lose control. We begin to trade like a wild man on steroids, all rational thought begins to leave our brains; we begin to reverse trade, we start to jump on every little move in the market with ever larger and larger size all in an attempt to get green! Saying:

"If I could just get green once again, everything will be okay!" (Let me remind you, what is the color of the Incredible Hulk?)

How did Bruce Banner keep from turning into the Incredible Hulk? How did he keep from going on a mad rampage? He never allowed himself to get angry in the first place.

As a trader, how do we control our anger, how do we keep from turning into the Incredible Hulk and destroying our accounts, trying to win it back, trying to get green?

We must give ourselves strict rules, and we must adhere to those rules. As traders, we must realize that we're going to have losses, we're going to have losing days, the key is to not allow those losing days to turn into catastrophic failures.

On the following pages, I've outlined several strategies to keep your inner monster from bursting out, follow these rules, and learn to squelch your angry passenger.

Futures & Forex, an Quick Introduction

On a previous page, we introduced you to pattern day trading rules, now remember, there are basically three different retail markets that you can trade, there is the Stock Market, which is traded primarily out of New York City, there is the Futures Market, sometimes referred to as the Commodities Market, which is primarily traded out of Chicago, and there is the Forex Market, which is where we trade foreign currencies, and is a world-wide market.

There are NO pattern day trading rules when trading Futures and Forex, which is why these markets will often times draw in the small speculator who is interested in day trading. Remember, in the Stock Market, if you want to day trade, you must have $25,000 in your account, otherwise if you enter the market, and exit on the same day, you can get your account suspended for a period of 90-days; this is not the case when trading Futures and Forex, you can open an account in these markets with as little as $2,000.

Futures and Forex are what I like to refer to as, "The last bastion of pure capitalism on earth today," a quote taken directly from the movie 'Trading Places.' You can buy and sell as often as you want, you can go long and short as often as you want, and there are no interest penalties, or additional fees for doing so, no easy or hard to borrow, none of that stuff is required when trading Futures and Forex.

The Futures and Forex markets are designed specifically for active traders, in fact, they have dozens of markets referred to as mini and micro-mini accounts just for beginner traders.

Now, just like in any industry, there are a few differences that you'll need to be aware of before jumping in and opening up your Commodity Futures or Forex accounts; when trading in these markets, we basically speak a different language, so you'll need to brush up on the differences and understand what they are before entering these markets.

The Forex market is pretty simple and straight forward, and is pretty close to the Stock Market, in that the price charts are one long continues chart for each currency that you're trading, now this summary is not meant to be a full on discussion of the differences between these three markets, but just a quick overview.

When trading Forex, you're trading the exchange rate between two countries, for example, EUR/USD is the symbol for the Eurodollar against the US Dollar, and we don't call each move between the currencies pennies, we call them Pips, and we don't trade shares, like in the stock market, we trade Lots.

The Futures market on the other hand trades Contracts, not Lots, or Shares. One Contract is the minimum size position size you can take, and one Contract in Corn for example, represents 5,000 bushels.

Since most traders could not afford to cash purchase one contract, or 5,000 bushels of corn, just to speculate on the rise or fall of the price of corn, all trading in the Commodity Futures Market, just like in Forex, is done on margin; each account opened is a margin account, therefore, to trade one contract of corn, you would need to only have $1,141.25 in your account (at the time of this writing) to trade one contract, or 5,000 bushels of corn, yet your profits and losses would be as if you owned the full 5,000 bushels.

These are just a few of the superlatives that makes trading Futures and Forex so attractive. For details about how to get started trading Futures and Forex, visit www.CommodityTradingSchool.com

Futures and Forex traders extraordinaire created by Lexica

Highly Effective, 7 Step, Day Trading/Scalping Strategy

Step 1:   Setup two charts, side by side; one five minute, the other a one minute. Five minute chart setup: Turn on Bulls 'n Bears, 72, Progressive, Blue Lights on. It's the five minute chart where we calculate the Elliott Wave trend and Fibonacci projection and retracement patterns; use Bulls 'n Bears and the Blue Lights.

Step 2:   One minute chart setup: Turn on and set ATR indicator to 1, 1.0. This is a very tight, risk averse setting, therefore the market must trend to be effective, follow rules learned on trading trending markets.

Step 3:   One minute chart setup continued: Turn on Heiken-Ashi. Only add Heihen-Ashi to the one minute chart, not the five. Heiken-Ashi is an indicator in itself, which smooths the price bars; this is why you're able to use such a tight setting with the ATR; without Heiken-Ashi you cannot use the tighter ATR stop settings. (No Bulls 'n Bears on one minute chart.)

Step 4:   Trail ATR Stop for entry. (You can setup OCO orders to do this.) This is a swing trade strategy, you'll be entering the market by trailing the ATR. Employ ABC pattern strategy; wait for A to rally, buy on B dip, anticipate a C rally.

Step 5:   Trail one or two price bars back until break-even. (OCO Orders can do this.) Once you enter the market, trail two price bars back until break-even, or trail the ATR dots, whichever is more aggressive. (Smallest loss if you're wrong. You can trail one price bar back, but sometimes this is too close; use good judgment to decide.)

Step 6:   Trail ATR until exit. (This is a manual switch within OCO settings.) Once you switch from Price bars back to ATR, then trail ATR all the way to exit. If you get stopped out halfway through a trend, on a small rebound, consider a re-entry, not a reversal, then continue trailing ATR. (Only reverse on the ATR flip.) Take profits along the way by dollar cost averaging into your winning position. (See profit taking strategy for details.)

Step 7:   Rinse and repeat.

Can the Track 'n Trade Autopilot do this? Yes, with some differences. Autopilot cannot trail to enter, it must take arrows for entry.

Sometimes, markets will move a rather large distance before triggered, consider using the Thrust Bar Signal Preventer to help alleviate this issue.

Autopilot takes every single arrow, or trade, regardless of other factors. Be smart, don't take every single arrow, be selective based on the knowledge you've gained from other strategies.

Dollar Cost Averaging. How to Build a Large Position Size with Less Risk.

When most traders think of Dollar Cost Averaging, they think of buying into a position as market prices fall, or what we call, averaging 'down," increasing size and risk. In my opinion, this is a recipe for disaster. A market can stay irrational longer than you can stay liquid. (There are some advanced strategies where we do this in a very controlled environment; strategies I call "The Flea Flicker," and the "King Tut." See my trading course for details.)

My favorite way to dollar cost average is to dollar cost average 'up,' not down.

For example:

A1: Enter the market with initial position size, let's say 4 contracts, or 400 shares.

A2: This is where we would 'add-on' or 'dollar cost average up,' by adding 2, or 200 shares.

A3: This is where we would once again average up, adding 1 contract, or 100 shares.

Notice how as we add onto our position at A2 and A3 (Possibly even A4, A5), we reduce the quantity. This is done in an attempt to never bring our average cost above our trailing stop order. Don't spend all your profits on new shares or contracts.

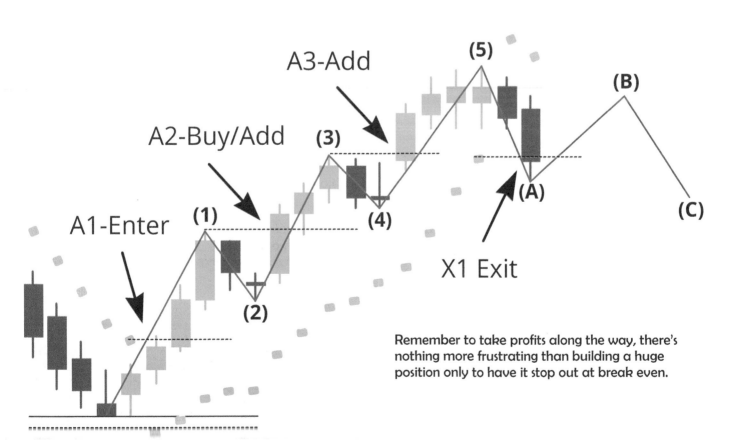

Remember to take profits along the way, there's nothing more frustrating than building a huge position only to have it stop out at break even.

How To Take Profits

Taking profits seems to be one of the most confusing events traders struggle with. When is it time to get out of the market? You don't have to completely exit a market to take profits, but also remember, if we never liquidate our positions, we never bank any earnings.

In previous chapters and discussions, you've heard me say, take profits along the way. So, in this section, we're going to talk about how to bank profits, while still remaining in the trade.

Let's say, for example, that we entered the market with 100 shares at A1, and the market moved in our favor. Let's also say we held onto our position through A2, & A3, but now we're receiving a new B1 signal, and we want to add onto our position, as well as take profits.

Step #1, determine your new stop loss position.

> Imagine you were getting into the market for the first time on the new B1; where would you put your stop loss order to get out if you were wrong? (Hint, behind a recent area of support, probably close to where we broke the X1, or maybe even on the Blue Light.)

Step #2, start adding onto your existing position incrementally.

> Dollar cost averaging your position up adding into a winning trade. (In Track 'n Trade, this is super easy, because as you add to your position, the new dollar cost averaged order line moves to the new price level right on the chart.)

> Add shares until your new position is set just beneath where you determined your stop order should be. (If you're not using Track 'n Trade, then you'll need to do the math by hand.)

> Let's say that during this process, you dollar cost averaged up another 75 shares. Now you're long 175 shares from your new dollar cost average location, which is just below your new stop loss order point.

Step #3, take profits!

> Now, liquidate 75 shares, and there you have it, you still have 100 shares of the stock, while also taking profits on 75 shares.

> Don't forget, once we establish our new dollar cost average position, we can also enter several stops at various price levels as well. Important note, never average your position above your stop loss order(s), which would put a winning trade into jeopardy of becoming a losing trade.

> This might take a bit of practice to understand, but once it clicks, it will be one of those wonderful "Ah Ha" moments of learning how to trade.

When performing this strategy, if I enter with an initially large position size, larger than usual, I'm very timid. If the market does not immediately move in my favor once the trigger is executed, I just remove the position, or significantly reduce the size.

Once a trigger is hit, the market should immediately move in your favor, if it does not, it's probably a weak trigger point, or a weak market, and probably not a trade you want to be in anyway.

Reevaluate Your Market Entry Strategy

If you keep getting stopped out because you bring your stop to break-even too quickly, it's probably not your risk management, or your stop strategy that needs work, it's probably your entry strategy.

> Before you enter into a position, always ask yourself, "what makes me think this market is going to take off and run right now?" Why do you think the market is going to suddenly make a large and significant move?

If it's a weak trend prior to the breakout, it will probably remain a weak trend; if it's a strong trend prior, it will probably remain a strong trend.

Ask yourself these questions:

- Did I enter on a significant breaking point of the trend? Am I drawing my trend lines?

- Did I chase the trend? Did I get in late? (Getting in late is the same as being wrong.)

- Am I jumping on every one bar rally?

- Am I chasing the reversal?

- Did I enter at a significant decision point?

- Were my indicators in line with my decision to enter?

- If taking a buy/sell, was my RSI/Stochastics in the oversold/overbought region?

- Where am I in the Elliott Wave count?

- What is the Fibonacci projection and retracement? Where is price on the Fibonacci scale?

- Am I just randomly jumping on mid-stream trend reversals?

- Do I continually reverse my trades? Reversing in and out randomly, trying to chase the trend?

- Did I wait for a signal from my primary indicator, ATR, Bulls 'n Bears, Blue Light, PSAR?

- Am I continually taking counter trend trades? (The trend is my friend.)

- Am I taking too small, or too large of a position size for the size of my account?

- Am I trading at the right time of day? (Goldilocks or Power hour.)

- Did I ask my girlfriend if I can take this trade? Actually, don't ask anyone, when you click that mouse button, it's all you; take responsibility.

Note: Right when you think the market is going to go down, is probably when it will go up, and right when you think it's going to go up, it will probably go down, and right when you think you've got the bear by the tail is when it will turn around and bite you; always use stops, prepare to be wrong.

In a weak market, you can go long and short and lose money on both trades. (Ask me how I know...)

How to Take Scalping Profits

The obvious answer is to exit the trade once you're in the money, right? Wrong!

What if you want to take some profits, but also stay in the trade, or do as Lan Turner always says, "take profits along the way?" How do you take half your profits if you're only in the market with a single contract, or share?

Here's the trick; let's say you're trading the mini S&P500 and your long the market with one contract.

The market starts to move in your favor, hurray, finally, you're showing a profit, but now you're scared the market might reverse and take that profit away, which makes you want to jump out, but wait, Lan Turner said to let your winners run, because we're also greedy, and we also want to stay in the trade to see if the market will continue to move further in our favor; how do you do both, stay in and get out at the same time?

Here's what we do; we dollar cost average into a winning position, then immediately take that position back off; for example, if you're long one, add a second position, which will move your average entry up by 50%, then immediately take that one position back off; now, you've just taken half your profits without exiting the trade.

Doing this locks in 50% of your profit, and only costs you one round-turn commission.

Let's say you get into a trade with a single contract, and the market really starts moving in your favor, you caught a whale of a trade, the big panda, but you only caught it with a single contract.

As that market blasts off in your favor, continually add on more positions to your trade, while also taking them back off; "taking profits along the way."

Here's an advanced strategy.

Enter with a larger initial size, for example, enter with quantity six contracts/shares.

By starting with multiple contracts, rather than just one, when you dollar cost average into the winner, and start removing contracts to take profits, you are far less likely to get knocked out of the trade.

If you dollar cost averaging two positions, each move will bring you 50% closer, while dollar cost averaging six positions, adding and subtracting one contract/share at a time, will only move your average position 13% closer to the current market price, which makes it less likely to get stopped out.

I like to try and dollar cost average into a winning trade while also staying behind my trailing stop, once the market moves to that point, try to never dollar cost average above/below your trailing stop.

Flea Flicker & King Tut.

> "Identifying Recurring Price Patterns, Setups, Triggers and Indicators
> is not trading. Trading is executing orders in a sequence designed
> to take advantage of those patterns and indicators."
> -- Lan Turner

As a day trader, it's important to have a strategy in place to manage your risk and potentially increase your profits. One way to do this is through dollar cost averaging. This involves dividing your total investment amount into equal parts and investing those equal amounts at regular intervals over a period of time.

By investing smaller amounts over time, we can take advantage of fluctuations in the price and potentially purchase contracts/shares at a lower price during market downturns and a higher price during market upturns.

The Flea Flicker is a dollar cost average strategy where we take an initial small entry, and rather than place a stop order for exit, we place a limit order to add onto our position, dollar cost averaging, building a pyramid from the top down (or bottom up if going short.)

> My favorite time to trade these (super advanced) Flea Flicker and/or King Tut strategies are at i, ii, X1, or X2 signals; of course, these strategies can also be executed at A1, B1, or C1 as well.

When we get our entry signal, enter the market with a single contract, or small share size. This is the tip of the pyramid. As the market continues to fall, dollar cost average in, by doubling the initial entry, so if we went in with 50 shares, then, at the next support level we would add another 50 shares, then, at the next support level we would add 100 shares, and so on.

At some point we need to yell uncle, and stop pyramiding; place a stop exit order and take our lumps if the market does not turn and rally in our favor; usually after three add points.

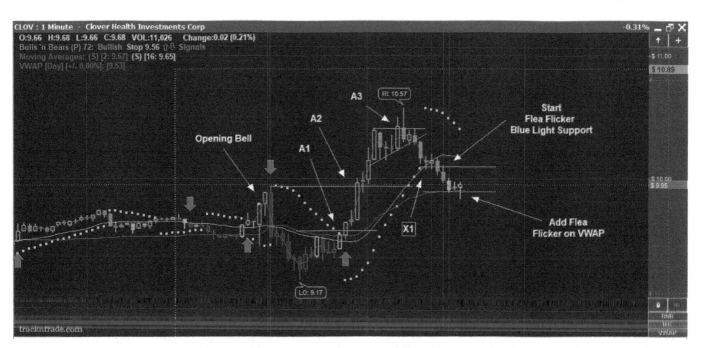

Using the skills we've learned from previous strategies, we can use the Flea Flicker to help build a larger position size and provide more staying power than what otherwise might be accomplish.

Heiken Ashi Scalping Rules & Strategy

Heiken Ashi bars are a type of chart that helps filter out noise. They are constructed using the open, high, low, and close prices of a given time period. Ashi bars are similar to traditional candlestick charts in that they display the same information, but they differ in the way the data is plotted. Heiken Ashi bars are calculated using the average of the open, high, low, and close prices, which can help to smooth out fluctuations and make it easier to identify trends.

Rule 1:   Turn on Heiken Ashi bars.
Rule 2:   Turn off ALL indicators other than Stochastics or RSI; your choice.

Long Strategy:

Only take LONG positions when Stochastics or RSI is oversold, (in the buy zone).

1.   Enter long on first green bar.
2.   Place stop one bar back.
3   Trail stop to break even.
4.   Exit on first red bar after RSI or SSTO reaches the Overbought; Sell Zone.

Short Strategy:

Only take short positions when Stochastics or RSI is overbought, (in the sell zone).

1.   Enter short on first red bar.
2.   Place stop one bar back.
3.   Trail stop to break even.
4.   Exit on first green bar after RSI or SSTO reaches the Oversold, Buy Zone.

If trading multiple positions, trail out according to the Cat's Meow, or Triple Sow Cow.

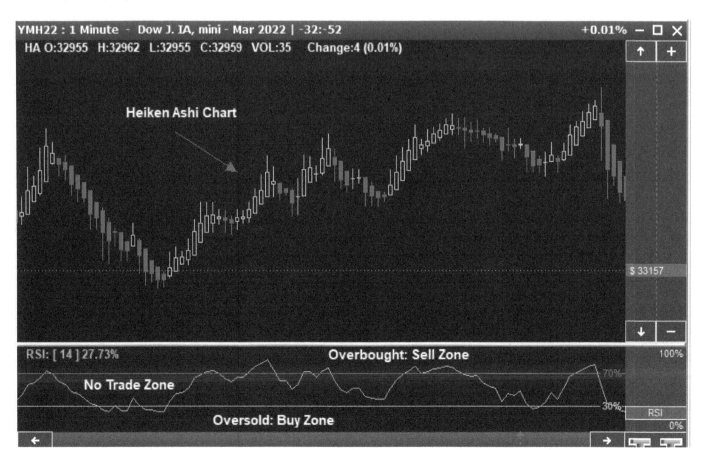

The Double Dip. Buy The Dip 9 and 20 EMA (Exponential Moving Averages)

This strategy is an extension of the Flea Flicker, where we buy the dip during a rising market; with this strategy we use the 9 and 20 period EMAs as our target points for; buying/selling the dip/rally!

> An exponential moving average (EMA) is a type of moving average that gives more weight to recent prices in an effort to make the average more responsive to new information. It is calculated using a formula that places a greater emphasis on the most recent data points, while also considering all data points in the period being considered.

Only take long positions if the market is trading above the 20 EMA, and only take short positions if the market is trading below the 20 EMA

During an uptrend, as the market pulls back, and hits the 9 period EMA, that would be a buy/entry, if the market doesn't bounce and rally, but instead continues to fall, we would then Flea Flicker, adding our second position at the 20 Period EMA.

Of course, if the market continues to fall below the 20 EMA, we need to pull the rip cord and take our lumps in anticipation of a trend reversal.

One popular strategy for final exit is to use a 28 Period Simple Moving Average, if price falls below the 28 Simple MA, then exit. Unfortunately, this only works in a few circumstances; I prefer to look for previous levels of support, or resistance, based on price.

For me, I'm not one to linger through a large draw-down, therefore if the add at the 20 Period EMA doesn't immediately work out for me, I pull the exit rip cord; I'll add on at the 20 EMA, but I need to see the close of each bar stay above the 20 EMA to be considered a viable trade.

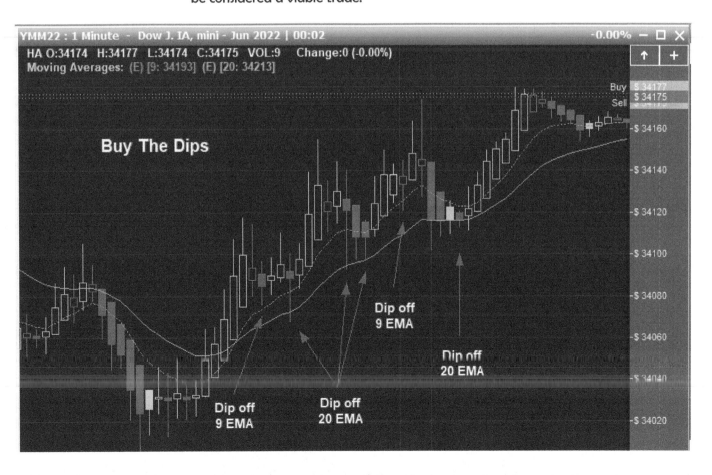

50 Period Simple Moving Average Strategy

As a day trader, watch the 50 period simple moving average as a tool to identify areas of support and resistance, as well as trigger points for market breaks and trends. I personally like to use the 50 and 100 simple moving averages on the two minute chart, which is my long-term reference for my day trading and scalping activities, which I do on the one minute chart. I've noticed that the 50 and 100 simple moving averages are highly effective on many time frames, meaning they are well respected by retail traders.

One of the main benefits of the 50 period moving average is that it smooths out short-term price fluctuations, making it easier to spot underlying trends and patterns. When the market breaks above the 50 period simple moving average on the long side, it's often a sign of strength and there's a good chance the market will continue trending, potentially targeting the 100 period moving average as a target price. (Keep an eye on the 50 period exponential moving average as well, as many traders prefer to follow it rather than the simple.)

On the flip side, when the market breaks the 50 period simple moving average to the short side, it's often seen as a sign of weakness and the market falls to the 100 period moving average for support.

Overall, the 50 period simple moving average can be a useful tool for day traders, but keep in mind that it's just one indicator and you should always consider a range of technical and fundamental factors before making any trades. I like it best when the Bulls 'n Bears Blue Lights match together with the 50 Period Simple Moving Average, those seem to be the best signal points.

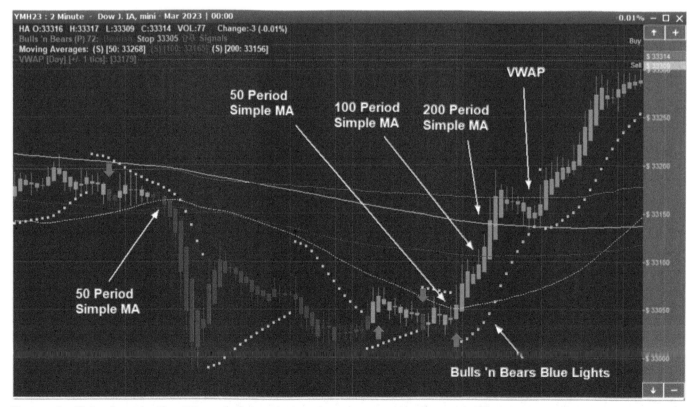

Example: Price breaks the 50 period simple moving average then runs to the 100 moving average.

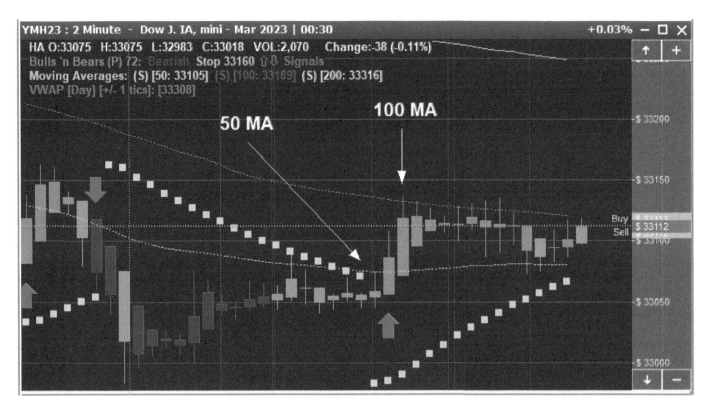

You'll often hear me talk about one indicator or another, but no indicator should be used in isolation, it's best if we can have one indicator confirm the other. In the case of the 50 period moving average, I like both the Bulls 'n Bears Blue Light System and the 50 Period moving average to line up together. These seem to be the best setups for me, and have found this strategy to be very effective.

Note, the fifty period moving average on the two minute chart will line up with the 100 moving average on the one minute chart. For the long(er) term moving averages, 50, 100, 200, I like to use the simple calculation, but when using the short(er) averages, 9, 21, I like to use exponential.

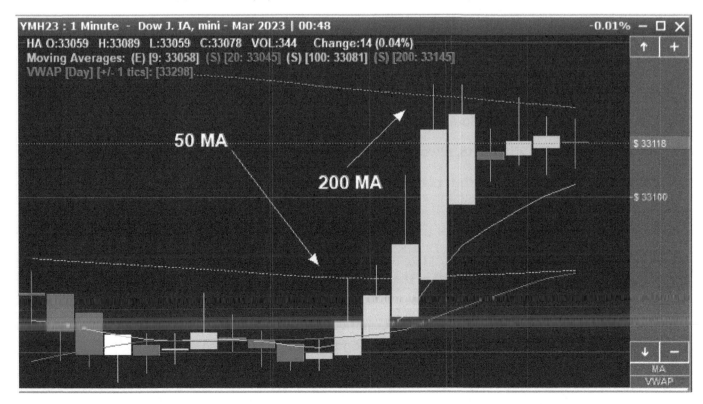

How to trade like a market maker. (Reverse Psychology Scalp Trade)

What is a market maker? A market maker is a financial institution or individual that actively buys and sells securities in order to facilitate trading and provide liquidity to the market. Market makers are typically responsible for maintaining a bid-ask spread for a particular security, meaning that they quote both a buying price (the bid) and a selling price (the ask) for the security. The difference between the bid and ask prices is known as the spread, and it represents the market maker's profit on the trade.

> Market makers play a crucial role in the financial markets by helping to ensure there is always a buyer and seller for a particular security, even during times of low trading volume. This helps to ensure that the market remains efficient and allows investors to buy and sell quickly and easily.

> Market makers generally use their own capital to take on positions in the markets in order to maintain liquidity and facilitate trading. They usually use their own proprietary trading algorithms to automatically execute trades, therefore 99% of the time that you take a trade, you're trading against a market makers algo, not another human.

Being a market maker seems like easy money, but market makers are also subject to certain regulatory requirements, such as minimum quoting and trading requirements, in order to maintain their status and continue operating in the market, and they sometimes get caught in a losing trade just like you and I, where they have to work to mitigate their losses.

Keeping this in mind, I want to teach you one of my favorite strategies; a strategy I call Trading Like a Market Maker.

Here's the typical rules given to all new traders. Do these sound familiar?

1. Don't trade lazy basing sideways markets or between lunch hrs Eastern & Central Times.

2. Place your STOP entry order for a LONG position above resistance. (Or, a SHORT below support.) Wait for a new break above "the perfect" previous high, or low.

3. Get a good fill! (Don't get in late and chase the market.)

4. Have a two to one (2/1) risk vs. reward ratio.

5. Place your stop loss order one bar back behind your entry bar. (Don't put stop too close.)

6. Place a profit taking limit order for that 2/1 risk reward ratio.

It's said that 80% of traders lose money. How many times have you executed the above strategy, and had it fail? 80% of the time?

Guess what? The market makers know these rules too, and since they're the one's taking the other side of your trade, and If new traders lose 80% of the time, how about we trade like the market makers, and win 80% of the time instead?)

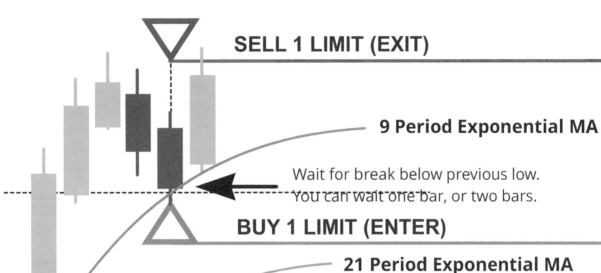

SELL 1 LIMIT (EXIT)

9 Period Exponential MA

Wait for break below previous low.
You can wait one bar, or two bars.

BUY 1 LIMIT (ENTER)

21 Period Exponential MA

BUY 1 LIMIT (ENTER) Flea Flicker

SELL 2 STOP (EXIT ALL)

Reverse Psychology Scalp (Trade like a market maker.)

1. Trade lazy basing sideways markets. Trade between lunch hrs eastern & central times; when markets are less likely to trend. (This is when we generally tell you not to trade.) Never trade like this near news events.

2. Wait for a break above the previous high. (Chase the A1). Trade on the backside of the trend, as indicated by the MACD indicator.

3. Place a LIMIT order for a SHORT entry above the previous high point of resistance, or above the first green candle to break a new high; A1. (The same place you would generally enter to catch a new trend.)

4. Get in late, get a "bad" fill. (chase the market.)

5. Place your profit taking limit order where you would normally place your stop loss order when taking a long position. (This is how you get "stopped out" with a profit. (Remember to put it too close, continue to trail behind the market like you would a trailing stop.)

6. If you get stuck in a trending market, Flea Flicker (dollar cost average) your way out. (Make sure to have an ALL OUT stop loss.)

7. Don't confuse this strategy with the CAFK (Catch a Falling Knife). This is not that, this is in fact, the reverse of Lan's Secret Sauce.

Once you've experienced a successful trade, and you've taken your profit from the Reverse Scalp strategy, don't setup and immediately take the second break of the next new break; the second attempt of a new trend is the A2, and often a great place to enter a position to catch a new trend.

Reverse Psychology Settings

In Track 'n Trade Live, we have the ability to "program" our Q-OCO buttons. Q-OCO stands for Quick-One-Cancels-Other. (Of course these are also OTO orders as well; One-Triggers-Other.)

We don't actually have to write any code to "program" our buttons, we simply fill in the blanks as you see in this example; easy cheese.

In this strategy I'm using the buttons as both, OTO as well as OCO, and the picture you see here are of my settings for my reverse psychology strategy.

You'll notice the very first line is nothing more than a label; not settings. It's a name tag that reminds you what this setup does. I like to give my strategies a number; I've used #20 for this particular strategy.

I also label the other Q-OCO buttons with the #16 as well, if my strategy allows for multiple variations.

As you can see, I've tagged this my Default Strategy, which tells Track 'n Trade to list this one as my default for this particular Q-OCO button.

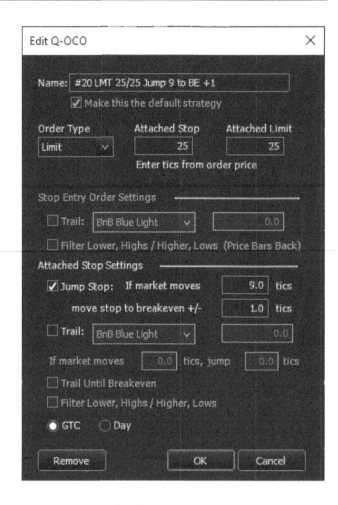

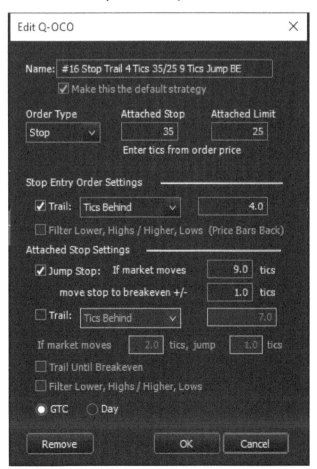

Example 2: Advanced auto-trail to enter.

I'm setting the Attached Stop and Attached Limit both to 25, these are just drop zones, or starting points, they both will be moved to more appropriate areas of support and resistance once the initial Limit order is filled, and we know where we've entered the market.

In example two, you see we're using a more advanced strategy with an auto-trailing stop, which follows the market 4 tics back until filled. Placement of the advanced tool is critical, as you'll want to drop and release it just as the market breaks the low, where we might otherwise have a static Limit order. The auto-trailing stop may catch a better fill.

The Jump Stop is set to jump to break-even, plus 1, automatically if the market pulls back nine (9) tics in your favor, protecting your downside. The plus 1 tics is so we cover commissions and fees if we get knocked out of the trade.

With either strategy, the static Limit entry in figure one, or the auto-trailing stop entry in figure two, once we've entered the market, I'll drag the profit taking Limit order to my target profit zone, usually one bar back from the entry bar; a quick scalp.

Fishing With Lan; Hook, Line, and Sinker Scalping Strategy

The Hook, Line & Sinker strategy is based on the breaking of higher highs, or lower lows. This is a quick profit taking scalping strategy using OCO/OTO (One Cancels Other / One Triggers Other) orders. This is not a trend trading strategy, you will never catch the BIG ONE with this methodology; this strategy is based on the belief that a lot of small pan fish are good eaten too. (See my Scalp & Trail strategy for an advanced version of this setup, using multiple quantities.)

The Hook, Line & Sinker strategy uses a static stop order as the hook, a very close OCO Limit order as your bate, and an OCO stop order as your sinker; the line is the the all important OCO connecting line between the three orders. Here's an example of the Hook, Line & Sinker strategy setup. (In Track 'n Trade you can set this with a simple mouse click.)

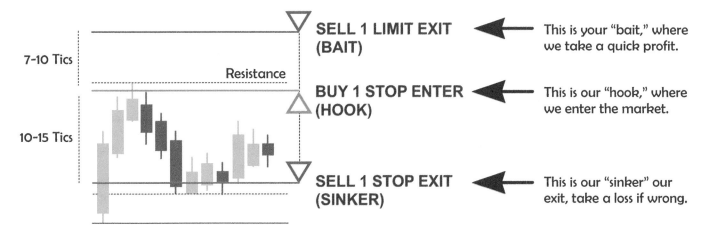

Notice that the "Hook," or Stop entry order is placed just inside the area of resistance, this is done in anticipation of the break above. If we place the hook on the outside of resistance, many times we get too much slippage on our fill, since this is where most stop orders are sitting; we want to jump ahead of those orders, getting filled first. (The downside to this is that we sometimes get filled on a double top, and never get the needed break and push above resistance that we need to profit, only to get stopped out with a loss instead when the market falls back down and hits our sinker.)

Remember, it's the markets job to fill orders. The market does not know if you profit or take a loss when your order is filled, all it knows is that you placed an order, and its job is to fill that order for you. The logic behind this strategy is that we place our Hook just inside resistance in anticipation of a break above. Our Limit order is the bait, we want the market to break resistance as it attempt to fill all the stop orders placed there by other traders, just above resistance, this is often referred to as 'hunting for stops,' therefore we're taking advantage of the fact that the market is out hunting for stops, only in our case, we want it to also hunt down our Limit order as well, which will result in a quick scalp profit for us. (Small pan sized fish.)

The key to this strategy is where we place the Hook, Line & Sinker. There are many places where you can place your hook, the more prominent a high, or low, the more likely your bait will be taken. The concept is that we're going to place our hook where everyone else is placing their stop orders, therefore you need to think like a trend trader, and try to imagine where they're placing their stops; these are the primary places that we want to place our hook and bait.

Advanced Strategy; as a market moves through a trend, highs and lows become established break points, consider placing a hook after each high or low of the previous trend. I call this ghost fishing, where we place a half dozen or more hooks along the way in anticipation of a trend reversal, each break of a previous support or resistance point will result in our hook being hit, and hopefully our bait being taken. You can also place hooks out in front of a trending market, as it makes micro pullbacks against the major trend. (Elliott A2, A3, B2, B3, C2, C3)

50-100 Tics ———————————— ▽ SELL 1 LIMIT EXIT (BAIT) ◀— This is your "bait," where we take profits.

Fishing With Lan; Scalp 'n Trail Strategy

The Scalp 'n Trail strategy is an advanced version of the Hook, Line & Sinker Strategy, (See my Hook, Line & Sinker strategy Cheat Sheet for details.)

The Hook, Line & Sinker strategy uses a static stop order as the hook, a very close OCO Limit order as your bate, and an OCO stop order as your sinker; the line is the the all important OCO connecting line between the three orders. (In Track 'n Trade you can set this with a simple mouse click.)

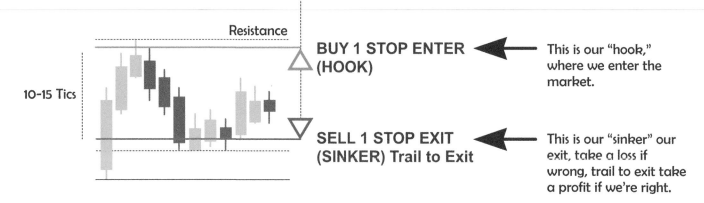

10-15 Tics

Resistance

BUY 1 STOP ENTER (HOOK) ◀— This is our "hook," where we enter the market.

SELL 1 STOP EXIT (SINKER) Trail to Exit ◀— This is our "sinker" our exit, take a loss if wrong, trail to exit take a profit if we're right.

The Scalp 'n Trail Strategy is almost exactly the same setup, with one difference. We don't place a close in Bait order, our Limit for Profit taking order is set much further away from the entry point, or from the Hook, and our Sinker is setup to trail the market in any number of ways, such as Tics Back, Bars Back, or follow a mathematical model like the Blue Lights, the PSAR, or the ATR. This is the Trail Part of the Scalp 'n Trail in an attempt to catch a trend, (Big Fish!)

The Scalp component is placing both a Scalp OCO, as described in the Hook, Line & Sinker strategy at the exact same price and time that we place the Scalp 'n Trail Strategy; we actually place them one on top of the other. The key is that these are two separate order setups, not just a quantity increase of one or the other.

If we try to simply increase the quantity of the Hook, Line & Sinker strategy, we don't get the advantages of the trail strategy, if we just increase the quantity of the Trail Strategy, we don't get the advantages of the Scalp; therefore these two strategies should be used one in combination with the other, each are setup individually within Track 'n Trade.

Notice that the "Hook," or Stop entry order is placed just inside the area of resistance, this is done in anticipation of the break above. If we place the hook on the outside of resistance, many times we get too much slippage on our fill, since this is where most stop orders are sitting; we want to jump ahead of those orders, getting filled first. (The downside to this is that we sometimes get filled on a double top, and never get the needed break and push above resistance that we need to profit, only to get stopped out with a loss instead when the market falls back down and hits our sinker.)

Advanced Strategy; as a market moves through a trend, highs and lows become established break points, consider placing a hook after each high or low of the previous trend. I call this ghost fishing, where we place a half dozen or more hooks along the way in anticipation of a trend reversal, each break of a previous support or resistance point will result in our hook being hit, and a trend to ensue. You can also place hooks out in front of a trending market, as it makes micro pullbacks against the major trend. (Elliott A2, A3, B2, B3, C2, C3)

Fishing With Lan; The Break-In Strategy

I call this the Break-in Strategy. We've all heard of the break-out strategy, where we buy on a break above a previous high, or sell on a break below a previous low.

I call this the Break-In Strategy because rather than buy on the break of a previous high, or sell on the break of a previous low, we simply anticipate the break, but we don't actually trade the break.

As a market approaches a previous high, or a previous low, many traders will stack their orders just outside of resistance or just outside support. We call these break-out orders bait, because their baiting the market to rise above, or fall below the level of support and/or resistance.

In the Break-In Strategy we place our hook and bait just inside resistance and/or support, in anticipation that the market will "gun" for those stop orders sitting outside support and/or resistance, and in our case, will be forced to go through our orders to fill those orders.

Here's the setup:

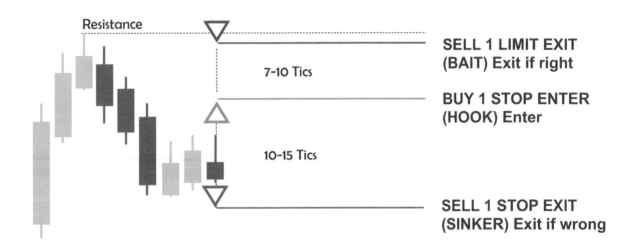

Place your OCO/OTO order system seven to ten tics below the previous high, or seven to ten tics above the previous low of the market. (Consider using larger quantities with higher probability setups.)

Remember, when we setup this up using the Track 'n Trade Q-OCO orders, the Bait and the Sinker do not become active until the Hook is set.

I've also used this strategy very effectively against the VWAP, anticipating that the market would reach down/up and bounce off of VWAP, so I placed my Bait / take profit order just above VWAP when short, and just below VWAP when long, anticipating that traders would push the market up to VWAP, or down to VWAP. (To be profitable, the market didn't have to break VWAP, it only had to test it.)

Also be mindful of Dollars and Half Dollar psychological resistance points, the market has a tendency to use these psychological price levels as support and/or resistance levels; consider placing your Bait just above/below these levels.

Fishing With Lan: Today is Backwards Day

I know we talked about this strategy in an earlier section, but I wanted to cover it again with a different twist, as part of our Hook, Line & Sinker series. Did you ever play the game of backwards day as kids? Where you would do everything just backward from what you normally would do? Put your pants on backwards, wear your shirt backwards, walk backwards. What? You didn't know that was a thing? Go search it on YouTube, it's a thing.

How many times have you said, "If you want to make a butt-load of money, just do exactly the opposite of what I do and you'll be rich, rich, rich!" Or, "I'm super good at losing money, I know exactly what to do to lose a lot of money!" Or, how about this one, "Every single damn time I get into the market, I get stopped out, I swear they can see my stops, and know exactly where I put them every single time!"

Well, if you're so good at losing money, then why don't you play opposite day, and do exactly the opposite of what you think you should be doing?

Think like a 'market-maker.' Yes, market makers can see your stops, and they're very smart about knowing where traders place their stops, and they use these points of support and resistance to 'gun for stops.' Don't be the fish, be the fisherman.

How do Market Makers make their money? They fill orders, that's their jobs. A market maker doesn't know if you make money, or lose money when they fill your order, all they know is they did you the favor of filling your order. Now most of us hate that, right? We're all angry, "Damn market came back and stopped me out!" But wait, that's what the market is supposed to do, it's supposed to fill your orders. So, stop being the fish, and start being the fisherman.

The most common stop loss dollar amounts are $50 and $100; so for example, most traders will trail their stops $50 behind the market, (or $100 depending on the market.) Most traders will buy on a break above a previous high, or sell on a break below a previous low, then bring their stops to break even, once they bring their stops to break even, the market (market makers) see those stops, and they don't come and "get you" like some say, or like some think, but they allow the market to fall, or rise by pulling their orders off the table, allowing the market more freedom to drop/rally which takes out your order, or fills it, which is what you asked for, right? (not really). So trade like you're a Market Maker, and not a trader, be the fisherman, not the fish.

Remember, these orders are setup as OCO/OTO orders, therefore the Bait and Sinker will not become active until the Hook is set. If market price moves through their price levels, nothing will happen.

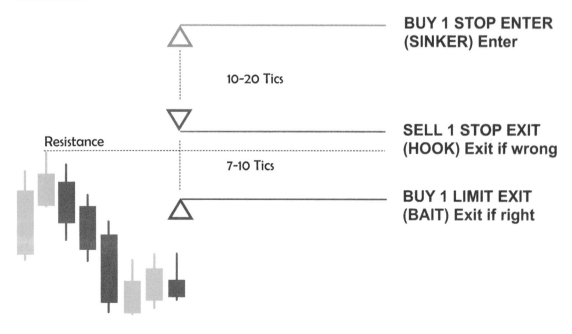

BUY 1 STOP ENTER
(SINKER) Enter

10-20 Tics

SELL 1 STOP EXIT
(HOOK) Exit if wrong

Resistance

7-10 Tics

BUY 1 LIMIT EXIT
(BAIT) Exit if right

Lan's Secret Sauce
A trend reversal strategy

I have two versions of this strategy, the older, simpler version, which I'll describe first, then the second version is an updated more advanced strategy that I've been using since we received an update to the software that allows me slightly different setups. (I like trading this strategy primarily on the Futures Stock Indexes.)

Version 1: The Swing Trade version: This is very simple. We're going to use Track 'n Trades ability to trail price bars back for entry. Step 1: Trail for entry one price bar behind the market. (Lately, I've been using Heiken-Ashi on a one minute chart, which works like a charm.)

Once the initial order is filled, we then enter another trailing stop, one price bar back, for quantity two, (or double the amount we initially went in with.) This is a reversal order, that will reverse your position with each new price bar high, or low; in essence, catching every new trend of the market.

Version 2: The modified, or advanced version of this is to switch off between the ATR (Average True Range) trailing indicator, and the high/low price bars. I like to use the high/low price bars when entering the market, but then switch off to the ATR, for trailing to exit/reverse; I'll move my orders back and forth between the two depending on which one is giving me the better signal at the time.

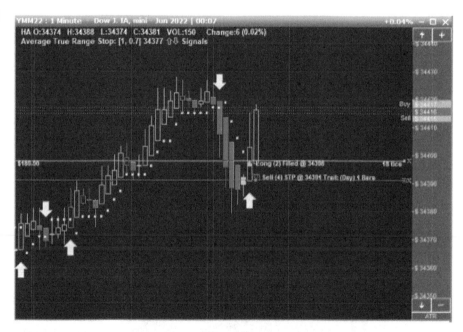

I set my ATR very aggressively, generally (1, 0.7) within the settings; (Heiken-Ashi bars only) This will take a little time, practice, and focus to master; where I've taken my biggest losses is when I get distracted, and the market reverses without me noticing, or I enter the wrong quantity for the reversal, and it takes off without me, or in the wrong direction, and I miss the reversal. Pay attention, order execution is key.

I think it goes without saying, in an actively trending market, this strategy kicks ass! In a non-trending quiet sideways market, this method kicks your ass.

As with any strategy, execution is key here, make sure you stay focused, and once you've caught the trend, stay in, it will often trend much longer than you think it will, don't jump out prematurely, let the system work it's magic. (You can do a slightly modified version of this with the TnT Q-OCO orders as well.)

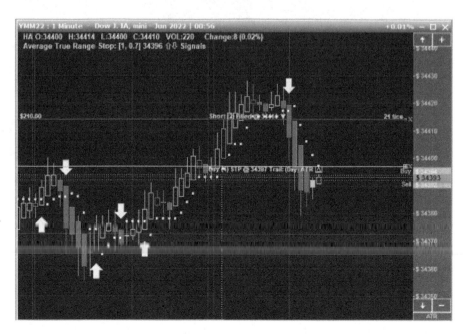

Setting up Q-OCO orders; Trade King Tut

The King Tut strategy is a combination of Pyramiding and Pillaring. Pyramiding and pillaring are two closely related trading strategies that involve increasing the size of a position as the price of the security moves in favor of the trade. Pyramiding involves adding to the position all at once, while pillaring involves adding to the position at regular intervals. Both strategies can be used to potentially increase profits, but they also involve taking on additional risk, as the size of the position is increased.

This is how I setup my Q-OCO order tools for trading the King Tut Strategy. The initial price bars back for the stop order may need to be adjusted slightly for different markets. For example, the Nasdaq and S&P may need a larger stop, while the Dow and Russell may be fine with a smaller initial stop. Practice in whichever market you chose to trade in the demo account to double check your settings and make sure everything is tuned in correctly.

Q-OCO 1   Q-OCO 2

Edit Q-OCO ×	Edit Q-OCO ×
Name: #1 Buy: Trail 1 PBB Exit	**Name:** #1 Sell: Trail 1 PBB Exit
☑ Make this the default strategy	☑ Make this the default strategy
Order Type / **Attached Stop** / **Attached Limit**	**Order Type** / **Attached Stop** / **Attached Limit**
Buy Market ∨ / 50 / 100	Sell Market ∨ / 50 / 100
Enter tics from order price	Enter tics from order price
Stop Entry Order Settings ——	Stop Entry Order Settings ——
☐ Trail: BnB Blue Light ∨ / 0.0	☐ Trail: BnB Blue Light ∨ / 0.0
☐ Filter Lower, Highs / Higher, Lows (Price Bars Back)	☐ Filter Lower, Highs / Higher, Lows (Price Bars Back)
Attached Stop Settings ——	Attached Stop Settings ——
☐ Jump Stop: If market moves 0.0 tics	☐ Jump Stop: If market moves 0.0 tics
move stop to breakeven +/- 0.0 tics	move stop to breakeven +/- 0.0 tics
☑ Trail: Price Bars Back ∨ / 1.1	☑ Trail: Price Bars Back ∨ / 1.1
If market moves 0.0 tics, jump 0.0 tics	If market moves 0.0 tics, jump 0.0 tics
☐ Trail Until Breakeven	☐ Trail Until Breakeven
☐ Filter Lower, Highs / Higher, Lows	☐ Filter Lower, Highs / Higher, Lows
● GTC ○ Day	● GTC ○ Day
Remove / OK / Cancel	Remove / OK / Cancel

The name at the top is just a title for reverence when you save the strategy. Pay close attention, notice that the first section is how the orders will behave on initial entry. Order Type and the Attached Stop and Limit. The second section is how the attached Stop order will behave. Will it trail, if so, how? Will it jump, will it follow mathematical models like the ATR, Blue Light, or PSAR, or any number of other methods?

My advanced strategy uses trailing stops for entry, and trailing stops for exit

Setting up Q-OCO orders; Trade King Tut

Q-OCO 3 & 4 are my Stop entry and Limit entry strategies. These are a bit more advanced than the simple Market order entry strategy. For example, the Stop entry strategy, (Q-OCO 3) automatically trails behind the market based on mathematical modeling, such as Blue Light, PSAR, or ATR, Price Bars Back, or any number of other models.

This is a nice strategy because it takes the entry point decision out of your hands, and puts it into the hands of the computer to execute on your behalf when a certain set of criteria is met. This removes a lot of the emotion out of trading, and reduces the number of trades you may possibly take.

The primary concept behind the King Tug is that we enter the market with either a single contract, and add on as the market moves in our favor, or we enter with multiple contracts and removed positions as the market moves in our favor.

Q-OCO 3	Q-OCO 4

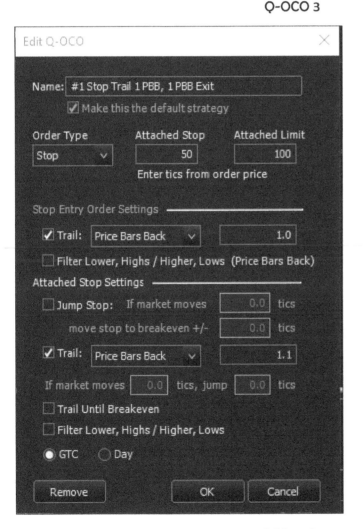
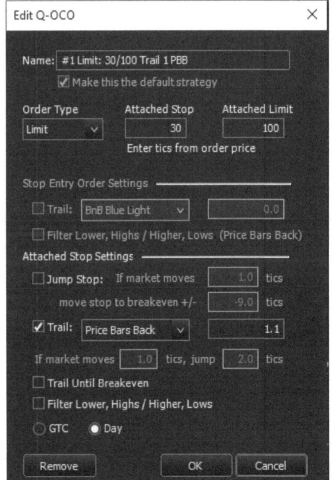

We use our OCO orders to enter the market, when the market moves in our favor, we add onto our position, which is Pyramiding (Building a larger position), then we remove positions, taking profits along the way, which is Pillaring out of our Pyramid.

I like to start my pyramid with multiple contracts, so when we dollar cost average into the winning trade, our average entry doesn't jump too close to the current market price, which can get us stopped out prematurely, then taking profits as the market pushes into new highs; sizing down the pyramid.

Fishing With Lan; The Martingale System

Let's talk Martingale. What is the Martingale system or strategy?

Martingale is very simple, it's a risk management methodology that's generally used, in an effort, to help increase our chances of recovering from a losing trade, or from a losing streak. The Hook, Line and Sinker strategy, especially the Break-In strategy, lends itself to the Martingale methodology very well.

The Martingale involves doubling up on losing trades, and reducing winning trades. We're basically playing the odds that if we just had a loser, our next trade is more likely be a winner, (This is actually a gamblers fallacy, but let's suspend disbelief for just a minute.) The idea here is that if we double up on the next trade, we have the opportunity to win back our losses. (If you're experiencing dozens of losses in a row, you need to work on your entry strategy.)

The anti-martingale works just the same, only in reverse, for winning trades. If you enter the market with three contracts, and your trade is a success, your next trade would be reduced in size to two contracts, and if you find success a second time, you would drop down to only a single contracts for the third trade.

Many traders have blown up their accounts attempting to continually employ this strategy incorrectly.

Therefore, it's for this reason that we MUST set limits to our Martingale, for example, if you're going to Martingale, it's imperative that you limit yourself to three attempts to recover, if we lose three times in a row, pull the rip cord and stop trading. Either come back another day, or start a new run. (Many traders think of each Martingale "run" as one trade, therefore the scenario below would be considered, by some, as three trades.) So, if you're limiting yourself to only three trades a day, then...here you go, this is a way of sneaking in a few extra trading opportunities.

Let's run a quick scenario:

1. Our first trade starts with Qty-2 contracts, and we win.

2. Our next trade would be Qty-1 contract, and we lose.

3. Our next trade would be Qty-2 contracts, and we win.

4. Our next trade would be Qty 1 contract, and we win.

That's run one, (one trade) now we start again:

1. Our second trade starts with Qty-2 contracts, and we lose.

2. Our first recovery trade would be Qty-3 contracts, and if we lose.

3. Our second recovery trade would be Qty-4 contracts, and if we lose.

4. Our final recovery trade would be Qty-5 contracts, and hopefully we win.

That's run two, (two trades) let's start again: (Of course, any strategy depends on stop loss and profit taking limit placement as well, if your risk of loss is greater than your potential for profit, then this strategy would not return all losses; suffice it to say, when trading, there are many moving parts, think it through, and make wise decisions.)

1. Our third trade starts with Qty-2 contracts, and we lose.

2. Our first recovery trade would be Qty-4 contracts, and if we lose.

3. Our second recovery trade would be Qty-6 contracts, and if we lose.

4. Our final recovery trade would be Qty 12 contracts, and if we lose.

5. Runaway, runaway, runaway!

Fishing With Lan; that will be a dollar fifty please. What is the "Dollar Fifty Strategy?"

Watch your areas of support and resistance, and you'll notice that they have a tendency to bounce around right along the even dollar and the half dollar points of the price scale. You'll also notice that recurring price patterns and Elliott Waves have a tendency to form and turn at these points as well.

We call these dollar, and half dollar levels psychological areas of support and resistance, but it goes beyond that, they're not only psychological, they're programmatic. I can tell you, as the owner of a software engineering firm, and someone who works with software engineers on a regular basis, and who also designs mathematical trading systems, that we, as mathematicians, love to create trading strategies that take dollar and half dollars into consideration.

Most trading activity, (volume) in the indexes, and large popular stocks in particular, comes from automated algorithmic trading systems. For the most part, you and I, as small speculators, are primarily trading against the computer bots, which is why the best time to trade is during the first hour of the morning, and the last hour before markets close, since that's when you get the most active retail traders, and the bots have less control.

Generally speaking, the more retail traders, and the less bots, the more likely the market will be to respect the rules of technical analysis. (This is why small caps are popular with retail traders, less bots, more live traders.)

For me, I love trading the futures market, due to the many additional advantages we get from trading futures. My personal favorite markets are primarily the indexes, Dow, Russell, Nasdaq, and S&P; but one of the disadvantages is that the indexes are littered with bots.

As a retail trader, you need to think like a computer programmer, like an algorithm, like a bot. Ask yourself, if I were a computer algo trading system, what are the most important numbers I have available to me to help me make my trading decisions? (Remember, many bots are market makers, they can see your orders, so gunning for stops is real.)

A computer is going to track current price and volume, along with current trend highs, current trend lows, daily highs, daily lows, along with dollar and half dollar price levels. These are the most important numbers to a computer algo trading system, therefore the algo is going to play off of those numbers.

It's for this reason that I suggest you pay very close attention to the Dollar and the Half Dollar price points within the trend; watch these levels very carefully, and consider building your trading strategy to include those price points.

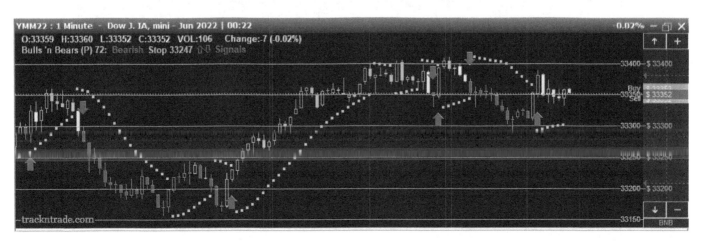

Return to Home! VWAP
What is Volume Weighted Average Price

The volume-weighted average price, (VWAP) is the average price of the market as it trades throughout the day. This is an intraday only indicator, we generally use VWAP when day trading on a small time-frame chart, such as five minute, or even one minute.

It's generally considered that if price is above VWAP, then the market is bullish, if it's trading below VWAP, we think of the market as bearish; but consider this too:

Think of VWAP as a rubber band, the market will be pulled back toward VWAP, either from the bullish side pulled down, or from the bearish side pulled up. Therefore VWAP acts like an area of strong support and resistance, a magnet; traders also look for price to bounce off of VWAP and begin to trend once again.

In the mornings, you'll often notice that the market will fire off and create a nice rally, either bullish or bearish, but then return right back to VWAP. (See the example below.)

Consider using VWAP as a *'return to home'* strategy, wait until the market is as far away from VWAP as it seems to be able to get, using other extreme point indicators, such as Stochastics, or RSI, registering in the extreme overbought, or extreme oversold regions, and then look for the market to '*return to VWAP.*'

Once it returns to VWAP, this is where we can also see a lot of consolidation and stagnation. It's where a lot of traders lose their shorts, looking for new trend breakouts, but instead, the market just whips back and forth crossing back and forth above and below VWAP, taking traders money.

Be careful, VWAP is a multi-edged sword, you can use it to your advantage as support and/or resistance, but it can also be a danger zone of stagnation.

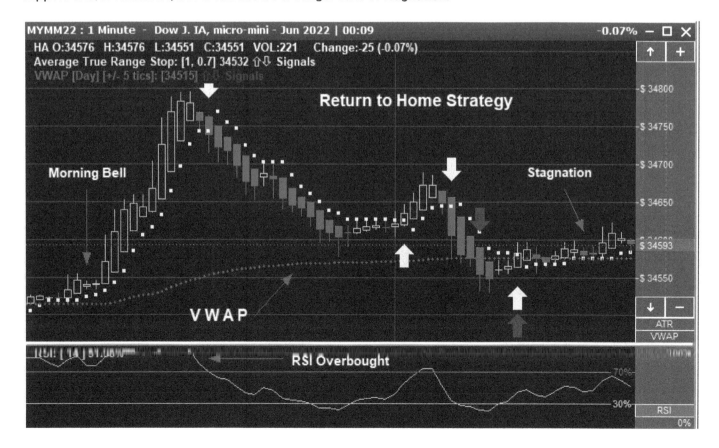

VWAP Autopilot Trading
Auto Trading Volume Weighted Average Price

In Track 'n Trade we have the Autopilot, which is a feature that will continually monitor the market for you, and execute trades based on the instructions you've given it. You can build a trading plan that you might otherwise not be able to execute on your own, due to your human limitations; lacking the ability to continually monitor the market over a longer period of time, and waiting for the perfect setup. The Autopilot can do this for you, waiting until that event occurs, then execute your trading strategy on your behalf; one such strategy is called the VWAP strategy, outlined here:

The volume-weighted average price, (VWAP) is the average price of the market as it trades throughout the day. This is an intraday only indicator, we generally use VWAP when day trading on a small time-frame chart, such as five minute, or even one minute. It's generally considered that if price is above VWAP, then the market is bullish, if it's trading below VWAP, we think of the market as bearish.

Track 'n Trade has the ability to display a bullish arrow when the market rises above VWAP, and a bearish arrow when market prices fall below VWAP.

The Autopilot has the ability to signal off of these VWAP bullish/bearish arrows, and use them as buy or sell signals, putting you into the market either long, or short; it's a simple strategy that can be very effective.

The concept is simple, we just need to admit to ourselves that we don't have any clue which direction the market is going to move on any given day, or by how far, and turn the decision for entry and exit over to the Autopilot, allowing it to enter into a position long if market crosses above VWAP, and short if the market crosses below VWAP.

The exit strategy can be two fold. First, we can simply close out the position fifteen minutes before the end of the day, again, using the Autopilot to manage that for us, or we can manually intervene at any point throughout the day and take profits.

A second, and more robust strategy, might be to diversify across multiple markets: For example, turn on the Autopilot VWAP strategy on four separate charts, Dow, Russell, Nasdaq, and S&P, then use Limit orders to exit when specific target prices are hit, for example, we might use no limit order for exit on the Dow, letting it run until the end of the day in an effort to catch the entire day's move. We might use a limit order of 50 points on Russell, a Limit of 100 on Nasdaq, and a Limit of 200 on S&P. (These are just examples, they've not been back tested for historical accuracy.) In doing this, you've diversified your strategy across multiple markets, using multiple variations for exit.

Be careful, VWAP is a multi-edged sword, you can use it to your advantage as a bullish and bearish indicator, but it can also be a danger zone of stagnation. The downfall of the VWAP Autopilot Strategy is that markets can sometimes stagnate around VWAP, and when this occurs, the Autopilot will continually enter you long, then short, then long, then short, possibly chopping up your account.

It may take multiple days of trending markets to break away from VWAP to cover the costs of a single day of stagnation. (This is a multi-day strategy, and should not be considered a quick one-and-done system. Consistency over time is the key to any trading strategy, this one in particular, and obviously it goes without saying, but I'll say it anyway, there is never any guarantee that this, or any trading strategy will consistently profit every time.)

Scalp Trading: Trading 25's 50's 75's and 100's

What is the difference between buying a dip, and scalp trading? Basically, it's the entry strategy. Remember, a scalper trades based on the 'action-bar,' the current active bar, while a day trader will only make new trading decisions based on closed bars, and let the action bar trigger his entry or exit. (It's a fine line, but a line that must be respected.)

Traditionally, when trading the dip, we wait for the market to break above the high of a previous bar, we use a stop order placed above the market in an attempt to catch a rise in market price, generally the first candle to make a new high.

When we scalp trade the dip, we don't use a Stop order to buy a rising market, instead, we use a Limit order to buy a falling market. We place our limit order at or below a strong area of support, where the market must break that support level to fill the order.

Strategically placing our orders at even price levels is another key strategy for limit order entries, placing our limit orders at .25, .50, .75, and/or 1.00 levels. Markets have a tendency to use even price levels as support and resistance. I like to place my limit orders one or two pennies inside those levels, such as .27, .52, .77, 1.02. This insures that my order will be filled if the market hits the exact even price level and bounces.

This is where it gets tricky.

If the market continues to fall, and does not bounce off the support level immediately after your order has been filled, you may need to flea-flicker (dollar cost average) into a larger position as the market continues to break through lower key support levels. (See flea flicker strategy for additional details.) Always make sure you calculate your risk vs. reward, and where you'll pull the rip cord for final exit if the market does not bounce.

Once the market hits your key level of support, and fills your Limit order, anticipate a quick bounce and reversal of the trend, which actually does happens sometimes, so be prepared, and be ready to quickly 'scalp' half your profit from the position on the rebound bounce.

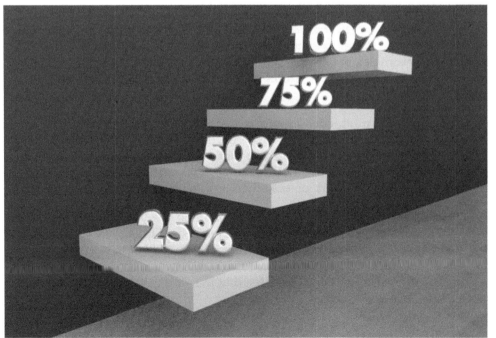

For example, let's say the market is falling after making new highs, creating a pull back that we calculate to be a dip trade of the Elliott A drive, anticipating a rise into the Elliott B drive. We place a limit order for 500 shares of the stock at a strategic area of support, let's say at the 10.52 per share price. When the market hits our limit order, and bounces back up to 10.75, we exit 50% of the position, take the quick 'scalp' of $57.50, drop our stop at break-even, then look for the market to continue higher with our remaining 250 share position, where we can now begin to pillar up.

Timing of a Limit Scalp Entry

When is the best time to put on a Limit order (scalp) entry?

We generally will only put on a Limit entry order strategy, or start a Flea Flicker, or King Tut strategy at market extremes. Either extreme highs for a short position, or extreme lows for a long position for obvious reasons.

Limit order entries require the market to be going "in the wrong direction," it requires that the market be falling to enter long, and rising to enter short.

When a market is falling, it tends to continue falling, and when a market is rising, it tends to turn and fall. (This is why many traders find greater success trading short rather than long.) See my Heisenberg Strategy Course for details.

> Many trading accounts can't take short positions, such as a retirement account, such as a self directed IRA, or 401K, there are also many stocks that are simply not shortable, or easy-to-borrow, therefore taking long positions is the only alternative.

So how do we know when a market is trading in an extreme high, or an extreme low? This is generally calculated using oscillating mathematical indicators such as Stochastics, RSI, or CCI. These indicators are designed to indicate when a market is considered to be in an extreme, overbought level, or an extreme, oversold level. (See my Understanding Indicators course for details.)

When the Stochastics, and/or RSI indicator is in the oversold region, generally below the 20% threshold, this is the time to start the Flea Flicker and/or King Tut Limit Order (scalp) entry strategies, the market is already oversold, therefore you have a higher probability of catching a reversal than at any other time.

Reverse that logic for a short position, only start Flea Flicker, and/or Balaams Ladder strategies when Stochastics, and/or RSI are in the extreme overbought regions, above the 80% threshold.

Always be mindful of where you're at in the Elliott Wave count, as well as where the breaking of the Blue Light, and/or the PSAR might come into play.

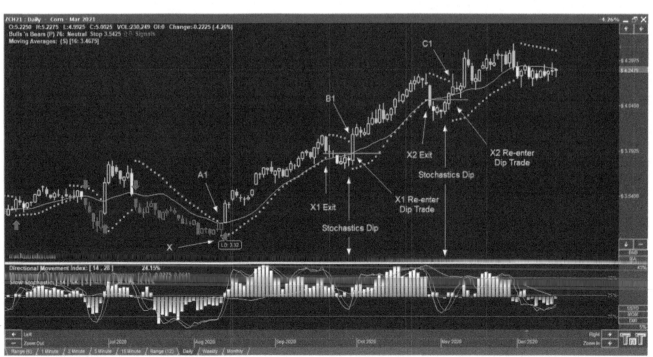

Building Pyramids; Pyramiding vs. Pillaring

When trading, there are a number of different methods for building a large(er) and larger position as the market moves in your favor, or against you.

> Managing market sizing can be the difference between turning trading into a career, remaining an amateur your whole life, or simply blowing up your account altogether.

There is no "one-way" of building larger positions sizes, there is never a one-size-fits-all solution when it comes to trading, but there are 'best practices' that most winning traders adhere to, and especially new traders need to be extremely conscious of.

> I've seen traders lose enough money, in just one trade, to have purchased a new house, because they didn't follow 'best practices,' when it came to account sizing.

When building larger and larger positions, my favorite method is to Pyramid my trades, you'll often hear traders say, "Don't Pyramid," you've probably even heard me say that, or publish it in my other work. What we're referring to is "UPSIDE DOWN," or negative Pyramiding, or Pyramiding into loosing trades something I've dubbed the Flea Flicker, since it's so dangerous.

Pyramiding and pillaring are two closely related trading strategies that involve increasing the size of a position as the price of the security moves in favor of the trade. Pyramiding involves adding to the position all at once, while pillaring involves adding to the position at regular intervals. Both strategies can be used to potentially increase profits, but they also involve taking on additional risk, as the size of the position is increased.

> An upside down pyramid is when you start with a small share size, and as the market moves in your favor, add-on larger and larger positions; for example, don't ever start with 100 shares at A1, add 200 shares at A2, then add 300 shares at A3. That's a recipe for disaster! New traders seem to love doing this.

A Pillar is when you Start with 100 at A1, add 100 at A2, then add another 100 at A3; this is a much "safer" method than upside down pyramiding, but still not my favorite. See the Flea Flicker, and King Tut sections of this guide for an exception to this rule, where I teach proper upside down Pillaring and Pyramiding strategies.

My favorite sizing method is the standard pyramid strategy; slowly build a larger and larger position.

For example: Start A1 with 500, at A2 add 250, then at A3 add 100. (Trail to exit all.)

Ideally, your average position size will never exceed your trailing stop order.

Pillaring out, or taking profits along the way is what I call the King Tut.

Castling Your Trade

A risk management strategy of taking profits without reducing position size.

"Trading is like playing chess, most players know how all the pieces move, but they don't know a single strategy for pinning the king in the corner to win the game." -- Lan Turner

In chess, there are three unique moves, one of which is where a player is able to switch places with their king and a pawn; this is called Castling.

When trading the financial markets, you'll often hear me say, "Take profits along the way!" I also say, "Increase your position size as the market moves in your favor." But wait, those two statements are inconsistent with each other, aren't they? How can you take profits and also increase your position size at the same time? We do this through a strategy I nick-named Castling, after the famous chess move.

How to "Castle" your trade.
When a market is moving decisively in your favor, and you want to take profits, but not reduce the size of your position, take action by placing a stop entry order just inside your profit taking limit order. This will add to your existing position at nearly the exact same time as taking one position off. (It's imperative that the new position is added first, prior to taking the profit position off.)

- Adding the new position prior to taking the profit will insure that your average (dollar cost) will not increase as aggressively as it would if you took profits first. If you take the profit first, then add onto your position, this will more aggressively advance your dollar cost average, mathematically bringing it closer to the current market price, creating a higher probability that you will get stopped out prematurely.

The key takeaway from this concept is that you must add to your new position prior to taking a profit, which then maintains your current position size, and does not aggressively advance your average entry position.

Sometimes, in a fast moving market, you can perform this strategy using market orders. Simply click the Buy Market button, quickly followed by clicking the Sell Market button.

Here's a quick diagram of how this trade might look in the setup.

Keep in mind, you want to always try to keep your average dollar cost average position behind your trailing stop order.

This strategy works hand-in-hand with the King-tut strategy.

Don't Feed The Trolls (Break out or bail out.)

When trading, we're continually looking for setups and triggers. These are patterns that have consistently, in the past, been profitable points of entry. You're probably familiar with many of these patterns; triangles, wedges, head and shoulders, breaking of high points, breaking of low points, and trend lines.

There are many setups and triggers, including mathematical modeling, such as buy and sell arrows from indicators such as RSI, Stochastics, MACD, etc.. For me, I always try to combine these elements of trading to establish a higher probability entry point, such as buying on a break of a triangle, or wedge formation when the RSI, Stochastics, or MACD matches with a buy signal.

Of course, my three favorite matching indicators are the Bulls 'n Bears Blue Light, the ATR (Average True Range), and the PSAR (Parabolic Stop And Reverse.) When one of these three overlay indicators buy/sell signal corresponds with a break point of a recurring price pattern, along with an overbought oscillating indicator such as RSI, or a momentum indicator such as MACD, these setups generally seem to be my best entry points. The more of these tools that match up, the higher likelihood the market will "break-out," and continue to trend in my favor. (Keep in mind 'time of day,' as well.)

That said, not all setups succeed, surprise! In fact, we're lucky if we can get better than 50% of them to succeed. (I know, hard to imagine, right?) Markets are fickle, they sometimes have no rhyme or reason for doing what they do. We have a saying in this industry, "Markets can stay irrational longer than you can stay liquid."

The primary point of this lesson is to warn you not to take unnecessary risks. Wait for the very best setups, take the trade, and if it does not IMMEDIATELY move in your favor, just get out, and wait for another setup; we call this strategy, Break-Out or Bail-Out.

Where most traders lose money, and blow up their accounts, is because they won't get out when they're wrong. We have another saying, "Cut your losers short, and let your winners run." This is not just a cute mantra, it's commandment number one of the traders ten commandments; break out or bail out.

Feeding the trolls.

When you stay in a losing trade, holding on for dear life, hoping the market will reverse once again, to come back and save your sorry ass; I call this feeding the trolls. The trolls are the market makers and apposing teams orders that sit on the other side of your trade, stealing money from your pockets.

Don't feed the trolls.

Why Am I Always Playing Catch Up?

Why does it seem like I'm always trying to play catch up, just continually working to recover losses? It feels like that because that's the game you're playing, it will almost always be that way for your entire trading career, the question is why?

Why are we continually playing catch up, always trying to recover losses? Why is it so difficult to make gains? Understanding the dynamics of trading will help you manage your emotions, and control your inner desire to revenge trade.

When we enter a trade, the first thing we do is establish a loss amount, how much are we willing to lose to find out if we're right, if this market is going to move in our favor. Let's say you're wrong 50% of the time, that in itself is the defining factor in taking losses, half the time you enter the market, you're going to be wrong, and lose money. The key is to recognize that you're wrong, and get out fast, and not take ever larger losses. (If the market does not immediately move in your favor on entry, then get out.) If you're always getting stopped out, we need to work on your entry strategy.

When we say cut your losers short, and let your winners run, this is not just a cute saying, if you're wrong, get out! I would rather take ten tries at the market and lose $20.00 on each try, than take one shot at the market, and lose $200. (Wait for small risk entries, and only take those.)

Unless you're a scalper, we are, as trend traders, continually looking to catch a trend, remember the 33.33.33 rule, this means we're going to be wrong 66% of the time, therefore we have to cut our losers short very quickly.

Yes, trading is frustrating, many times price breaks your decision trigger, getting you into the market, only to flash back down, take you out, and then take off and run once again. Yes, it happens all the time, but how do you know it's going to do that? You don't, because the same exact setup could also be a trend reversal pattern; we just need to recognize that fact, and learn to deal with it.

We just have to realize that we're going to get caught in those whipsaw patterns, and that's why it feels like we're continually playing catch up, always trying to cover losses...because we are!

That's why it's so imperative that we set risk parameters, as well as number of trades we're willing to take in a day. This is what's called Risk Management, and it's more important than trade setups, patterns, and indicators. Risk management is Strategy Number One! (Go study risk management!)

First and foremost, we need to be trading explosive markets, markets with high volume, and a lot of movement. Never trade flat, low volume, sideways markets. Trader's often think, "Oh, I'll catch the break-out of this sideways trend!" So, they continually buy into every one bar breakout. Don't do that! It's a sure fire strategy for failure; leave that strategy to other traders.

As trend traders, we want to only trade explosive markets, markets that are already trending, markets that are on the move. Jump on the moving train, in the direction the train is headed. (...and if the train stops moving in your direction then jump off, and wait for the next train.) I call this train trading, or "How to trade like a hobo." ;-) Don't feel bad if you caught a train that left New York, headed to Las Angeles, and you jumped on in Chicago and only rode it as far as Denver. That's okay, be a hobo!

Day Trading News

Day traders often trade based on news events and economic reports, as these can have a significant impact on the price of financial instruments. It is important for day traders to stay up-to-date on the latest news and to be aware of any upcoming economic reports that may affect the markets.

In addition to paying attention to the news, it is also important for day traders to use technical analysis to identify potential entry and exit points in the market. By combining fundamental analysis, which involves considering the underlying factors that may influence the price of a security, with technical analysis, day traders can potentially make informed decisions about when to enter and exit trades.

Here's an example of a government report GDP Growth Rate QoQ. Notice it's set to have a high impact on the market when the news releases. The charts are an example of how the market reacted to that news event.

The strategy, of course, is to watch these scheduled news events, then trade them using entry and exit points based on technical analysis. (I never listen to the main-stream media for tradable news, they know nothing.) There are several great news sites, this example comes from DailyFX.com/calendar)

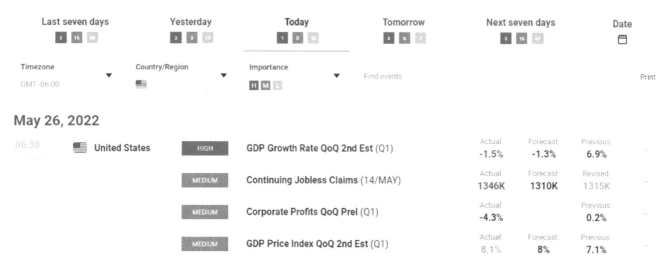

May 26, 2022

06:30	🇺🇸 United States	HIGH	GDP Growth Rate QoQ 2nd Est (Q1)	Actual: -1.5%	Forecast: -1.3%	Previous: 6.9%
		MEDIUM	Continuing Jobless Claims (14/MAY)	Actual: 1346K	Forecast: 1310K	Revised: 1315K
		MEDIUM	Corporate Profits QoQ Prel (Q1)	Actual: -4.3%		Previous: 0.2%
		MEDIUM	GDP Price Index QoQ 2nd Est (Q1)	Actual: 8.1%	Forecast: 8%	Previous: 7.1%

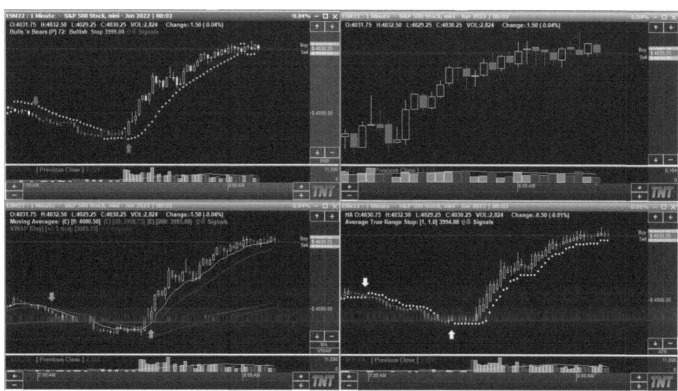

Why trading seems like we're playing a carnival game. The 33, 33, 33 rule

As a trader, does it feel like you're always wrong? Does it feel like every time you get into the market, the market goes the opposite direction?

You're not alone. The fact is, trading the financial markets is like playing a carnival game where the odds are continually stacked against you.

Have you ever noticed when you go to a carnival that the basketball hoops are just a tiny bit smaller and not the same height as a normal hoop?

Or, how about the baseball toss, where it looks so easy to just toss a baseball into the apple basket, but for some damn reason, you can never get it to stick!

Why? Because the odds are stacked against you.

How many times have you walked through a Carnival and seen someone carrying around one of those giant stuffed animals? Almost never, right?

Same thing when trading, taking home a giant stuffed panda every day is extremely difficult.

The 33, 33, 33 rule says that markets can only do three things, they can go up, they can go down, and they can go sideways, therefore it doesn't matter which direction you pick, since you can only pick one, the odds are 66% stacked against you being right.

The biggest mistake most traders make is believing that the market is going to trend.

Just because the market fell hard and created a beautiful downtrend, that you missed, does not now mean that it's going to reverse and rally back up, and visa versa, just because the market rallied hard does not mean it's now going to turn and fall; don't chase the reversal! (The problem with this game, is that sometimes it does reverse, yes, which is what sucks you into the carnival game, but it's not a general rule.)

Use stops, and don't over trade, jumping on every little one bar rally in anticipation of a trend reversal is how the carnival game takes your money; wait for setups & triggers.

Prepare yourself for a flat non-trending market, and always remember, as a new trader, you're probably going to be wrong 66% of the time; plan for that! (Your goal is to get and stay above 50%, super-de-duper traders hover around 60%).

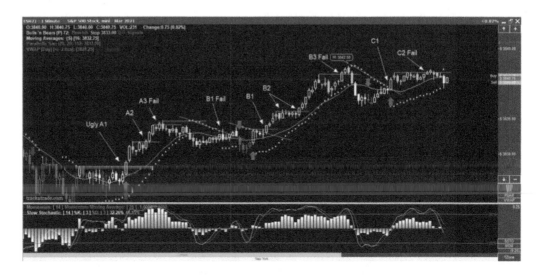

Are you an Olympic Athlete?

Maybe you are an Olympic athlete, but are you a top formula one racer? How about a PGA golf contender? Wait, what? Are you not the best of the best of the best in this world at doing something? Anything? Oh my god, how can you live with yourself?

Look, the fact is, 99% of us are not top contenders in anything, and you know what? That's okay. It still doesn't make it any less wonderful to go out onto the golf course and hit balls, working to get a little bit better each and every day. But why? Why do we do it? If we know darn good and well that we're never going to be a PGA golf champion, why go out and play golf? Why even bother practicing?

Did you drive your car today? Did you go 200 miles per hour around an oval for 500 miles? Why not? You know how to drive a car; why aren't you a Formula One racer? What? You mean to tell me all you ever use your car for is to get milk from the grocery store and to drive to work and back? Oh my god, how can you live with yourself? You're such a loser, my god, if you can't drive your car 200 miles an hour for 500 miles, you must be such a tool. Not only that, you probably have tiny hands.

Can you ride a bike? Are you a racer in the Tour de France? What? You're not? Oh my god, I can't believe you! You can ride a bike, yet you don't race the Tour de France? What's the point of even getting on your bike, then?

For some reason, in the financial markets, when it comes to trading, everyone thinks they need to be one of the top contenders in the world. What the hell am I doing this for if I'm not? My god, I didn't make $10,000 today day trading; why the hell am I even doing this? I'm such a loser! I quit! I give up!

We, as traders, need to stop already with the unrealistic expectations. We see the markets in hindsight, and we say, "Oh my god, look at that, had I bought right there and sold right there, I'd made thousands of dollars! And, if I'd traded 50 contracts or 100,000 shares, I'd be rich, rich, rich beyond my wildest dreams!

Of course, we never do trade 50 contracts, or 100,000 shares, because we don't have the balls of steel to pull the trigger on those sizes. Am I right? We're scared to trade one contract sometimes, "Oh my god, I just lost $14, god I hate this; I'm never going to get good at this!"

Is this you? "Oh my god, I just paid $80 to play 18 holes of golf, and to add insult to injury, they made me actually rent the cart, WTF! I even had to buy my own clubs! God, what's next? They're probably going to make me pay for balls too! I've played this goddamn game six times already, and I'm not making millions on the PGA! God, I hate this stupid game. I don't know why I even keep trying! Why isn't golf free? Why do they charge me for the cart? Why do I have to pay for clubs? If I lose a ball, they make me pay for new ones!

God, don't they know it should all be free? How will I ever be a PGA contender if it's not free?"

We are our own worst enemy when it comes to trading. We keep believing all the kids on YouTube, who are NOT traders (who are producers of videos), when they tell us, "How easy day trading is, and oh my god, if you're not day trading like me, making millions, buying Lamborghini's, then you're such a loser!" Trust me, 99% of them are lying to you.

Trading the financial markets is like anything else in life. It takes time, it takes work, and it takes dedication, and, yes, it takes an investment in tools, education, and practice. Some days we win the game, and some days, we lose the game, but all in all, we're having fun, hitting par on more holes than we don't, and work every day to get better and better. We're never "there!" Being the trader we want to be is always just one step away; that's called progress.

Nobody expects you to be a world-class PGA golfer when you walk onto the golf course for the first time, just like nobody expects you to be a professional trident trader when you start doing a bit of day trading.

You often hear highly successful people say, "It took me ten years to become an overnight success!" To be a successful day trader, you need to do it because you love it, and yes, in the beginning, there will be some start-up costs. Just like with golf, or bicycling, or race car driving or flying airplanes, you'll have to pay to learn.

Trading does have the potential to provide an income, even a substantial one. Just like playing golf offers the prospect of income--someday. Yeah, you could ultimately become a world-class PGA golfer and cash in one of those giant checks; that would be cool, right? I say we keep that as something fun to aspire to, but hey, in the meantime, how about we grind away at the community course, hitting balls for fun, and maybe even compete in local tournaments for cash and prizes? We do it because it's what we love, and if you're not willing to approach trading with the same mindset, you should not trade. Go back to scrolling Facebook, watching other people do fun things.

The greatest secret you can reveal to your friends when they ask is:

"Yeah, I'm a day trader and I do okay at it."
"Oh, Really? What's your secret?"
"I know how to stop when I'm ahead."

Which will be the title of our next article, "How to know when it's time to stop trading for the day."

Up, Down, or Sideways

How to differentiate between trending days and range days. Strong trending days are easy to recognize, whether up or down, one side dominates the other. Some key factors that can help you define a strongly trending market are:

1. In a strong uptrend, the chart is filled with more average to large sized green price bars, where the close of each bar is at or near the high. At a glance, there are simply more green than red bars.

2. In a strong downtrend, the chart is filled with more average to large sized red price bars, where the close of each bar is at or near the low. At a glance, there are simply more red than green bars.

3. In an uptrend, red retracement, or pull back bars are generally small, and short lived, generally have narrow bodies, and long wicks at the bottom. The long bottoming tails, or wicks is a representation of the markets rejection of an attempts to push prices lower.

4. In a downtrend, green retracement, or pull back bars are generally small, and short lived, generally having narrow bodies, and long wicks at the top. The long topping tails or wicks is a representation of the markets rejection of an attempt to push prices higher.

5. During a strong uptrend, we look for long wicks at the bottom of green bars, not on top, again indicating that selling is being rejected, and price is being pushed up. During a strong downtrend, we look for long wicks at the top of red bars, not on the bottom, indicating that buying is being rejected.

    a. Heiken-Ashi bars are an exception to this rule. With Heiken-Ashi bars we want to see topping tails on all the green rally bars, and no bottom tails, and just the opposite for red bars; this is because Heiken-Ashi employ a mathematical smoothing component not seen in traditional candlestick bars.

6. In a bull market, the green bar bodies are larger than the red bars, in a bear market, the red bars bodies are bigger than the green bars.

    a. Higher highs, and higher lows. In an uptrend, each individual candle should adhere to this rule. Each high should be higher than the previous bars high, each low should be higher than the previous bars low; ideally, each close should be higher than the previous bars close. This same rule applies to a downtrend as well.

7. Markets rarely move straight up and straight down, they generally move through waves, creating price corrections, either a rally, or a fall, the market will then generally move sideways, before it rallies, or falls once again. These pivot points, or levels of price hesitancy or stagnation are where we find many internal price patterns or continuation formations such as wedges, triangles, flags, or pennants.

    a. The highs and lows of these points of stagnation are where we draw our connecting trend lines, up or down, which establishes our high and low levels of support and/or resistance.

8. Sideways trends, or non-trending markets are identified by price bars with large topping tails and large bottoming tails on most of the price bars, as both buying is being rejected, as well as selling is being rejected, often causing back to back trend failures.

    a. To take advantage of range days, look for long candle wicks, or bottoming tails around trend lows, where sellers are rejecting lower prices, while looking for topping tails or long wicks around the highs of a sideways trend, where buyers are rejecting higher prices, ride the internal sideways trends from top to bottom of the overall longer term daily sideways patterns, with trend lines draw across points of support and resistance as entry and exit levels.

    b. Candle wicks represent failure; topping tails means buyers failed, bottoming tails means sellers failed.

Lan H Turner

Trading is Just a Big Video Game

Yeah, okay, I said it; day trading and scalping is nothing more than playing a video game for real money.

Go take a look at your iPhone or gPhone App Store, inside the App Store, you'll see two lists, one list is for free games, the other is for paid games.

Notice that all the best games, the award winners, are all on the paid list, while all the crap shit games are on the free list. Why do you suppose that is? Think about it. Do you think it might be because it actually costs money to make great software?

Yeah, but Lan, there's lots of free trading platforms. Do you know what I say to that? Yeah, there are, but all the great award winning trading platforms cost money, why do you suppose that is? Just maybe, because it costs money to create great trading software too? I know, hard to believe, right?

If you want to go risk your life savings with a free shit trading platform, then by all means, knock yourself out, but you should also realize that the company who's promoting that 'free' business model is not in the business of providing great trading software, they're in the business of getting you to churn and burn your trading account. They don't make money selling great trading tools, they make money from getting you to trade as often as they can; the more you click that buy button, the more money they make.

Ask yourself, is that really the company you want to be associated with? Do you really want to be associated with a company that makes all their profits off of your trading activity, rather than from providing you with great trading tools? Think about it, it's up to you.

I don't care if you use free software or not, I'm just saying, you need to realize, companies need revenue to survive, and if you think you're saving money by trading with free software, then those companies are making money from you somewhere else, if they weren't, how could they survive?

That said, there are lots of great computer video games in this world, there's not just one answer to all video games, some players like World of Warcraft, some players prefer Mario Brothers, other's like to play Tetris.

It's the same in the world of trading, some traders like to play Track 'n Trade, some like to play TradeStation, and other's like to play Robinhood.

The problem with traders, is they think they can start off playing Track 'n Trade, and because they couldn't make money with that platform, they can just jump over and start trading with TradeStation, and they should suddenly be rich, because they're now trading a different platform. Obviously, it doesn't work that way; whatever platform you use, you need to master that tool, yes, some are easier to master than others.

Just because you master Tetris, doesn't mean you can suddenly be great at Call of Duty. You would never think like that when it comes to video games; so where do traders get that mindset in trading?

Each platform is unique, special, and has different capabilities, allowing you to perform the function of trading in different ways. You need to spend time mastering the software, the gaming platform, as well as the concepts behind trading. Trading concepts may be somewhat universal, but the gaming platform, or trading platforms approach to trading is often wildly different, having a wide spectrum of capabilities.

If you spent as much time mastering the art of trading, as you spent learning how to master World of Warcraft, or Tetris, then just imagine how you could eventually become unstoppable when trading.

Do The Math!

Calculating Batting Averages & Win Loss Ratios

Rule number one, take no big risks!

- In the beginning, count on being wrong 70% of the time. (Initially, plan on winning only three out of every ten trades.) Hopefully, we can achieve higher, obviously, but don't plan on it in the beginning as a new trader.

Cut losers short, let winners run...

- For example, let's say you lose, on average, $50 per trade. Lose 7 out of 10 trades = Loss of $350.00; you must win 3 out of 10 trades, each trade must average = $117.00 to break even, not including commissions & fees, the point being, don't expect to win all your losses back on one trade.

How to Calculate Your Batting Averages.

- Winning Trades: 30
  Losing Trades: 20
  Total Trades: 50
  Batting Average: 30/50 = 60% Winning Ratio

Batting Average is not enough, what if your losers are bigger than your winners? We must also calculate our Win Loss Ratio.

- Winning Trades: $150, $750, $38, $235
  Losing Trades: $275, $320, $75, $50, $85

- Average Winning Trades: $293.25 ($1173/4)
  Average Losing Trades: $161 ($805/5)

  Win/Loss Ratio: 1.821 ($293.25/$161)

Win Loss Ratio is your personal performance score, use it to gauge if you're doing better or worse over time; compare your performance against other traders.

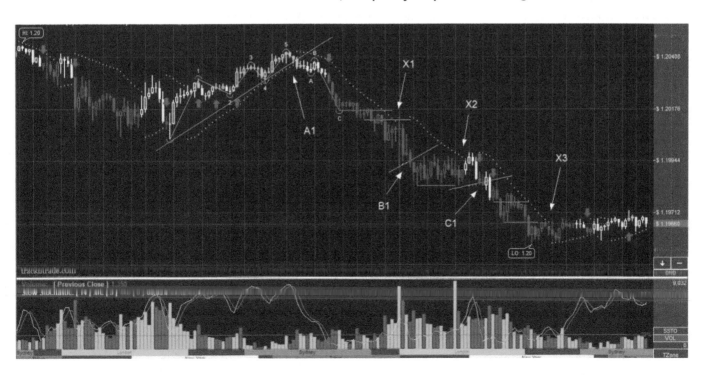

When to Take Profits?

Believe it or not, it's a rare event for traders to actually take money out of their trading accounts, it seems most traders are continually putting money in; so when should a trader take money out? For me, this is a general rule of thumb, which of course, I would expect you to modify for your own purposes, this concept is a building block to work from.

I recommend, when day trading the futures market that we open our trading accounts with $5,000, in my opinion, $5,000 is a good starting point, it's not too much to ask for most people to invest, and affordable to most beginning traders. (When trading stocks, you'll need at least $30K to avoid pattern day trading rules.)

$5,000 is also enough money that you won't be severely under leveraged, anything less is probably too little. If you can start with more, should you? There's no right answer to this, but in my opinion, no, it's not necessary.

In the beginning, you need to practice trading with real money, and learn how to build your account through trading and not from putting more money into the account; although this may also be necessary a couple times as well.

A second advantage of starting with a smaller amount is most new traders will experience a point where they begin to revenge trade, where suddenly you lose all emotional control and start risking your entire account on stupid trades in an attempt to "get your losses back!" If you only have $5,000 in your account when this occurs, the max you can lose is your $5K. If you start with $50K and this feeling of despair takes hold, you could lose a much larger amount before you finally throw the towel in and walk away.

Here's my general rule for building your trading account, and also when to take profits; they don't have to be mutually exclusive.

Stage 1: Start with $5,000, build your trading account to $10,000; this is the most critical time for a trader, it's when you're working to learn to trade with real money, and how to control your emotions, and how to walk away each day profitable. You will have red days along the way, and during this building phase, you need to learn how to control your emotions on those days, everyone has losing days, it's part of the process; you need to learn to deal with it.

Stage 2: Build your account to $10,000. Once you've achieved this first goal, take you and your significant other out to dinner in celebration; I believe it's important to celebrate milestones, even if it's just a small reward.

Stage 3: Continue to build your account. After you reach your goal of doubling your account from $5K to $10K, it's time to start taking profits. Every two weeks, once you've earned $1,000 in profit, (In this first case, that would be $11,000) contact your broker and have them send you $500, or half of your profits over and above the $10K.

Stage 4: Continue this strategy until you reach your upper goal of having a $50K trading account balance, at which point, I believe is a great target point for then taking 100% of your profits thereafter.

Stage 5: If your account balance falls below the $10K, or $50K thresholds stop taking profits until you bring it back.

Risk Management Cont. Options

Although this document is not specifically written with options trading in mind, the basic entry and exit strategy are basically the same.

- The most common options strategy is to buy an option 'at-the-money,' or as close to the current market price as possible.

  - If you think the market will rise in price, buy a call option, if you think the market will fall, buy a put option. Pay close attention to volume and open interest; try to get 100 volume, and 1000 OI. (If you can't find the volume, don't trade it!)

  - Buy an option with twice as much time to expiration as you think you'll need to complete the trade; always error on the side of caution by adding extra time rather than less, this lowers your daily time decay; theta.

  - After purchase, if your option loses 10-15% of it's value, kill it, dump it!

    - Make adjustments as needed, your percent loss should match closely to where you would otherwise have a hard stop if trading shares.

  - If your option reaches a Delta value of .80 consider taking profits; roll position.

  - If you follow these simple rules, you'll have 75% of option trading mastered.

Now that you have the basic concept of options under your belt, use the same methods you've learned here in this document to know when to buy and liquidate your options positions; buy Calls at A1, B1, C1, and liquidate calls, and/or buy Puts at X3, X4, X5.

At this point, buying and selling options becomes very systematic, take profits just as you would with shares, cut losses just the same.

With stocks, one option represents 100 shares, in futures it represents one contract, you can purchase an option for about 20% of the cost of the shares/contract; that's your leverage.

Many traders take this as a sign that if they were equally willing to invest $5,000 into a stock, that they should then invest the same dollar amount into buying options, therefore controlling 5X the number of shares, or futures contracts.

Just remember, if leverage can work in your favor, and make you more money more quickly, then it can also work against you, and you can lose more money more quickly as well.

What is the differences between intrinsic and extrinsic value?

In this scenario, we're going to talk about intrinsic value, and extrinsic value from several points of view, the first being real estate, the second being the financial markets.

Intrinsic Value: If you pay $100,000 for a condo, the intrinsic value is $100,000. If you hold that piece of property for five years, and it increases in value by $10,000, you've increased your intrinsic value to $110,000, an increase of 10%; wonderful, usually, we expect that to occur in seven years, and in this case you did it in five, nice job!

> Extrinsic Value: Over those same five years, you rented your condo for $500 per month, therefore you earned $6,000 per year, multiplied by five years, equals $30,000 in extrinsic value.
>
> Now, let's talk about intrinsic value, vs. extrinsic value as it applies to the financial markets.
>
> Let's say you purchase 100 shares of Amazon's stock at $100,000. If you hold that stock for a period of five years, and it increases in value by $10,000, you've increased your intrinsic value to $110,000, an increase of 10%. (Same exact scenario as our real estate model.)
>
> So, where does extrinsic value come into play within the stock market? Options.
>
> When we buy an option, we pay for that option with two types of value, intrinsic and extrinsic value.

If we purchase one Apple option priced "at-the-money," how much intrinsic value is there in the option? Zero! Why? Because, the underlying stock itself is trading at the same price as the option was purchased, therefore if the underlying stock does not increase in value, the option will have zero increase in intrinsic value, but, if the underlying stock increases by $10, the option itself would then have $10 of intrinsic value. (Actually, it's a bit more complicated than that, given the Delta, but for this simple example, just go with it.)

> Extrinsic Value: The question has to be asked, if I'm buying an option at-the-money, and it has zero intrinsic value, why am I paying a premium for the option? Why does it have any value at all? Because, it has time, and opportunity value, or the amount of time it has left for the opportunity to turn a profit.

Let say you purchased the option with six months until expiration, this means you have six months of time value, or what I like to refer to as opportunity value. This is how much extrinsic time we have, or the opportunity for that option to increase its intrinsic value. Therefore, in the financial markets, in this scenario, we don't receive extrinsic value like in the real estate example, since we can't rent out our stock, therefore extrinsic value is something we must buy, or pay for, and it immediately begins to decay the minute we purchase it, which makes our extrinsic value a decaying asset, therefore the intrinsic value of the option must increase fast enough to cover the cost of the extrinsic (time/opportunity) value that we purchased.

Now, there are options strategies (covered calls) that we can employ to help us increase our extrinsic value, (rent out our stock) which is something we'll talk about in a future class, or cheat sheet.

Trading While Sick

We always advise traders, never trade when sick. Can you imagine? How clearly are you thinking when hopped up on pain meds, or cold medicine?

If you're like me, when all drugged up, I certainly don't think very clearly.

Very often, traders need to think quickly, and make wise decision in a split second, and if you're compromised cognitively, then that's not usually going to fair well for you.

As many of you know, I recently suffered a debilitating heart attack, which landed me in the hospital for two weeks. As you can imagine, I had no access to my trading platform, and could not manage my positions.

Fortunately, each one of my positions were properly setup, using stop loss orders as protection, as well as several options positions that were tendered properly as well, not to mention, I also have my brokerage team to watch out for me as well.

My friend, and member of our trading club, unfortunately, was not so fortunate.

He went into the hospital for, what he thought would be, a very simple in and out, same day surgery, when for some reason, he had a reaction to the anesthesia.

Six weeks later, he walked out of the hospital to discover he had lost 50% of his sizable portfolio value; this was a hard lesson to learn.

First and foremost, always, always trade with stops, make sure you protect yourself against a market down-turn.

Second, always have a friend, a spouse, or a professional member of your support team able to get into your account in case of an emergency to manage your positions for you. Make sure to leave them detailed instructions on what you want done, usually just "liquidate all positions," would be the expectation.

You can always come back and reassess your status once you're feeling better.

As a futures brokerage firm, we've had clients die with open positions on the board, causing some stress for the families.

Don't leave your loved one's in this vulnerable state, and don't risk your account in that way, make sure to consider a backup plan in the event of an unforeseen tragic event.

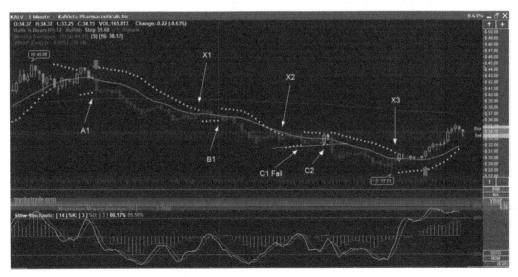

Pre-Market & Post Market Trading

In the stock market, we have what is known as Pre-Market, and Post Market trading. This is where traders trade before the morning bell, and after the closing bell.

There are several hours before and after that traders can still actively trade the markets, but beware, there are special rules for this trading time-frame.

Why are there special rules, different than the regular hours?

Well, because then it wouldn't be different, it would just be extended regular hours, and that's no fun, this is a game, and we need different rules to make the game fun and interesting, right?

So, here they are.

Pre-market trading, in the stock market, starts at 4:00am Eastern time, while regular market hours start at 9:30am Eastern.

In the pre-market hours, you can trade, but the only acceptable order types are Limit orders, therefore the market must tick up to take a short position, and tick down to take a long position. (Check with your broker to confirm that these rules apply to you.)

We have basically the same rules in the post-market hours, where you can trade after the market closes, but again, only with Limit orders, therefore the up tick and down tick rules still apply. The post market starts at 4:00pm Easter, and ends at 8:00pm Eastern.

Be very careful trading pre and post market hours, usually the volume is very light, making it difficult to get orders filled, usually resulting in wide spreads.

Also, due to the fact we we are only allowed to use Limit orders, which require an up tick, or a down tick to enter and exit, you could potentially get your order filled, but since you can't use stop orders, only Limits, the market could take off and run against you, and never look back, never giving you that up tick to let you out of the market...resulting in a large loss. (Ask me how I know.) Buyer beware.

> Weird, I know, but, those are the rules. again, if we didn't do crazy things like that, then what would be the point of having pre and post market hours? (You might as well be trading in the Futures Market, where we can trade up to 23 hours a day, and where there are no crazy restrictive rules like that.)

Time Management

Managing your time as a trader is also a key element to our trading plan. I've devised a quick trading / time management system, and provided it here. Use this time management system for helping brainstorm new systems and strategies, and what time of day these systems have performed well.

Feel free to copy this time management system and use it as your trade journal.

How to know when the stock market will go up?

That's the million dollar question, isn't it? Everyone wants to know how they're supposed to know if the market is going to suddenly rise or fall. How do we catch the beginning of that big new trend?

The short answer is, we don't, and never will. We don't have any way of knowing for certain when a market is going to make a significant move. And, as small speculators, because we can't know, we really should never plan on, much less continually try to catch the beginning of that big move, and here's the reasons why.

The first thing we must understand is, what drive a rising and falling market? What makes a market suddenly break out and take off for the moon? The short answer is, large speculators. It's large banks and hedge funds that move the market in significant ways, not small speculators. Individually, we're way too small to be able to significantly move a market. (Now, that said, we small speculators can, as a group, push a market higher/lower once the trend has been primed, if we all join in together, (Think Wall Street Bets). But, primarily, for the purposes of this discussion, it take a power house to significantly move the market.) We, as small speculators, for the most part, are just along for the ride.

So, our struggle is knowing when those big speculators, banks, and hedge funds, 'Power Houses,' are going to suddenly start their buying spree, right? Before entering a trade, we need to always ask ourselves, what makes me believe that a large Power House, (Or, a significant number of small speculators), are going to jump into the market at this particular point in time and significantly move the market? If we can't answer that question, then we should NOT take the trade.

Large speculators generally buy at strategic times, they're purchases are not random, and are not generally based on technical analysis like we small speculator might do. If they are using technical analysis, it's generally on a longer term time frame as outlined by Elliott Wave, and the Wyckoff theory. (Mastering those concepts will serve you well.)

Large banks and large speculators are continually looking for fundamental reasons to enter a market, either long or short. Most banks and hedge funds make their profits from buying and going long, holding for a long(er) period of time. They don't generally scalp like you and I might do, they generally accumulate positions for a long(er) term investment strategy. The big boys don't go all in, or all out at once. This is why you'll often times see small bursts of energy in a market, a single ten or twenty bar rally, followed by stagnation once again.

These "random" ten or twenty bar rallies are large bank and/or hedge fund adding, or taking away from, an overall larger position, accumulating, or dispensing of additional shares for one reason or another.

When a bank, or hedge fund does this, it will often 'prime the pump,' which causes a large number of small speculators to jump onboard and help push the market higher, or lower, but knowing when large speculator is going to make that initial purchase is nearly impossible without some sort of nefarious insider trading information. (See Nancy Pelosi and Mitch McConnell)

It's for this reason that we, as small speculators, never intend to catch the beginning of a new trend. It's just too dangerous to continually jump on every one bar rally, hoping it will "be the one" that takes off and runs. The prudent small speculator will wait until a market has already made a significant move, has already made that three, six, or ten bar rally, who will be patient, and wait for a micro pull back (A2) in the active trend, or catch the second leg (B1), what we call the C,D leg of an A,B,C,D rally. If you'll do that, you can significantly tip the odds of success in your favor.

When entering a market at its initial breakout, it's important to be cautious and not jump into every single rally. The wise trader will wait for confirmation before making a move. Sure, the initial breakout may be a sign that the market is starting to trend in a certain direction, but it's not always a reliable indicator of what's to come. The price of a security can change dramatically for various reasons in the short term, so it's crucial to wait for confirmation before acting. A good way to confirm an initial breakout is to wait for the follow-through move, like a second rally or a sustained trend in the direction of the breakout. By being patient and waiting for confirmation.

So, the answer to our previous question, why am I entering the market now? Because, it's already made its first significant move, and I'm just trying to catch the continuation. Let a market first prove to you that it wants to trend before you jump aboard.

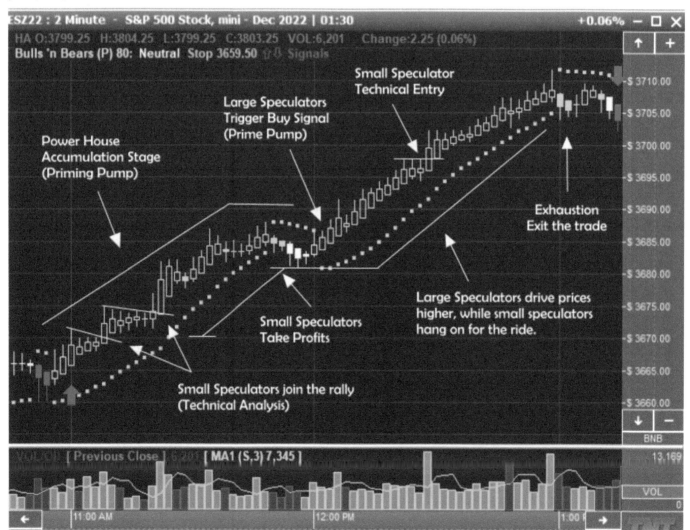

BARRON'S

TECHNOLOGY

Apple Rules the S&P 500 With Highest Weighting for Any Company Since 1980

As of Tuesday, the world's largest company by stock market value, at $2.7 trillion, accounted for 7.3% of the S&P 500 index. That is the highest weighting for any stock in the index based on records going back to 1980, according to S&P Dow Jones Indices.

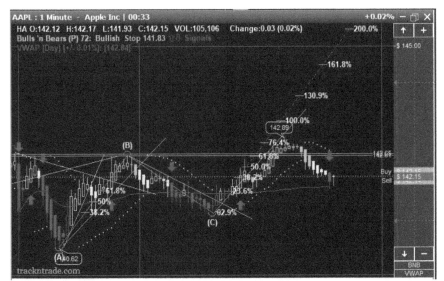

I follow Apple on my left screen, using Track 'n Trade Stocks. I'm not actually trading the stocks version of Apple, I'm using it as an indicator.

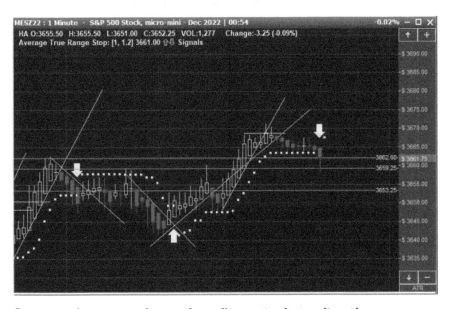

On my right screen, this is where I'm actively trading the futures indexes. I trade the indexes based on the action of the Apple stock. If Apple is active and trending, then I can generally expect the same from my futures indexes.

My Secret Weapon

When I day trade the futures market indexes, I most certainly do have a secret weapon. Here it is:

As you can see in the article by Barron's Technology, Apple is the king of the roost, holding the highest honors, or weighting within the S&P 500. This has been true since 1980, and will probably not change anytime soon; until then, let's just stick with Apple.

Never forget the old adage; as goes Apple, so goes the S&P 500. This is true for the NASDAQ, as Apple also holds the highest weighting within that technology heavy index as well.

On my right side screen, my active trading screen, I have my Track 'n Trade Live Futures trading platform, where I watch both the one minute, and two minute Charts of the S&P and/or NASDAQ.

The two minute chart is where I watch the Bulls 'n Bears, and do my Elliott Wave and Fibonacci Counts and measures.

My one minute chart is where I execute my trades, based on patterns and setups.

It's on my second monitor (left side for me.) where I have Track 'n Trade Live Stocks running. As I day trade, I continually watch, analyze, and perform my counts and measures on the one minute Apple chart.

If Apple is NOT giving actively strong trends and trade signals, then I won't take positions within the S&P or NASDAQ.

When trading the DOW, the largest weighting goes to United Health Group, at 11.47%, so be mindful of other individual stocks that can be used as canaries in your coal mine as well.

Try it, you'll like it!

Bill Williams Fractals

Bill Williams is a well-known trader, author, and educator in the field of technical analysis who also developed several oscillating indicators, including the Alligator, and the Awesome Oscillator, both of which can be found within Track 'n Trade.

Bill's Fractals are a technical recurring price pattern used to identify potential reversal points in the price movement of an asset. Williams took the famous pattern known as Pivot Points, (In Track 'n Trade, it's known as the Dart tool), then based on his own observations, created rules for trading Pivots Points, or Darts. He provides insight on which points to ignore, how to enter, exit, and how to manage the trade, then named his strategy "Fractals."

Bill's Fractal consists of five or more bars, which includes the two bars before and after the Pivot Point, where the middle, pivot bar, has the highest high or lowest low of the group, and the two bars on either side have lower highs or higher lows. A bullish fractal occurs when the middle bar has a higher high than the two bars on either side, and a bearish fractal occurs when the middle bar has a lower low than the two bars on either side.

Bullish Five Bar Fractal Pattern

The rules for trading with fractals can vary depending on the trader's strategy and the market conditions, but here are some general guidelines:

1. Identify the fractal: Look for five or more bars with the middle bar (Pivot Point) having the highest high or lowest low of the group. A bullish fractal occurs when the Pivot Point has a higher high than the two bars on either side, and a bearish fractal occurs when the Pivot Point has a lower low than the two bars on either side.

1. Determine the trend: Fractals are most useful in trending markets. Determine the trend by using other indicators such as the Bulls 'n Bears indicator within Track 'n Trade.

2. Enter a trade: If the market is in an uptrend, look for bullish fractals and consider going long when the price breaks above the high of the fractal. If the market is in a downtrend, look for bearish fractals and consider going short when the price breaks below the low of the fractal.

3. Place a stop loss: Place a stop loss order below the low of a long trade or above the high of a short trade to limit potential losses.

4. Take profit: Fractals can be used to set profit targets by identifying the next level of resistance for long trades or support for short trades.

5. Manage the trade: Once in the trade, monitor the market and adjust the stop loss and profit targets as needed.

Bearish Five Bar Fractal Pattern

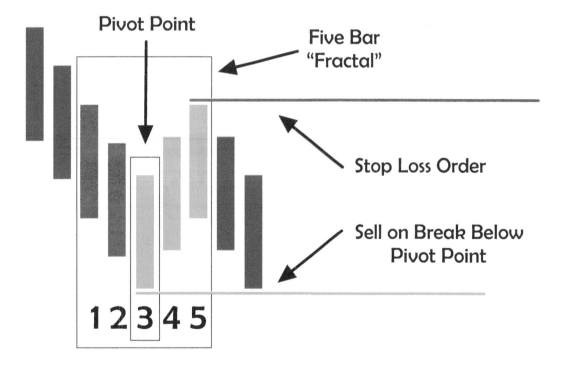

It's important to note that trading with fractals should not be the only factor in making trading decisions. Traders should use fractals in conjunction with other technical indicators and market analysis to make informed trading decisions.

On the following page are several "real-world" examples of where you might find Fractal Pivot Point setups.

"Real-World" Fractal Patterns
I've identified a few, can you find more?

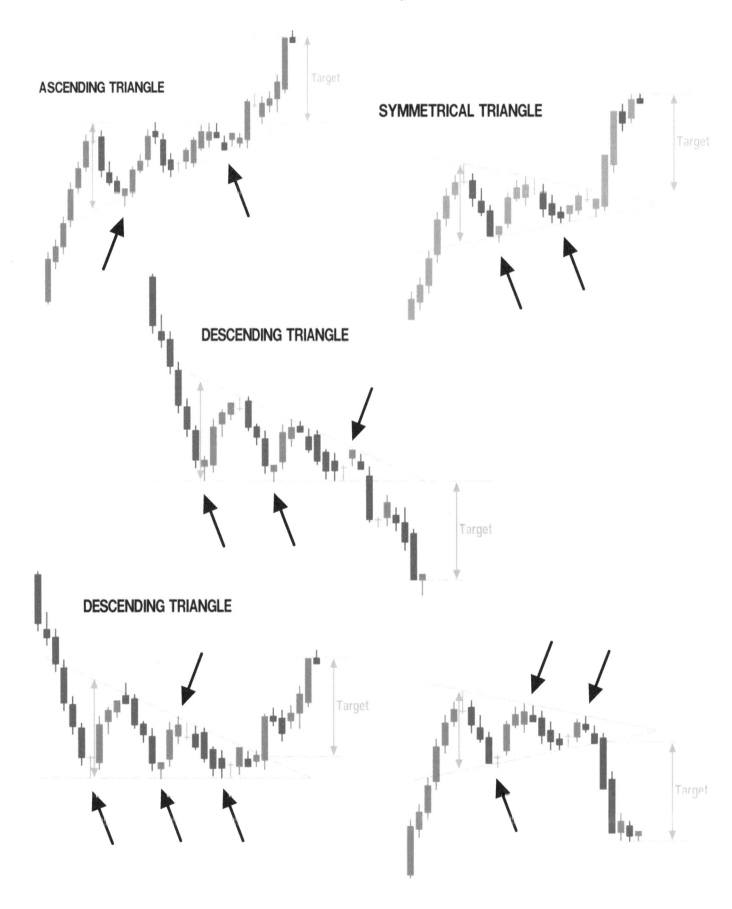

The Trend is Your Friend Until it Bends or Ends

Higher highs, and Higher Lows is the definition of an uptrend, while lower highs and lower lows is the definition of a downtrend. Being able to identify when a market is trending, either bullish or bearish is a learned skill, and the very first skill a trader needs to master.

A changeover from bearish to bullish, or bullish to bearish creates a series of recurring patterns, we give them names like ABC, or 123 Tops & Bottoms. These patterns help traders identify potential entry and exit points in the market. In a trending market, we look for these price reversal patterns that signal a shift from bearish to bullish or bullish to bearish. This shift occurs from bearish to bullish when the market moves from displaying lower lows and lower highs to exhibiting higher lows and higher highs, or the other way around for bearish.

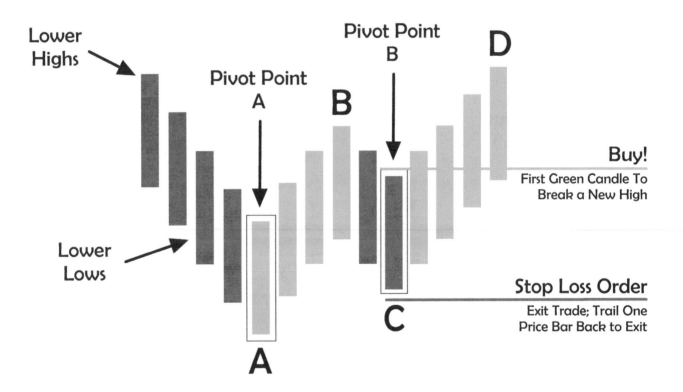

Often I like to use Heiken-Ashi bars to help visualize the trends more effectively. Heiken-Ashi bars are a variation of traditional candlestick charts. Instead of using the open, high, low, and close prices, they use an average of these values to create a smoother chart, which reduces noise and makes it easier to identify trends and potential reversals.

Once a market begins to trend higher, after the above mentioned reversal pattern, we're looking for a market that is consistently forming higher lows. However, for a second entry strategy in a rising market, we want to see a topping tail where the highs are lower, this is what we call a flag or pennant pattern. This pattern indicates a brief pause or consolidation before the trend resumes.

Enter the market long when the price breaks out to a new higher high, while still maintaining the higher low trend. This breakout point signals a continuation of the uptrend and is an ideal entry point for a long position. (Reverse this concept for a short play.)
By identifying these patterns and understanding the concept of higher highs and higher lows for uptrends, and lower highs and lower lows for downtrends, you can make informed decisions when entering and exiting trades, increasing your chances of success in the market.

How To Re-Enter a Rising Market

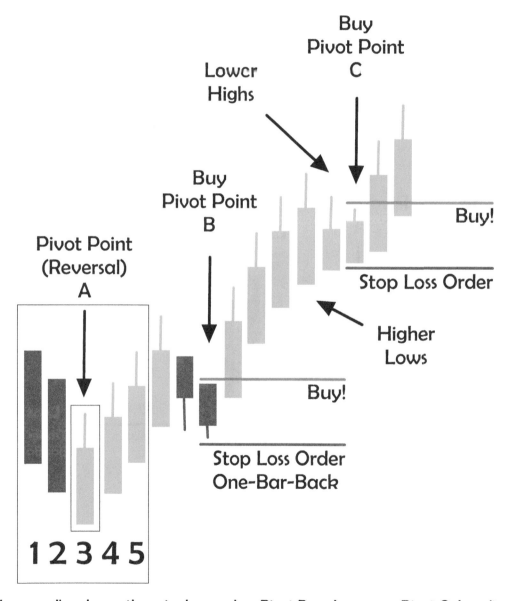

Just because I've drawn the price bars red on Pivot B and green on Pivot C doesn't mean that it must always follow this specific setup. The bars could be any combination of green or red. (Keep in mind this is just an example drawing.) The most important point to remember is we're looking for a micro pullback against the prevailing trend; lower highs on the topping tails. (In the case of Pivot C, green bars, we also want higher lows for our trailing stop, which should be auto-trailing one price bar back, followed by a break of the next high bar.) It doesn't necessarily matter whether the breaking bar is green or red; what matters is that we're looking for a continuation of the trend after the topping tails pull back, creating a pennant formation.

We can automate the process of entering the market by using the Track 'n Trade OCO pre-programmed action buttons. I like to auto-trail for entry, one price bar back, then automatically drop my stop at approximately 20 ticks behind the market. (This number will be different for different markets, but works well on the Mini-Dow.) Once I've dropped my stop, I want it to begin auto-trailing one price bar back until exit, with a limit order set at my first target price of 14 ticks.

I like to drop two, or even three of these "bots" all at the same time, then adjust the Limit order at varying profit zones. Here's my Track 'n Trade OCO (bot) setup for this strategy.

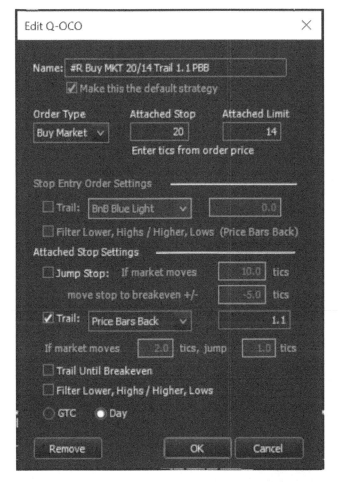
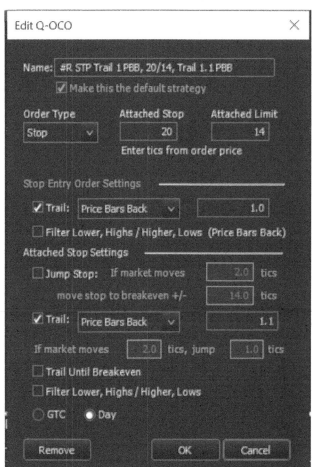

By trading with multiple quantities and taking advantage of dropping several automated One-Cancels-Other (OCO) "bots" at the same time, you can greatly enhance the flexibility and robustness of your trading strategy.

By implementing multiple OCO bots simultaneously, you can better manage risk and capitalize on various entry and exit points in the market.

This approach allows for more dynamic decision-making, as you can optimize your positions as market conditions change. However, one drawback of entering with several OCO bots at the same time, obviously, is the risk of incurring additional losses on the initial entry if the market doesn't follow through into a trend. It's for this reason that we need to be very careful and judicious about our entry points, based on the highest probability setups.

Size Matters

The question is always asked, given the choice between entering the market with high quantity and taking profits off as the market moves in our favor, versus entering with a single contract and adding on as the market rises depends on a number of factors, such as your risk tolerance, capital, and preferred trading style.

The approach of starting large, and reducing along the way may be better suited for traders with a higher risk tolerance and larger capital, while starting small and adding along the way seems to work well for traders with lower risk tolerance and smaller capital. The market conditions and the anticipated strength of the trend should also be taken into consideration when determining which approach to take.

It's important to take profits along the way as the market moves in your favor and approaching areas of resistance and even number price levels. (100, 150, 200, etc.) Place take-profit limit orders just inside these areas of resistance, which increases the chance of your order being executed just prior to the market reaches, or tests resistance.

In this example, we enter with quantity three contracts, take two off, banking our profits as the market tests levels of resistance, then let the final contract run, only exiting the trade once the auto-trailing stop takes us out. (I call this the hail-marry trade, just in case the market wants to go to the moon!) This is the simple version of the King-Tug, where we "castle" our trades, see my Castle & King Tut cheat sheets for details.

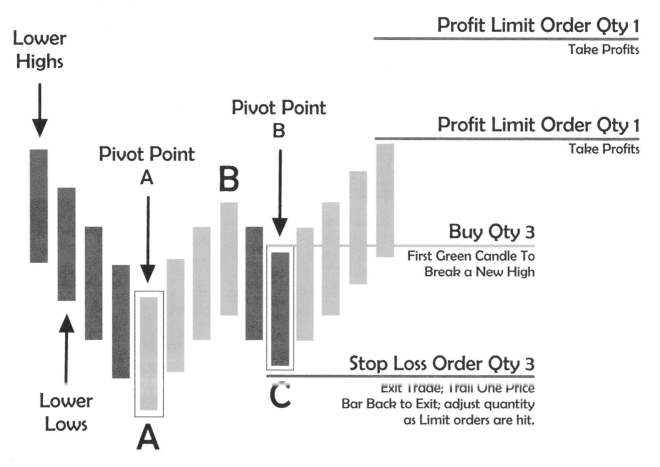

Risk vs. Reward: Considering Quantity Size on Entry.

Here are some Advantages and Disadvantages of Entering with High Quantity and Taking Profits Off Along The Way.

A. Advantages:

1. Greater profit potential at the beginning of the trade.
2. Quicker risk reduction as the market moves in your favor.
3. Provides a cushion against potential reversals.
4. Does not require a constant uptrend to be effective.
5. Increased overall profit potential; increased flexibility throughout the trade.

B. Disadvantages:

1. Larger initial risk exposure.
2. Higher capital requirements.
3. Psychological pressure.

Here are some Advantages and Disadvantages of Entering with a Single Contract and Adding as the Market Rises/Falls:

A. Advantages:

1. Lower initial risk exposure.
2. Trade management flexibility throughout the trade
3. Smaller capital requirements.

B. Disadvantages:

1. Smaller profit potential at the beginning of the trade.
2. Increased risk as more contracts are added.
3. Requires a consistently strong uptrend to be effective.

Ultimately there is no "right" answer, you'll have to choose what's right for you. Let's Consider the Better Approach and Suitable Scenarios:

A. Entering with High Quantity and Taking Profits Off:

1. Suitable for traders with larger capital.
2. Ideal when a strong market move is anticipated.
3. Effective for short-term trades where quick profit-taking is desired.

B. Entering with a Single Contract and Adding as the Market Rises/Falls:

1. Suitable for traders with smaller capital.
2. Ideal for trending markets with a higher probability of a sustained trend
3. Effective for longer-term trades where the goal is to maximize profits by scaling into a winning position.

What are Phantom Taxes?

Yes, the term "phantom tax" is a real thing, and it's a situation that can occur when traders have large gains in one year, but then experience losses in subsequent years.

Here's how it works: let's say a trader has a big gain from trading stocks in one year, and they pay taxes on that gain. Then, in the following year, they experience losses that wipe out their gains from the previous year, and then some. However, the tax code only allows traders to deduct up to $3,000 in net capital losses each year against their ordinary income.

So, in this scenario, the trader may have paid taxes on gains they no longer have, but may not be able to fully offset those taxes with losses in subsequent years. This results in a "phantom tax" - the trader paid taxes on gains that didn't actually translate into long-term profits, and they may not be able to fully recover those taxes with subsequent losses.

It's important to note that there are some strategies that traders can use to help mitigate the impact of phantom taxes. One such strategy is tax-loss harvesting, where traders sell losing positions to offset gains and reduce their tax liability. Another strategy is to spread out gains over multiple years to avoid being pushed into a higher tax bracket in a single year.

The Benefits of Trading Futures:

There are some tax advantages that futures traders have over stock traders. The main advantage is that futures traders are able to use a special tax rate called the 60/40 tax rule.

Under the 60/40 tax rule, 60% of any gains from futures trading are taxed at the long-term capital gains tax rate, and the remaining 40% are taxed at the short-term capital gains tax rate. This is a beneficial tax treatment because long-term capital gains tax rates are typically lower than short-term capital gains tax rates.

On the other hand, stock traders are subject to short-term capital gains tax rates on any gains they make from trading stocks. The short-term capital gains tax rate is the same as the trader's ordinary income tax rate, which can be as high as 37% for the highest tax bracket.

It's important to note that the 60/40 tax rule only applies to futures contracts traded on regulated exchanges. Other types of futures trading, such as contracts for difference (CFDs) and forex trading, are subject to different tax rules.

It's also worth mentioning that taxes are just one aspect of trading, and traders should not base their trading decisions solely on tax considerations. It's important to have a solid trading strategy and risk management plan in place, regardless of the tax implications.

Tax-Loss Harvesting

As a trader, managing taxes is an important part of maximizing returns. One strategy that I've found particularly useful is tax-loss harvesting.

Tax-loss harvesting is a strategy where traders sell losing positions in their portfolio to realize a loss, which can then be used to offset gains elsewhere in the portfolio. This can reduce the trader's overall tax liability and improve their after-tax returns.

Let me give you an example of how this works. Say I have a portfolio of stocks and I've realized a capital gain of $10,000 from one of my positions. However, I also have another position that has lost $5,000. Instead of holding onto the losing position and hoping for it to recover, I could sell that position to realize a capital loss of $5,000. I could then use that loss to offset the $10,000 gain, reducing my taxable gains to $5,000.

By doing this, I've reduced my tax liability by using the $5,000 loss to offset my gain. If I had not sold the losing position, I would have had to pay taxes on the full $10,000 gain. By selling the losing position and realizing a loss, I was able to offset part of my gain and lower my overall tax bill.

It's important to note that there are some rules and limitations to tax-loss harvesting. The IRS has a "wash-sale" rule that prohibits traders from buying a "substantially identical" security within 30-days before or after selling a losing position. Additionally, traders can only deduct up to $3,000 in net capital losses each year against their ordinary income.

Despite these limitations, I've found tax-loss harvesting to be a useful strategy for managing my tax liability and improving my after-tax returns. By identifying and selling losing positions, I can offset gains and lower my overall tax bill.

Spreading Gains Over Multiple Years.

As a trader, I've also found that spreading out my gains over multiple years can be a useful strategy for managing my tax liability. By doing this, I can avoid being pushed into a higher tax bracket in a single year and potentially save money on taxes.

One way to spread out gains is to strategically sell positions in different years. For example, if I have several positions that have realized gains, I could sell some of them in one year and then wait to sell the rest in a subsequent year. This can help me avoid realizing too many gains in a single year and minimize my tax liability.

Another strategy for spreading out gains is to use installment sales. This strategy allows me to defer the recognition of gains by selling an asset and receiving payments over time. By spreading out the payments over several years, I can avoid realizing all of the gains in a single year and potentially save money on taxes.

How to Establish Daily Market Boundaries

As a day trader, establishing areas of support and resistance is crucial for making informed trading decisions. By identifying these levels, traders can gain a better understanding of the supply and demand dynamics of the market and make trades based on that information.

> While the most common method of establishing support and resistance levels is to draw horizontal lines across previous highs and lows, in my opinion, there is a better solution: using option strike prices.

Option strike prices can act as magnets for the underlying asset price, causing it to move towards those levels as options traders adjust their positions. By taking option strike prices into consideration, traders can gain a more accurate picture of where these support and resistance levels are likely to occur.

For example, the Iron Condor strategy is a popular trading method that involves selling two options at different strike prices while simultaneously buying two options further out. Traders use the Iron Condor strategy to profit from a range-bound market. One way I like to determine the price difference between the two options sold, when putting on my Iron Condors, is to take the at-the-money option price and establishing a support and resistance level below and above the market based on that value.

These strike prices due to the volume of options traders who perform this strategy then become highly correlated with common support and resistance levels. By taking these levels into consideration, day traders can gain a better understanding of where the market is likely to move to, and adjust their positions accordingly.

> For example, let's say the market is currently trading at $100 and the at-the-money premium for a one day option is $1,000. To establish your daily area of support, based on option strike prices, you would first identify the nearest strike price that's $1,000 below the current market price, and use this strike price as your support level, since it's the level at which options traders are likely to start buying calls and selling puts to profit from a potential rally in the market.
>
> Next, since the at-the-money call, in this example, is also $1,000, then identify the nearest strike price that's approximately $1,000 above the current market price. This strike would then be used as your resistance level, since it's the level at which options traders are likely to start buying puts and selling calls to profit from a potential pullback in the market.

Setting boundaries when day trading by using option strike prices to establish areas of support and resistance is a powerful strategy for making informed trading decisions. By taking these levels into consideration traders can gain a more accurate picture of where the market is likely to move and adjust their positions accordingly.

Note: When placing my Iron Condors, I use this same methodology, but add an additional buffer of two to three strikes above and below our established areas of support and resistance for my sold puts and calls exactly because of this reasoning.

My Five Steps for Setting Daily Boundaries When Day Trading

As a day trader, it's important for me to establish daily boundaries to maintain a healthy work-life balance and prevent burnout. Here are five steps I follow to set my daily boundaries:

1. I set a schedule that includes specific times for when I'll start trading, take breaks, and end trading for the day. I'm realistic about the amount of time I can dedicate to trading each day and create a schedule that accommodates my other obligations.

2. I take regular breaks to maintain focus and prevent burnout. I step away from the computer every so often, take a 15-minute walk outside, do some stretching or meditation, or simply step away from the computer to grab a snack or drink.

3. I set financial goals to help me stay on track and avoid getting caught up in the ups and downs of the market. I set specific targets for how much I want to earn each day, week, or month, and stick to those targets. Having clear financial goals helps me avoid over trading or making impulsive decisions based on emotion.

4. I create a dedicated workspace that helps me set boundaries between my work and personal life. I set up a home office or trading desk that's separate from the rest of my living space. Having a dedicated workspace helps me focus on trading during trading hours and leave work behind when I'm finished for the day.

5. I develop a routine that helps me establish a sense of structure and predictability in my day. I start each day with a specific morning routine or end each trading day with a specific set of tasks. Having a routine helps me stay focused, engaged, and on-task throughout the day.

In conclusion, setting daily boundaries when day trading, for me, has been crucial for maintaining a healthy work-life balance and preventing burnout, which still happens sometimes anyway. But by setting a schedule, taking regular breaks, setting financial goals, creating a dedicated workspace, and developing a routine, I'm able to establish more clear boundaries between my work and personal life and avoid becoming consumed by the markets; which still happens anyway. ;-)

Lan's One-Bar Momentum Day Trading Rule

Timeframe: Typically 1-minute chart, Indicator: Heiken-Ashi bars, Elliott Wave ABCD Patterns
Market: Suitable for liquid markets, tight spreads (e.g., index futures, or highly liquid stocks)

Entry Rules:

Identify the prevailing Elliott Wave trend using Heiken-Ashi bars:

- For an uptrend, look for a series of higher highs and higher lows.
    - Long entry: Buy during an uptrend when a lower high is formed.
    - Ideally, we would like to see higher lows, and lower highs.
        - This pattern is known as a bullish pennant.
- For a downtrend, look for a series of lower highs and lower lows.
    - Short entry: Sell during a downtrend when a higher low is formed.
    - Ideally, we would like to see lower highs, and higher lows.
        - This pattern is known as a bearish pennant.

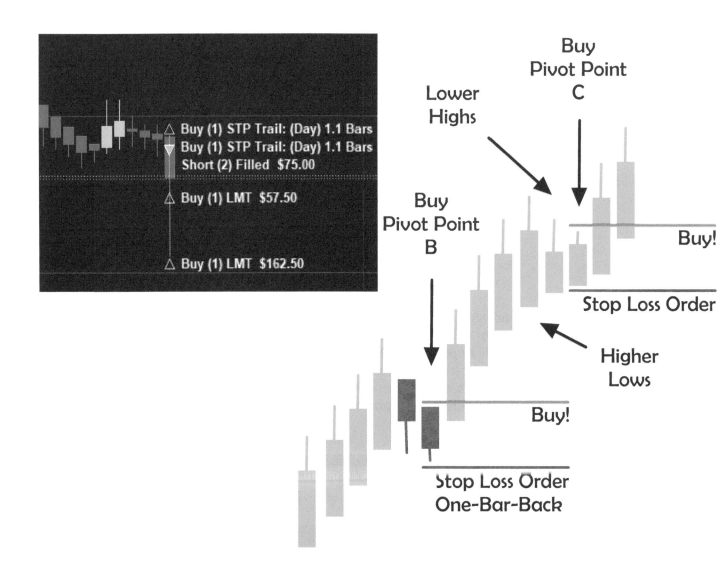

Enter the market with a single contract in the direction of the prevailing trend.

To automate this step, use the one-bar-back auto-tailing features within Track 'n Trades Q-OCO programmable buttons. [See example settings]

As soon as you see a lower high in the prevailing uptrend, or a higher low in the prevailing downtrend. (Ideally, we would like to see two to three lower highs, or two to three higher lows.) Drop the Q-OCO order into place, letting it begin auto-trailing (intercept) for entry.

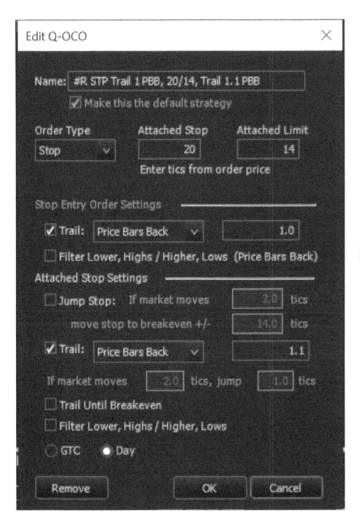

- If you're in an uptrend, you'll be dropping the Q-OCO order(s) above the market, where the software will automatically jump the order(s) to the desired price level and begin to trail for the intercept entry as soon as the market makes a new higher high.
- If you're in a downtrend, you'll be dropping the Q-OCO order(s) below the market, where the software will automatically jump the order(s) to the desired price level and begin to trail for the intercept entry on the first red candle to make a new lower low.

Risk Management:

In the setup of the Q-OCO order dialog box, (one minute chart) set your initial stop-loss order to drop at 20 tics. I like to set the limit order to take profits at 14. (This looks like a reverse risk vs. reward ratio, but remember, the 20 tic placement is just a placeholder, the stop order is going to immediately jump to the one price bar back level, and begin to auto-trail one price bar behind the entry bar. (20-tics back is a good average price level to start, adjust that level depending on the size and scale of the market(s) you are trading. I've found that 20 tics back for the initial drop works well on the mini-Dow.)

The One-Bar-Rule:

Here's where the "One-Bar-Rule" comes into play. If the trade remains profitable after one bar, add a second contract to the position. (If you get stopped out before the second bar, then you'll be stopped out with a single contract and a small loss. (You must resist the temptation to add the second contract too quickly.) This is why we wait for the next price bar to print, in an effort to prove that the breakout is holding before adding to our position. This also should move the stop loss order closer to our entry price reducing our risk-reward ratio. (Now can you see the beauty of this strategy?)

As the trend continues, Track 'n Trade will automatically move the stop-loss order to each new higher low (for long positions) or each new lower high (for short positions) as the next bar in the series forms.

Scale up the position if the trade continues to be profitable, adding additional contracts at predetermined intervals (e.g., every new price bar, or after a certain price movement in your favor). This can be done with any time frame from 1 minute, to daily charts.

Exit Rules:

Profit-taking limit order: Set a predetermined profit target for each trade based on your desired risk-reward ratio or specific market conditions. Again, I like 14 (when day trading) for the very first profit taking zone. (This is because historically speaking, 14 has been a high(er) average of profitable trades.) Once you drop the second, third, fourth, or fifth order into place, move the limit orders into place by clicking and dragging the on-screen triangle to the desired resistance point for profit taking.

Trailing stop-loss order: Exit the trade when the trailing stop-loss order(s) is/are hit, which would indicate a potential trend reversal or a loss of momentum. With this strategy, generally, all trailing stops are moving at the same price level, while limit orders are spread across multiple resistance points to achieve varying levels of profit taking.

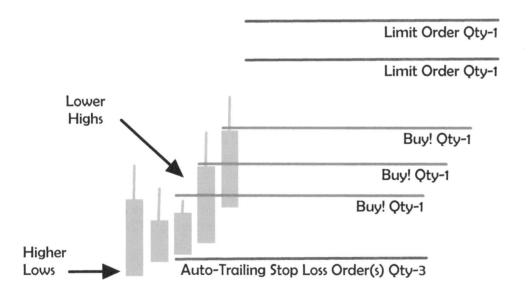

This One-Bar Momentum Scalping strategy combines Heiken-Ashi bars with Elliott Wave (Bulls 'n Bears) for trend identification with my one-bar rule for position scaling and risk management. By starting with a single contract and gradually adding to the position if the trade remains profitable, the strategy aims to minimize risk while capitalizing on strong trends. Remember, each trader's risk tolerance and preferences may vary. It's essential to test and adjust the strategy to suit your individual needs, and market volatility.

What is "The Stab"?

The Stab is a day trading strategy where traders look for opportunities to enter or exit a trade by capitalizing on the market makers' tendency to hunt for stops.

> Stop hunting refers to the practice where market makers push the price in a particular direction in an attempt to trigger stop loss orders set by traders. When these stops are triggered, the price often makes a dramatic move in the opposite direction. (Resuming the trend once again.) This can, for the savvy trader, create a highly profitable trading opportunity. (Market makers are more likely to "stab stops," during low volume trending markets.)

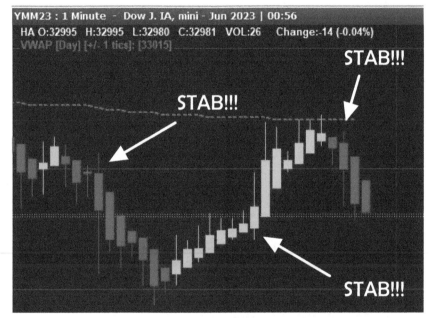

Why It Matters

The stab is crucial to understand because it often leads to a strong move in the market. Traders who recognize this phenomenon can benefit from the subsequent trend continuation, while those who are unaware may suffer losses.

> The Stab strategy focuses on identifying the point at which the market makers go hunting for stops.

In an uptrend, this is where price is making higher highs and higher lows, in a downtrend, it's where price makes lower highs and lower lows. Traders then look for a single topping tail or bottoming tail that breaks the trend for just one brief moment, taking out all the trailing stops before continuing in the direction of the overall trend once again.

Although the stab can be frustrating, there are a few possible ways to address this issue, to minimize losses and possibly even turn lemons into lemonade. How we can use "The Stab" to our advantage.

To use The Stab strategy, you need to have a good understanding of the market and the price action. You must know how to identify a trend, read the charts, and interpret the candlestick patterns. You also need to have a solid risk management plan that includes setting stop loss orders and taking profits at the right time.

Here are some steps we can follow to use The Stab strategy to our advantage:

1. Identify the trend: Look for a clear uptrend or downtrend in the market. Identify the support and resistance levels and the key price levels. Higher highs and higher lows, or lower highs and lower lows. (I like to use Heiken-Ashi bars for this purpose.)

2. Look for a stab: Look for a single topping tail or bottoming tail that breaks the trend for just one quick moment, taking out all the trailing stops.

3. Wait for confirmation: Wait for confirmation that the trend has resumed. Look for another price bar that confirms the trend. (Sometimes the resumption of the trend can be dramatic, be ready to take advantage of this quick and decisive move.)

4. Enter the trade: Once you have confirmation that the trend has resumed, enter the trade in the direction of the trend.

5. Set your stop loss: Set your stop loss order below the support level in an uptrend or above the resistance level in a downtrend.

6. Take profits: Take profits at key price levels or when the market reaches your target.

Challenges and risks associated with "The Stab" strategy

One of the biggest challenges of The Stab strategy is that it requires a lot of patience and discipline. Traders must wait for the right moment to enter and exit the trade and not get tempted by false signals. Traders must also be aware of the risks associated with stop hunting, which can result in losses if the market does not resume its trend.

Solutions to overcome these challenges

While the stab can be challenging to deal with, there are a few other possible ways to address this issue and minimize losses:

1. Wider Stop Losses: One solution is to use wider stop losses to avoid getting stopped out by the stab. This approach, however, may increase your risk exposure and should be carefully considered.

2. Partial Profit Taking: Another option is to take partial profits when the market is trending in your favor. By doing so, you can secure some gains and leave a portion of your position open in case the trend continues. (Take profits along the way.)

3. Stop Loss Management: Rather than using a "close-in" trailing stop, (one price bar back) consider employing a dynamic stop strategy based on indicators such as the PSAR, the ATR, and/or the Blue Light System. This method allows for a more flexibility and dynamic way of protecting your position from the stab, breaking your stops into multiple price points rather than placing all your stops at the same level.

4. Diversify Strategies: Experiment with Different Trading Styles: Day trading is just one of many trading styles. You might consider incorporating other styles, such as swing trading, position trading, or options, into your overall trading plan. This diversification allows you to take advantage of different market conditions and time horizons, reducing your reliance on a single trading style or strategy.

If you have questions, please don't hesitate to contact me, I'm here to help!

Rich, Rich, Rich Beyond Your Wildest Dreams!

I had a client ask me why I'm not sitting on a beach in Cancun if I have the Track 'n Trade Autopilot? I tried to explain it this way: I said, "The Track 'n Trade Autopilot's success, just like any solid trading plan, depends on the execution settings and the market conditions.

Sometimes it knocks home runs, and you scream to your wife to quit her job and pack her bags, thinking you're all going to be rich, rich, rich beyond your wildest dreams; then, sometimes, it loses its ass. It really depends on the settings and the market conditions.

The Track 'n Trade Autopilot is not a pre-programmed "system" where everything is predetermined for you, and you just click a button and get rich. It's a tool designed to trade your strategy, whatever strategy that might be, whatever method you set up within the Autopilot. You develop each strategy yourself; it doesn't come with pre-packaged, predetermined formulas.

(Although, if you take my educational course, I teach several 'systems' you can set up. I teach how to 'program' the Autopilot without the need to write code.)

That said, the Autopilot functions based on indicators from within Track 'n Trade. You can have it trade the Bulls 'n Bears, you can have it trade the ATR, the PSAR, the MACD, the SSTO, Moving Averages, RSI, CCI, or any number of other "systems/indicators."

You decide the quantity, what risks your willing to take, where to put your stops, and how to take profits. The great thing about that is you can make adjustments on the fly as market conditions change. (No programming language skills required.) But you must be smart enough to know what changes need to be made; training and education.

> The Autopilot has a historical back testing feature where you can test your theories. It has filters to help you avoid bad trades. It also back tests individual settings, like where to place stops, where to place limits, etc.

It's pretty robust, but can you just turn it on, run off to Cancun and come home in three months to be rich, rich, rich beyond your wildest dreams? No, I've been doing this for over 35 years and have never once seen anything able to do that, although many slick-Willie-style salesmen claim it. Those people constantly come and go but never last long in this dog-eat-dog industry; they fleece their clients, then run away and disappear, never to be heard from again.

> Suppose my Track 'n Trade Autopilot was a truly set-it-and-forget-it program that could make me money hand over fist without any effort. I'd spray-paint the windows black, lock all the doors, and kill all the phone lines. Do you think I would sell it to anyone, for any price? Not only no, but hell no!

Track 'n Trade's Autopilot is a tool that helps you automate your trading, but you still have to be a trader to understand it and make it function. Do I use it in my own trading? I use some aspects of the auto-trading features within Track 'n Trade almost daily; TnT has multiple tools for trade automation, not just Autopilot.

If I were to claim I had a set-it-and-forget-it program that could make you rich, rich, rich beyond your wildest dreams, because I'm registered with and regulated by the government, I would go to jail. And, since I haven't contributed millions in ill-gotten gains to the Democrat party, I'd never get the kit glove treatment of Sam Bankman-Fried."

Lan H Turner

Date:

TOP PRIORITIES FOR THE DAY	

BRAIN STORM	TIME BLOCKING	
	5	
	6	
	7	
	8	
	9	
	10	
	11	
	12	
	1	
	2	
	3	
	4	
	5	
	6	
NOTES	7	
	8	
	9	
	10	
	11	

Real Life Chart Examples
How To Read a Chart in Real Time

Lan Turner's Crash Course In Trading

Stocks * Futures * Forex

Real Market Examples - Daily Time frame

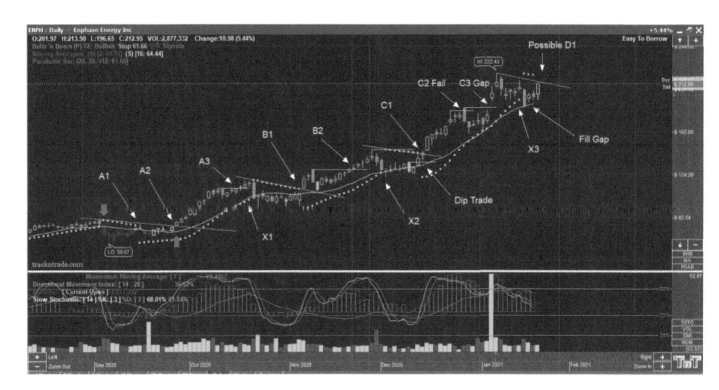

*Elliott Wave, and Fibonacci know no boundaries when it comes to time frame and which charts we can execute this trading strategy between. As you'll see in this as well as the following examples, you'll find the exact same setups, triggers, and follow-through methods work on all time frames; daily, hourly, and minute charts; time has little relevance.

As an options trader, I love using this strategy with options trading, picking up long call options at Major A1, B1, and C1 turning points, and then adding on by trading shares at A2, A3, B2, B3, and C2, C3 break-out points, dollar cost averaging into larger positions. (If volume allows, this same options strategy can be implemented on intra-day charts as well.)

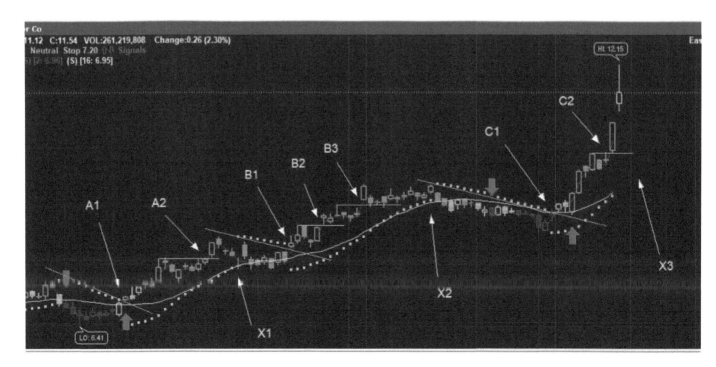

Real Market Examples - Intra-day

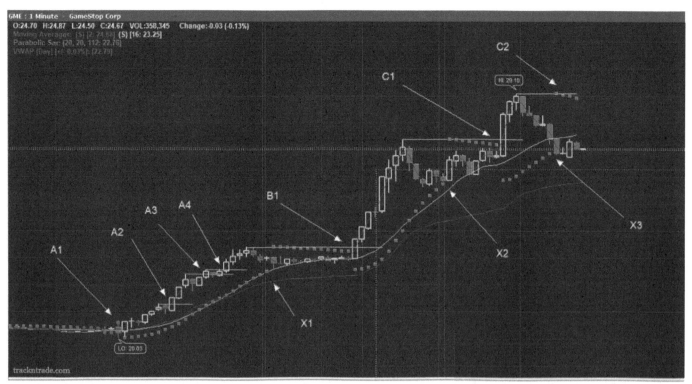

*Not everything is as clear and concise as this GameStop example, but whether you get the count off by one or not in the beginning isn't so important, the signals are still the same, label adjustments can be made as more of the trend becomes revealed.

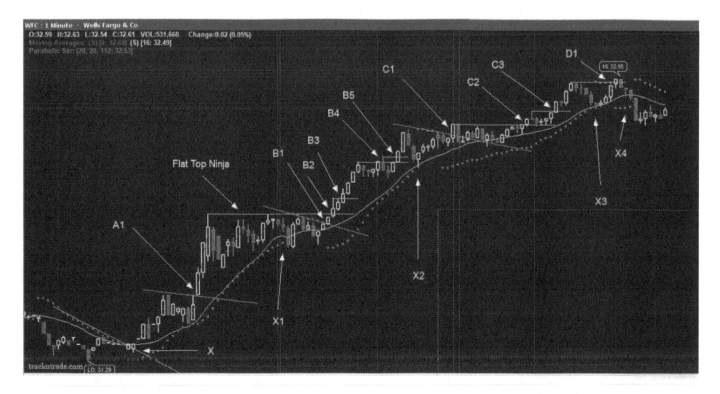

*Technically, the count might be considered "off" on this example, as A1 might be thought of as A2, and where X is identified would be A1. Hindsights is 20/20. Make adjustments as needed.

Real Market Examples - Intra-day

*Not everyone has access to the Bulls 'n Bears indicator, which is a real shame, since it is, in my opinion, the magic bullet of trading, I've been trading for 25-years, and this is the best tool and methodology I've found; if you find something better, please let me know.

Here's several examples of how the Bulls 'n Bears is key in understanding how the market moves through the Elliot Wave patterns, Setups and Triggers.

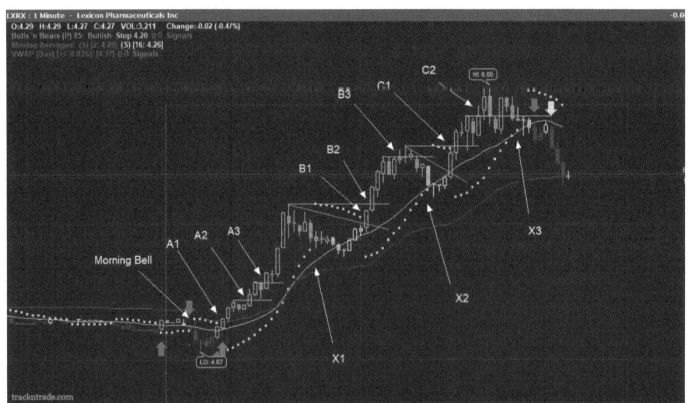

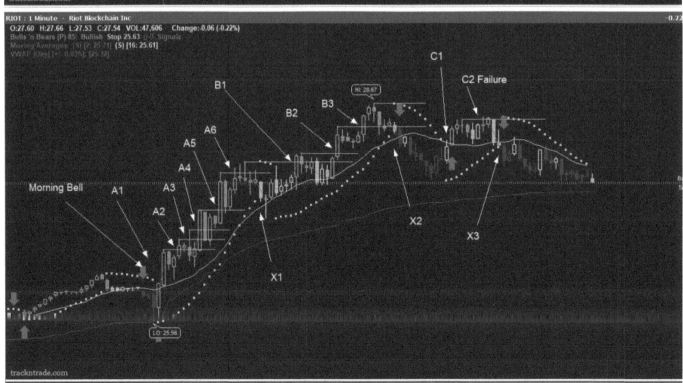

Real Market Examples - Bearish

Remember, Elliott Wave and Fibonacci are direction neutral strategies; meaning that we can employ the exact same strategies in a bear market as well. Here's a couple of examples of markets in a down-trend, where we apply all the same rules.

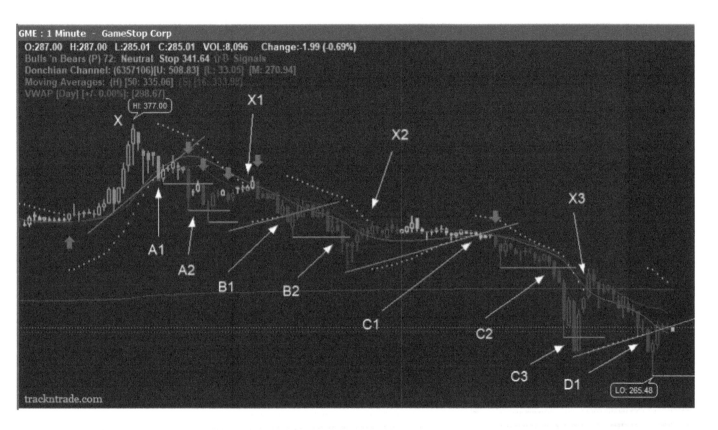

This is a Head and Shoulders Top Formation, always pay attention to traditional recurring price patterns as they also help predict market directional break points; Decision Point Trading.

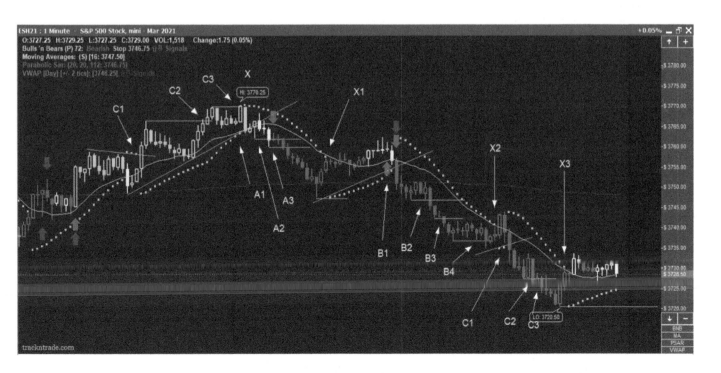

Real Market Examples - Intra-day

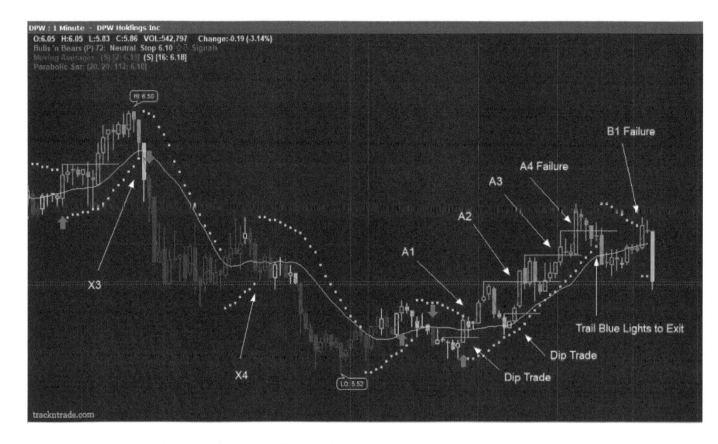

*This is an example of a couple nice Dip Trades, buying on the pull backs.

When using the Bulls 'n Bears Indicator, its much easier to identify the best Dip Trade entries, as the market breaks green above the yellow pull back zone; only ever take a long Dip Trade when the market is still above the Blue Lights.

> Don't confuse Dip Trades with X1, or X2 Dip Trades, although similar, a standard Dip Trade occurs above the Blue Lights, while an X1, or X2 Dip Trade occurs between the trend and the counter-trend break points.

Only take long positions when the market is above the Blue Lights, and only take short positions when the market is below the Blue Lights. Don't be too quick to bring stops to break-even, remember, the market machine likes to come back and take out everyone's stops who moved their stop orders to break even too quickly; this is often referred to as "gunning for stops."

Once the market begins to trend in your favor use your auto-trailing stop features within your software to manage your trailing stop for you; takes the emotion out. Attach your auto-trailing stops to the Bulls 'n Bears Blue Light System, Red Lights (PSAR), or Yellow Lights (ATR), or consider breaking stops apart, and trail on all three; getting the best of all three worlds.

Real Market Examples - Futures

Our Elliott Wave Count, Measure, Setup, Trigger and Follow Through methodology works in all markets, stocks, futures, and Forex, and on all time frames; agai, this is known as fractal.

Here are two examples within the futures market, where there are no pattern day trading rules.

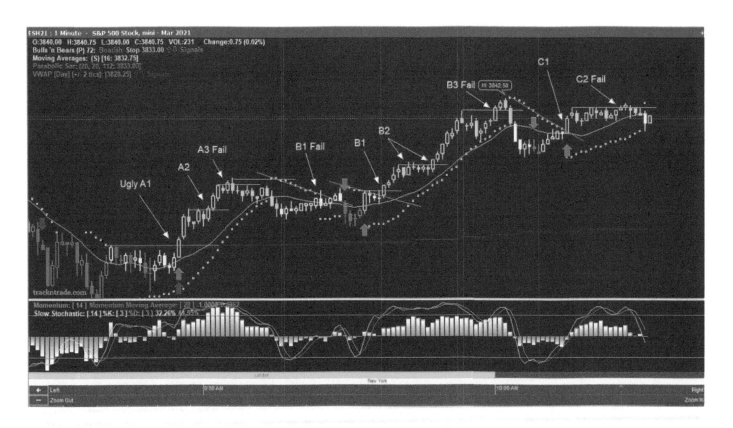

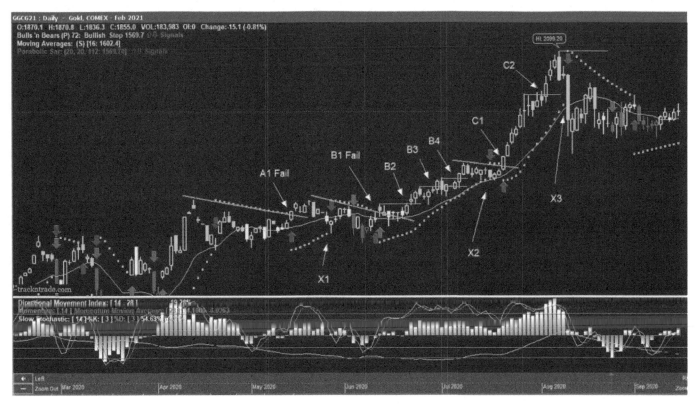

Real Market Examples - Futures

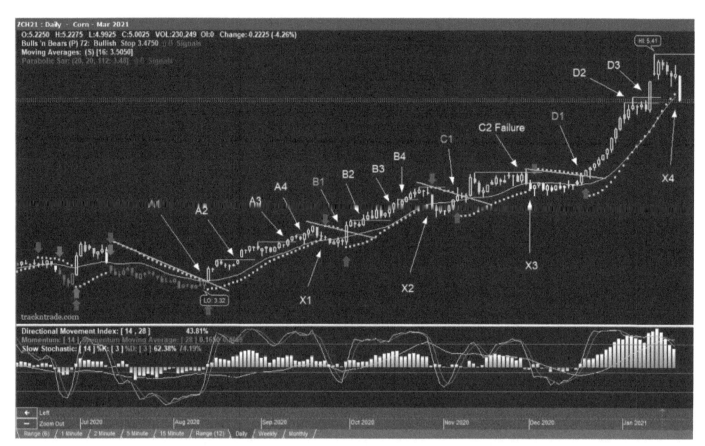

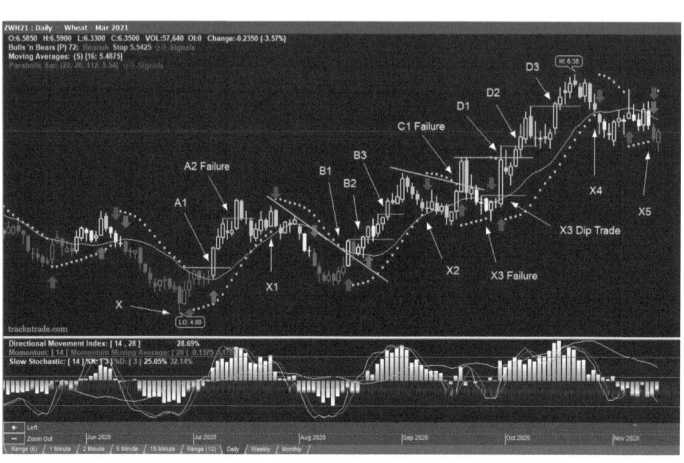

Real Market Examples - Forex

Trend trading in futures and trend trading in forex both involve analyzing charts and technical indicators to identify the direction of a trend, and manage risk. The main difference between the two is the type of market they are used in. Futures trading is the buying or selling of contracts for future delivery of a commodity or financial instrument, while forex trading is the buying or selling of different currencies. Despite the difference in market, the underlying principle and strategies used for trend trading in both futures and forex are the same. In both cases, traders use technical analysis to identify trends, and then make trades based on those trends to try to profit from market movement.

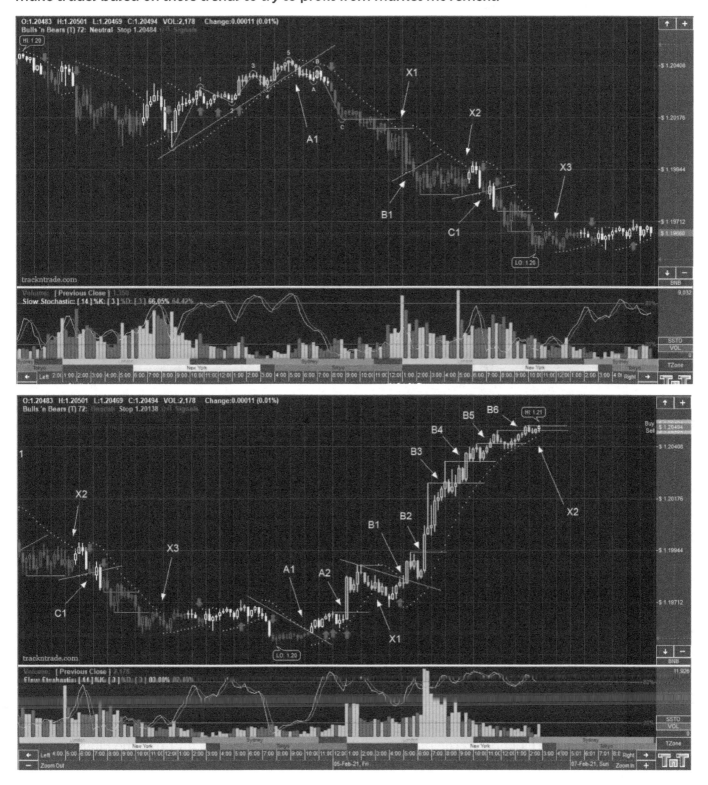

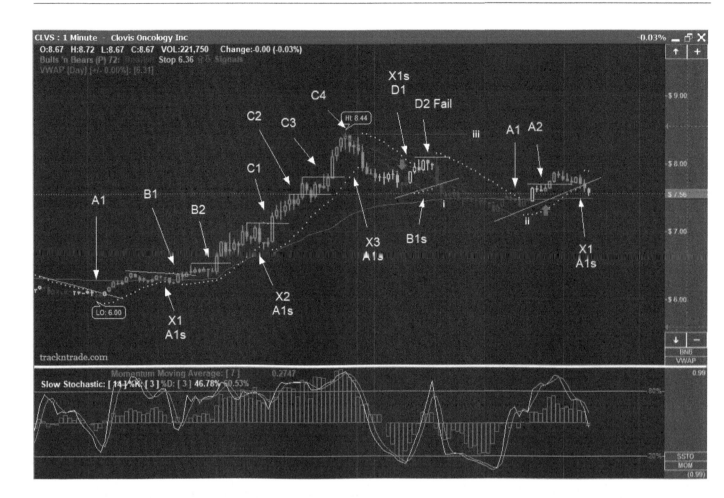

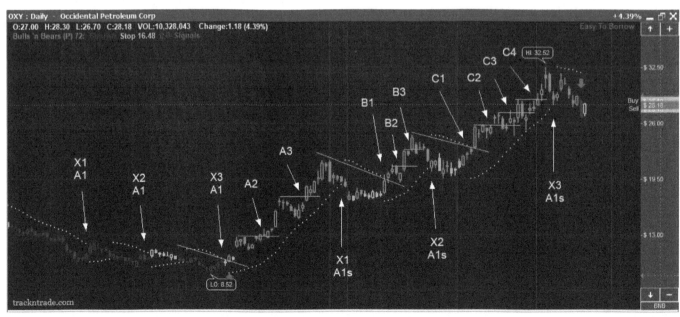

Elliott wave count and measure technique and the Fibonacci technique can be applied to a variety of markets including stocks, futures, and forex. The Elliott wave count and measure technique is a method of technical analysis that helps traders identify patterns in the market, and predict future market movements. This technique is based on the idea that market movements can be predicted based on repetitive patterns, and the use of Fibonacci ratios can help traders identify key levels of support and resistance. Similarly, the Fibonacci technique is a method of technical analysis that uses the Fibonacci ratios to identify key levels of support and resistance, and can be used to predict market turning points.

Resources

Trading Resources
Tools of the Trade

Lan Turner's Crash Course In Trading

Stocks * Futures * Forex

Why Trade Futures?

Watch the video at: www.CommodityTradingSchool.com

- Reason #1: NO PATTERN DAY TRADING RULES!!!
- Reason #2: Get started with as little as $2,000; no $25,000 min. requirements.
- Reason #3: Leverage, don't waste all day trading only to make or lose $8.00
- Reason #4: Trade all the fun stuff, like; Gold, Silver, Crude Oil, Corn, Wheat, Live Cattle, Cocoa, Coffee, Orange Juice, UL Gasoline, Natural Gas, EuroFX, Canadian Dollar, BitCoin, Australian Dollar, Bonds, Notes, plus all the stock indexes like S&P500, NASDAQ, Russell, and the DOW! (Just to name a few!)

How Do I Get Started Trading Futures?

Step 1: Download and install your futures trading and charting software.
  i. Visit www.Tools4Traders.ORG

Step 2: Open a futures trading account (Directly through the software, or...)
  ii. Visit www.GeckoFS.com

Step 3: Practice in your free demo account to learn, then...

Step 5: Trade to your hearts content!

Gecko Financial Services
Recommended Futures & Forex Brokerage Firm

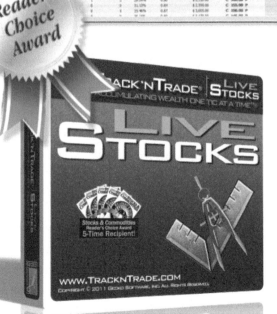

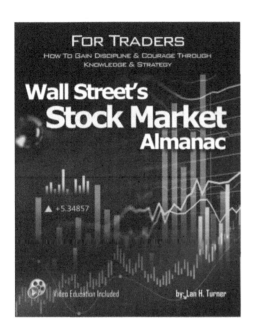

Wall Street's Annual Calendar of Trades
The Seasonal Nature of Markets
www.StockMarketAlmanac.com

Looking for a powerful tool to help you make more informed trades in the stock market? Look no further than "Wall Street's Stock Market Almanac." In this comprehensive guide, you'll find a wealth of data on seasonal trades that have been consistently profitable between two specific dates.

Whether you're a seasoned investor or just starting out, this book will help you identify key trends and patterns in the market, giving you a competitive edge and boosting your chances of success. From analyzing historical data to predicting future market movements, "Wall Street's Stock Market Almanac" is an essential resource for anyone who wants to make smarter, more profitable trades.

So why wait? Start using the power of seasonal trades to your advantage today. Pick up a copy of "Wall Street's Stock Market Almanac" and start seeing results! www.StockMarketAlmanac.com

The seasonal nature of markets refers to the tendency of certain financial instruments to experience certain price patterns or trends at certain times of the year. These patterns or trends may be caused by various factors, like changes in supply and demand, economic conditions, and investor behavior.

For example, agricultural markets may see seasonal patterns because of the natural growing and harvesting cycles of crops. On the other hand, the stock market may experience seasonal patterns due to things like increased consumer spending during the holidays or the tendency for stocks to perform better in certain months. It's important for traders to be aware of the seasonal nature of markets and to consider these patterns when making trades.

Wall Street's Calendar of Trades, Stocks & Commodities. Did you know:

- Caterpillar (CAT) between Oct. 4th and Nov. 9th, the past 13 years, has been profitable 85% of the time!

- Apple (AAPL) between Jul. 6th and Aug. 15th, the past 11 years, has shown profits 82% of the time!

- Travelers (TRV) between Oct. 4th and Nov. 8th, the past 13 years, have been profitable 85% of the time!

- Silver, between Nov. 8th and Nov. 23rd, the past 11 years, has been profitable 92% of the time!

- Feeder Cattle, between Aug. 4th and Aug. 29th, the past 10 years, has been profitable 90% of the time!

This book is filled with these types of trading opportunities; over 75 in all, including the 30 stocks within the DOW, twelve top commodities, and many additional stocks beyond the DOW.

I call them Wall Street's Calendar of Trades because, seemingly, every year, just like clockwork, Wall Street buys and sells the same stocks at the same time. Find details at: www.StockMarketAlmanac.com

Now, just because these trades have done this 80%, 90%, or in some cases 100% of the time over the past dozen(s) of years, give or take, doesn't necessarily mean they're going to do it again this year, but I can promise I'm going to be watching these stocks, are you?

In the included free video course, we discuss different strategies, everything from options trading, Elliott Wave and Fibonacci technical analysis strategies and more.

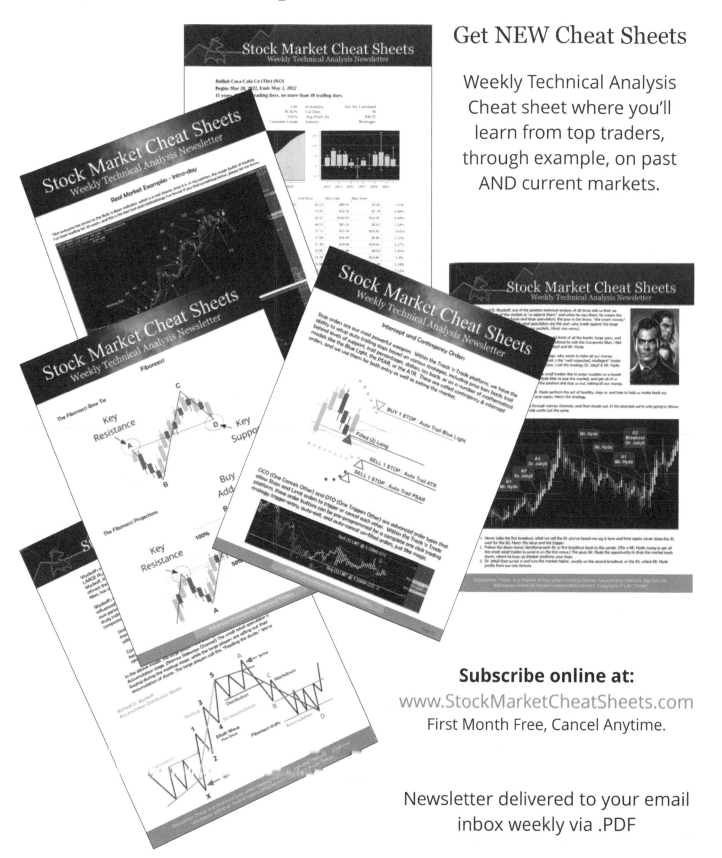

Technical Analysis Can Be Hard
Learn from experts in bite-sized summaries

What my friends think I do

What my girlfriend thinks I do

What my clients think I do

What society thinks I do

What I think I do

What I actually do

Disclaimer

All advice, trade examples, trading scenarios, and market information is fake; it has been conjured up to complete the novel's narrative and should not be considered trading advice.

There is a chance of substantial loss when trading stocks, futures, and forex; please search ruling government agencies for complete financial risk disclosures.

High Risk Investments

Trading Stocks, Futures, Foreign Exchange (Forex), or Options on margin carries a high level of risk, and may not be suitable for all investors. The high degree of leverage can work against you as well as for you. Before deciding to trade any of these markets you should carefully consider your investment objectives, level of experience, and risk appetite. The possibility exists that you could sustain a loss of some or all of your initial investment and therefore you should not invest money that you cannot afford to lose. You should be aware of all the risks associated with trading these markets, and seek advice from an independent financial advisor if you have any doubts.

Internet Trading Risks

There are risks associated with utilizing an Internet-based deal execution trading system including, but not limited to, the failure of hardware, software, and Internet connection. Since Commodity Trading School and any partners do not control signal power, its reception or routing via Internet, configuration of your equipment or reliability of its connection, we cannot be responsible for communication failures, distortions or delays when trading via the Internet. Our partners, employ back-up systems and contingency plans to minimize the possibility of system failure, and trading via telephone to the clearing firm is an additional option if such an event occurs.

Accuracy of Information

The content on this website is subject to change at any time without notice, and is provided for the sole purpose of assisting traders to make independent investment decisions. Commodity Trading School has taken reasonable measures to ensure the accuracy of the information on the website, however, does not guarantee its accuracy, and will not accept liability for any loss or damage which may arise directly or indirectly from the content or your inability to access the website, for any delay in or failure of the transmission or the receipt of any instruction or notifications sent through this website or by email.

Distribution

This site is not intended for distribution, or use by, any person in any country where such distribution or use would be contrary to local law or regulation. None of the services or investments referred to in this website are available to persons residing in any country where the provision of such services or investments would be contrary to local law or regulation or to the laws of the United States. It is the responsibility of visitors to this website to ascertain the terms of and comply with any local law or regulation to which they are subject.

Market Risks and Online Trading

The trading program(s) provide sophisticated order entry and tracking of orders. All stop-loss, limit and entry orders are generally deemed reliable against slippage, but slippage may still occur based on market conditions and liquidity. Trading on-line, no matter how convenient or efficient does not necessarily reduce risks associated with stocks, futures, forex, or options trading. All quotes and trades are subject to the terms and conditions of the End-User License Agreement and Client Agreement.

Testimonial Disclaimer

Unique experiences and past performances are not necessarily indicative of future results! Testimonials herein are unsolicited and are non-representative of all clients; certain accounts may have worse performance than that indicated. Trading Stocks, Futures, Forex, or Options involves substantial risk and there is always the potential for loss. Your trading results may vary. Because the risk factor is high trading any leverage markets, only genuine "risk" funds should be used in such trading. If you do not have the extra capital that you can afford to lose, you should not trade. No completely "safe" trading system has ever been devised, and no one can guarantee profits or freedom from loss. Commodity Trading School does not pay for testimonials, most of our testimonials are unsolicited and voluntary.

Commodity Trading School Market Opinions

Any opinions, news, research, analyses, prices, or other information contained on this website are provided as general market commentary, and do not constitute investment advice. Commodity Trading School is not liable for any loss or damage, including without limitation, any loss of profit, which may arise directly or indirectly from use of or reliance on such information. Commodity Trading School has taken reasonable measures to ensure the accuracy of the information on the website. The content on this website is subject to change at any time without notice.

Views, Opinions, and outside links

The views and opinions represented in any link to an outside website link and/or resources are not controlled by Commodity Trading School or by our associated firms. Further, Commodity Trading School nor our associated firms are responsible for their availability, content, or delivery of services.

DISCLAIMER: THE DATA CONTAINED HEREIN IS BELIEVED TO BE RELIABLE BUT CANNOT BE GUARANTEED AS TO RELIABILITY, ACCURACY, OR COMPLETENESS; AND, AS SUCH ARE SUBJECT TO CHANGE WITHOUT NOTICE. WE WILL NOT BE RESPONSIBLE FOR ANYTHING, WHICH MAY RESULT FROM RELIANCE ON THIS DATA OR THE OPINIONS EXPRESSED HERE IN.

DISCLOSURE OF RISK: THE RISK OF LOSS IN TRADING STOCKS, FUTURES, FOREX, AND OPTIONS CAN BE SUBSTANTIAL; THEREFORE, ONLY GENUINE RISK FUNDS SHOULD BE USED. STOCKS, FUTURES, FOREX, AND OPTIONS MAY NOT BE SUITABLE INVESTMENTS FOR ALL INDIVIDUALS, AND INDIVIDUALS SHOULD CAREFULLY CONSIDER THEIR FINANCIAL CONDITION IN DECIDING WHETHER TO TRADE. OPTION TRADERS SHOULD BE AWARE THAT THE EXERCISE OF A LONG OPTION WOULD RESULT IN A FUTURES OR FOREX POSITION.

HYPOTHETICAL PERFORMANCE RESULTS HAVE MANY INHERENT LIMITATIONS, SOME OF WHICH ARE DESCRIBED BELOW.

NO REPRESENTATION IS BEING MADE THAT ANY ACCOUNT WILL, OR IS LIKELY TO, ACHIEVE PROFITS OR LOSSES SIMILAR TO THOSE SHOWN. IN FACT, THERE ARE FREQUENTLY SHARP DIFFERENCES BETWEEN HYPOTHETICAL PERFORMANCE RESULTS AND THE ACTUAL RESULTS SUBSEQUENTLY ACHIEVED BY ANY PARTICULAR TRADING PROGRAM.

ONE OF THE LIMITATIONS OF HYPOTHETICAL PERFORMANCE RESULTS IS THAT THEY ARE GENERALLY PREPARED WITH THE BENEFIT OF HINDSIGHT. IN ADDITION, HYPOTHETICAL TRADING DOES NOT INVOLVE FINANCIAL RISK, AND NO HYPOTHETICAL TRADING RECORD CAN COMPLETELY ACCOUNT FOR THE IMPACT OF FINANCIAL RISK IN ACTUAL TRADING. FOR EXAMPLE, THE ABILITY TO WITHSTAND LOSSES OR TO ADHERE TO A PARTICULAR TRADING PROGRAM, IN SPITE OF TRADING LOSSES, ARE MATERIAL POINTS WHICH CAN ALSO ADVERSELY AFFECT ACTUAL TRADING RESULTS. THERE ARE NUMEROUS OTHER FACTORS RELATED TO THE MARKETS, IN GENERAL, OR TO THE IMPLEMENTATION OF ANY SPECIFIC TRADING PROGRAM WHICH CANNOT BE FULLY ACCOUNTED FOR IN THE PREPARATION OF HYPOTHETICAL PERFORMANCE RESULTS AND ALL OF WHICH CAN ADVERSELY AFFECT ACTUAL TRADING RESULTS.

Made in the USA
Las Vegas, NV
29 November 2023